175

INSTRUMENTS OF THE ORCHESTRA

THE FLUTE

THE FLUTE

*A Study of its History, Development
and Construction*

PHILIP BATE

LONDON · ERNEST BENN LIMITED

NEW YORK · W. W. NORTON & COMPANY INC.

First published by Ernest Benn Limited *1969*
Bouverie House · Fleet Street · London · EC4
and W. W. Norton & Company
55 Fifth Avenue · New York 3

© Philip Bate *1969*

Printed in Great Britain

510–36351–2

TO
Y. M. B.

Contents

Introduction

IN EMBARKING on an account of the orchestral flute as it is known today any student must, I think, begin by acknowledging a basic debt to two previous workers in particular—R. S. Rockstro and Dayton C. Miller. In 1890 Richard Shepherd Rockstro of London, a well-known professional flautist and teacher, published the first edition of his *Treatise on The Flute* which remains the most comprehensive study of the instrument yet written. That his views on certain matters were deeply prejudiced, and have in justice called for reassessment and correction by later writers (notably Christopher Welch), detracts little from the value of the book as a factual account, and in many respects Rockstro's huge volume remains a model for all time. It is an essential in the reference library of any woodwind historian.

During some fifty years Professor Dayton Clarence Miller of Cleveland, Ohio, compiled what is undoubtedly the world's finest assemblage of flutes and related instruments, cognate literature, pictures, and flute music, the instrumental part alone numbering over 1,500 specimens at the time of his death in 1941. This material is now deposited in the Library of Congress, Washington, D.C. Dr Miller was an astronomer and acoustician who made revolutionary contributions to both these branches of Science, and to his collecting he brought the orderly mind of the physicist; but he was in addition a good performing musician and a man of charm. The writer holds it a great privilege to have enjoyed his friendship and generous help over a number of years.

With no more than two such mines to exploit, and disregarding all others, the student will see at once that concerning the flute there is a mass of source material; but even so, there are unfilled gaps in its history. Authentic examples dating from before the mid-18th century are comparatively rare, though there are ample literary and pictorial references. Much of this material is, however, distributed through encyclopaedias, periodicals, pamphlets, and catalogues, and is not very easy to find. Sometimes references are contradictory, so the rôle of the historian becomes that of a sort of musical and scientific detective. Further, it is not unknown for successive writers to quote each other without either acknowledgement or attempt at verification. As a result, many statements which began only as suggestion or surmise (whether well or ill founded) have gained currency and are now accorded the respect due to proven fact. Much of our information about musical instruments is traditional, and tradition is to be respected. We should, however, be wrong always to accept tradition without reasonable and, if possible, unprejudiced enquiry.

The extreme popularity of the flute among amateurs from the 18th century on (even the egregious Dick Swiveller, we are told, fell under its spell) may perhaps account for its having been more 'written-up' than almost any other instrument, but the very quantity of this material makes a problem for the present-day student. Accepting the reliability of the best of former scholars, he may perhaps feel that he need not pursue every reference to its ultimate source; but if he takes this view he must select with discrimination and choose aptly in the light of his own knowledge. In preparing these pages the sources of at least two oft-repeated quotations have proved untraceable, and there must be many others in the same case. I have tried, therefore, to be as clear as possible as to my derivations, and in cases where I have offered my own conclusions or conjectures I hope this will be clear to the reader. I am aware that some of these may possibly be challenged, and in their defence I can only say that I have not set them down lightly.

The present book makes no pretence at being a treatise. Its object is to present a reasonably short conspectus which may interest the lay reader on the one hand and, on the other, encourage the potential specialist to further research. In line with other volumes in the Instruments of the Orchestra Series, stress has been placed on the flute as it is found in the orchestra today, and this limits our consideration mainly to the transverse or cross-blown instrument. The various vertically blown instruments, the recorders, flageolets, and whistles which in the broadest sense are classified as *flutes*, are treated mainly as they bear on our principal subject. A similar reservation has been applied to present-day Oriental and exotic cross-blown instruments, and I hope the discipline thus imposed may have helped to keep the general narrative from becoming intolerably diffuse.

From this point of view we may see that the modern orchestral flute had reached a definitive form over a century ago, and subsequent improvements and developments have been mainly concerned with materials or with mechanical matters. Those which appear to be of lasting importance I have dealt with in some detail, but it is to be noted that even while this book has been in preparation, work has been done on the standard Boehm flute which may before long prove of great value.

Since Rockstro's day the science of acoustics has advanced greatly with the acceptance of some entirely new concepts, and recently the characteristics of the flute—acquired empirically over the years—have been investigated and explained in terms of absolute mathematics. In the acoustics chapter I have attempted some account of this, though it can hardly be sufficient to satisfy the pure scientist, who is referred to the original papers listed in the Bibliography. In November 1966 the New York Academy of Science held a Conference on 'Sound Production in Man' at which Dr A. H. Benade of Case Institute of Technology, Cleveland, Ohio, and Dr D. J. Gans of the University of Illinois presented a report on 'Sound Production in Wind Instruments'. Their most comprehensive study has been going on for several years, and their results may well revolutionise present views of this branch of acoustics. As this page goes to press a full account of the conference is still awaited, but a pre-report in respect of this Section has been printed by the Department of Physics of Case Western Reserve University.

As to the general lay-out of this volume, a word of explanation is perhaps due. First, I should like to make it clear that the general descriptions presented in Chapter 1 apply to modern instruments, or those sufficiently recent that the reader is likely to find them still in use. We should remember that a player who has formed his technique on an instrument that was perhaps the latest thing at the beginning of his musical life and has served him well for many years, is not particularly prone to exchange this for a more modern one without very careful consideration of the pros and cons; and a professional career may well last for half a century. Again, the various essential features found in both main types of flute today are intimately bound up with certain immutable laws of physics. I have therefore thought it useful to place the chapter on acoustics near the beginning of the book, as this forms the basis of much that is described later. To the reader whose interest is chiefly historical I would suggest that he need not burden himself with it—at least at the outset. I should hope, however, that later on he might come to enjoy this very beautiful and complex science. As a result of this decision, which makes the section something of a separate essay, there will be found minor duplications between chapters. Other duplications arise inevitably from the consideration of some topics from different viewpoints, and I hope these will not be regarded as blemishes.

In respect of a previous book I have been both praised and criticised for the number of notes that I placed at the end of each chapter. In the

present volume I have again supplied extensive references and comments for the sake of the student, but I have deliberately kept them as
footnotes in the hope that thereby the reader will not find the historical
sequence too disconnected. Finally I must say that I know that there are
certain omissions—for one, I have made no attempt to list or criticise
the playing literature of the flute. The former task would be quite
beyond my capacity, and its magnitude is indicated by the 10,000 or
more titles accumulated by Dr Dayton Miller. The reader is, however,
referred to Vester's *Flute Repertoire Catalogue* (see Bibliography).
Artistic criticism I regard as the province of the professional critic who
by study has equipped himself for it. For the same reason I have made
little reference to the performance of living players. The general
Bibliography can only be strictly selective since, as already mentioned,
there is so much published material of varying quality and interest, and
for my selection I alone must take responsibility.

Again, considerations of space have forbidden the inclusion here
of biographical notes on flute players. A very full biographical section
to the year 1880, or thereby, will be found in Rockstro, and further
coverage was supplied by Fitzgibbon in the second edition of *The Story
of the Flute*, 1928. Many distinguished flautists, especially in America,
are noted in L. de Lorenzo's *My Complete Story of the Flute*, New York,
1951.

As a student of woodwind instruments during many years my object
in this volume has been to provide a generally useful reference book,
and to share with others the intense pleasure that the study has afforded
me.

Acknowledgements

IN PREPARING this book I have enjoyed the help and encouragement of many good friends. The Musicians, musicologists, and fellow students alike have made me free of their libraries, their collections, and their own researches, and I thank them all sincerely. I am particularly indebted to Mr A. C. Baines, Professor and Mrs Brian Boydell, Mr Albert Cooper, Mr Edward Croft-Murray, Dr H. Fitzpatrick, Mr Squire L. G. Grimes, Mr James Howarth, Mr A. Hyatt King, Mr Lyndesay G. Langwill, Mr William Lichtenwanger and Miss Laura Gilliam of the Library of Congress, Washington, D.C., Mrs S. T. Mackay (representing executors of the late Professor Bernard Hague), Mr Alex. Murray, Mr Guy Oldham, Mr R. Morley Pegge, Mr Maurice Porter, L.D.S., Mr Karl Ventzke—nor must I forget the many flautists, both amateur and professional, with whom I have had long discussions, often without even exchanging names. I have also to thank the editors of *The British Dental Journal* and *The Instrumentalist* and Messrs B. T. Batsford for permission to quote from their publications. The Curators of the Victoria and Albert Museum, the National Gallery, the Conservatoire royal de musique, Brussels, the Kunstmuseum, Basel, the Library of Congress, and the Glasgow Art Gallery and Museums have all been most generous in permitting the reproduction of treasures in their keeping, and I must acknowledge also the great help I have had from the staff of the National Library, Dublin, the Patent Office in that city, and the Assistant Pepys Librarian, Magdalene College, Cambridge.

In some most exacting photographic work I have had unstinted help from Messrs Neil Badger (illustrations from my own collection), Roy and Philip Byrne, Brian O'Raghallaigh, and John Henshall. I am grateful to them all.

Finally I have to thank Ralph Overall and my wife for their encouragement and patient work in checking and indexing.

PHILIP BATE

The tonality or pitch of an instrument is indicated by a capital, e.g. Flute in C, or G Flute. To save innumerable musical examples, the following method of staff notation has been adopted.

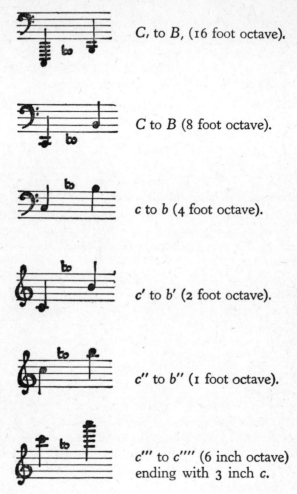

$C_{,}$ to $B_{,}$ (16 foot octave).

C to B (8 foot octave).

c to b (4 foot octave).

c' to b' (2 foot octave).

c'' to b'' (1 foot octave).

c''' to c'''' (6 inch octave) ending with 3 inch c.

In the body of the text a further convention has been used. A hole, key, or note when mentioned generally is denoted by a capital letter, but where a specific octave is intended it is distinguished by the use of upper or lower case letters with strokes as above.

List of Illustrations

In each of the following plates the group of instruments shown has been reproduced as nearly as possible to the same scale. Except where indicated all examples are taken from the Author's collection.

Following a convention recently adopted by a number of writers the flutes shown in these plates are presented with the head to the right, i.e. in playing position as seen by the observer. Text figures, however, which are mainly concerned with fingering, etc., are shown from the player's viewpoint.

PLATE I Flute Quartet, *c.* 1500 Urs Graf (1485–1527). Note implied offset of sixth finger-hole of Bass flute and 'fork-fingering' of discant (top right). *Kunstmuseum, Basel*

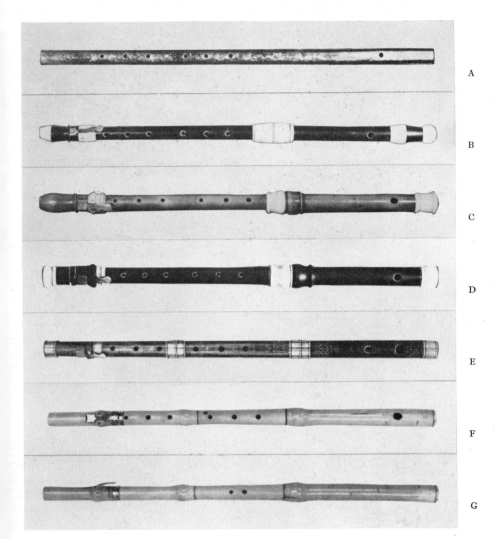

A

B

C

D

E

F

G

PLATE 4

A. Hotteterre-le-Romain. Portrait by Picart from *Les Principes* (1707). Compare with:

B. Head of standing figure from the Tournières? group, Plate 3.

C. Advertisement by George Brown, flute-maker of Dublin. From *The Dublin Courant*, Saturday, January 16th to Tuesday, 19th, 1747/48. The earliest illustrated advertisement so far recorded from an Irish newspaper. Note that, allowing for some crudeness in the drawing, the flute shown has some Baroque features though built in four sections. Note also the early reference to walking-stick flutes.

A   B

C

GEORGEBROWN Muſical Inſtrument Maker, dwelling at Mr, Hyens's, Cutler in Crane-lane, Dublin. has by his Skill and Induſtry, brought that Inſtrument call'd the German Fute to that Degree of Perfection, that the moſt Knowing in that Art can find no Defect in them, and by a new Machine of his own Invention, Gentlemen may with the greateſt Facility found all the Notes of the ſa'd Inſtrument, from the higheſt to the loweſt. He alſo makes excellent German Cane Flutes, for the Accommodation of thoſe Gentlemen that wou'd recreate themſelves abroad, and as he has been for this conſiderable Time paſt a ſucceſsful Practitioner in his Art, and has wrought for the moſt eminent Maſters in his Travels through Germany, Holland, Flanders and England, humbly hopes, Gentlemen, ſuch as have occaſion for ſaid Inſtrument will favour him with their Cuſtom, and they may be aſſured of getting as good Inſtruments from him as is poſſible to be made.

PLATE 5   One-keyed flutes, 18th and 19th centuries

A. Bizey, Paris. Ivory. 1716–52. Earliest four-joint type. F, G♯, and C keys added later.

B. Anon. Ivory. Early 18th-century type of key.

C. Cahusac, London. Ivory. *c.* 1755. G♯ key added later.

D. Suchart, London. Ivory. *pre*–1759. With three corps de réchange. Shown with longest in position.

E. Elberg, Copenhagen. Box wood. Profile suggests early 18th century. 'Register' on foot joint.

F. Proser, London?. 1777–95. (See p. 116.)

G. Potter, Richard, London. Box wood, *c.* 1760. With three corps de réchange.

H. Drouet, London. Stained box wood, ivory cap and mounts. Brass key. 1815–19. Possibly a cheap model.

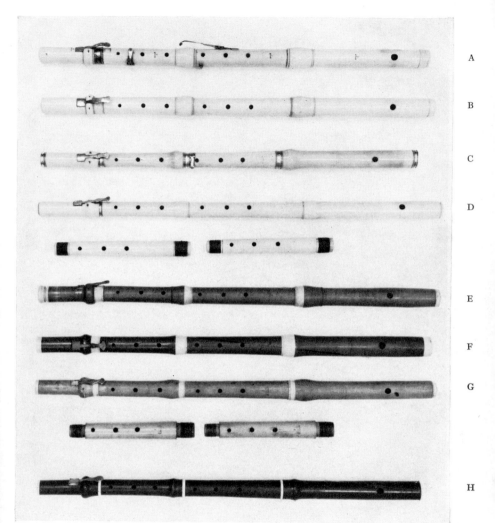

A

B

C

D

E

F

G

H

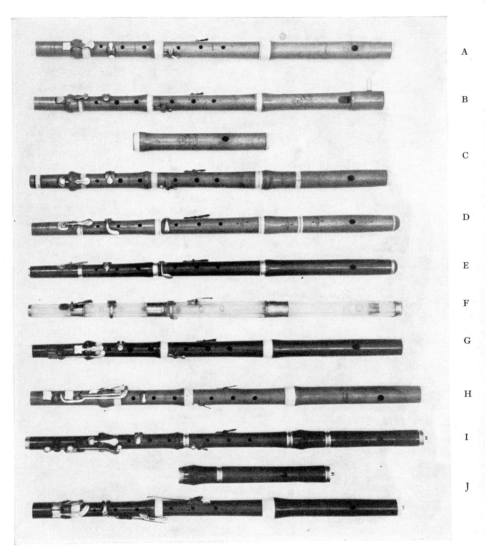

A

B

C

D

E

F

G

H

I

J

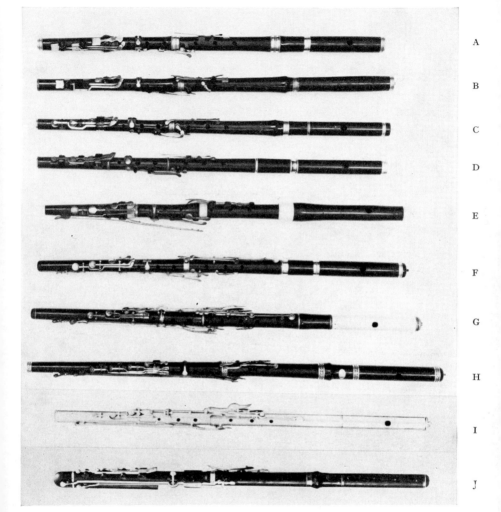

A

B

C

D

E

F

G

H

I

J

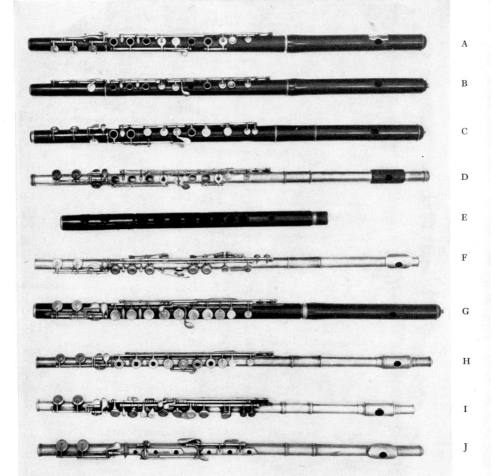

A

B

C

D

E

F

G

H

I

J

PLATE 9   Mechanised Flutes, etc., *post* Boehm
- A.   Cornelius Ward, London. Cocus wood. Ward's first model. Foot keys to left thumb by tracker wires, etc.
- B. & C.   Clinton & Co., London. Cocus wood. Two versions of Clinton's 'Equisonant' Flute.
- D.   'Whitaker from Rudall & Rose', London. Cocus wood. Card's system.
- E.   Siccama, London. Cocus wood. Typical Siccama 'Diatonic' Flute.
- F.   Lafleur, London, Rosewood or *Palissandre*? Tenon repaired. Cylinder bore, large holes adapted to 'old' fingering. Imported, probably Belgian make.
- G.   Anon. Cocus wood, silver mounts and keys. A superior quality instrument adapted to a left-handed player.
- H.   Wallis, London. Ebonite. Keyless Giorgi flute.
- I.   Schaffner, Florence. Plated metal. Giorgi-Schaffner flute. Probably made by Maino e Orsi, Milan, but bearing Schaffner's mark on an embossed plate.

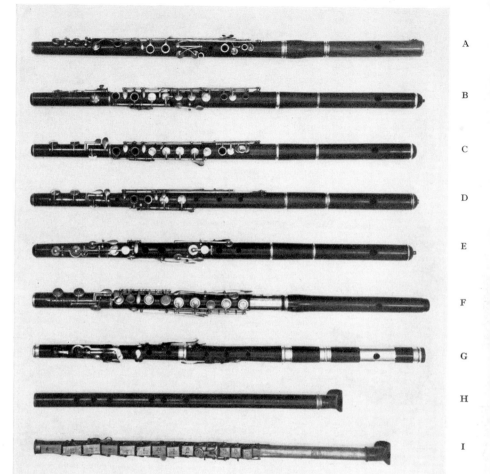

A

B

C

D

E

F

G

H

I

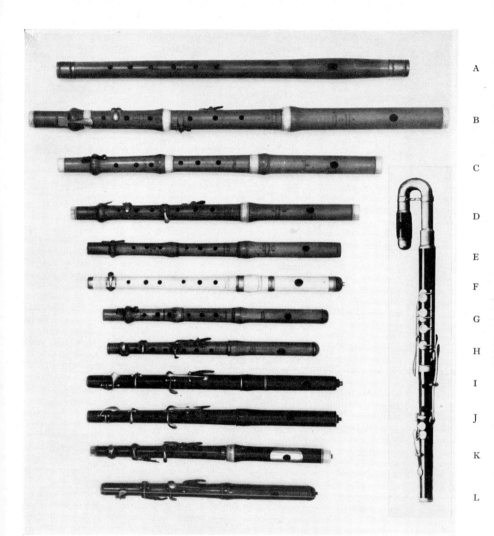

A

B

C

D

E

F

G

H

I

J

K

L

M

PLATE 11   Alto Flutes; experiments by Burghley, etc.

- A. Scherer, Paris? (maker of Frederick the Great's flute) Ivory. Alto flute. *c.* 1760.
- B. Clementi & Co., London. Box wood. Alto flute. *c.* 1810.
- C. Dr. Burghley, London. Experimental concert flute. Mahogany, ivory, and ornamental woods. Plain cork stopper. The sections of the head are movable.
- D. Dr. Burghley, London. Experimental concert flute. Mahogany, ivory mounts. Screw-cork.
- E. Dr. Burghley, London. Experimental bass flute in C. Mahogany, ivory mounts. (See p. 139.)
- F. Reffay, Paris?. Walking-stick flute. 18th century?.

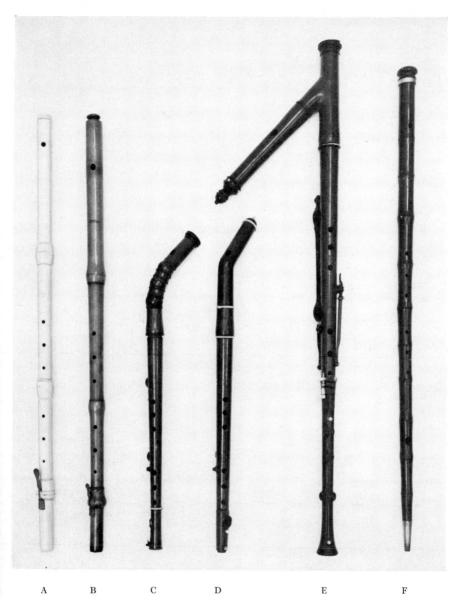

A   B   C   D   E   F

PLATE 12   Bass Flutes, 19th and 20th centuries.

- A. Albisi, A., Milan. 'Albisiphon', *c.* 1910. (See p. 189.) *Dayton C. Miller Collection.*
- B. Boehm, Munich (the mark is probably false). Bass Flute in C. *c.* 1890. (See p. 187.)
- C. Bartoli, G., Milan. Bass Flute in C. *c.* 1925. *Dayton C. Miller Collection.*
- D. Rudall, Carte & Co., London. Bass Flute in C. *c.* 1933.

A   B   C   D

General Considerations: Definitions and Descriptions

Flute. Cross Flute. German Flute (18th century), Transverse Flute.
(Fr. *Flûte, Flûte traversière, Traversière, Flûte d'Allemagne*; Ger. *Flöte, Querflöte*; Ital. *Flauto, Flauto traverso, Traverso*.)

THE MODERN transverse flute is in principle one of the simplest, in practice one of the most sophisticated of all orchestral instruments. In essence it consists of a tube of wood, metal, or man-made material, usually rather more than two feet long, and about ¾ of an inch in diameter, closed at one end by a cork or stopper. Near the stopper is a fairly large hole with a sharp edge—the mouth-hole, or in French the *embouchure*—and at intervals along the body of the tube there are a minimum of six more holes so placed that they can be opened and closed by the fingers, either directly or with the help of some mechanism. This, to the great majority of people, is 'The Flute', but here we have to be careful. The term *flute* is in fact a widely comprehensive one, and when we use it we must decide whether we are thinking as playing musicians, physicists, ethnologists, or even perhaps as glass-blowers, for the word flute is also applied to a type of tall narrow wine glass. To the ethnologist the word presents its widest connotation, and to him—paraphrasing Robert Donington[1]—'Flute is a species not a family'. In this sense the flute comprises a huge group of instruments both primitive and sophisticated and of many shapes, all having one common feature—an air column confined in a hollow body and energised by the vibration or 'fluttering' of a thin jet or sheet of air from the player's lips impinging on the sharp edge of an opening. This sharp edge may be that of a mouth-hole specially provided, or it may be simply the cut-off end of a tube, but in any case the process involved is what the physicist recognises as the generation of an 'edge-tone' (see Chapter 2). The jet of air may be shaped and directed by the player's lips alone, as in the modern flute, or it may be confined in a prepared channel and so directed positively against the necessary sharp edge or 'fipple'. This construction is typified by the recorders, flageolets, and whistles, as well as all organ 'flue-pipes'. In passing we may note that although all flue-pipes in the organ operate on this principle, the organ builder has a special terminology and only uses the word 'flute' for pipes of particular tone quality.[2]

As the jet of air from the player's lips energises the main air column by its flutter to-and-fro the term 'air-reed' has been coined for it by a loose analogy with the cane reeds of other woodwinds. It is not really a good term, however, as we shall see later on, but it is useful in making a first basic division in the great flute species—into 'Free air-reeds' and 'Confined air-reeds'. At one period the confined air-reed found its place in the orchestra as the Recorder or *flûte-à-bec*, and indeed in scores as late as Handel's time this was the instrument implied by 'flute' or *flauto*, while its growing and more powerful rival, the cross-blown instrument, was strictly specified as *traverso* or *flauto d'Allemagna*, etc. Today the recorder is undergoing something of a revival as an instrument in its own right as well as for the realisation of orchestral parts originally conceived for it.

Beyond this basic division the great group of flutes can be sub-divided in a multiplicity of ways according to secondary features, i.e whether the vessel enclosing the air column is tubular or of some other shape (the ocarinas, Chinese bird whistles); if tubular, whether it is cylindrical or tapered in some manner; whether it is open at both ends or closed at one end (pan-pipes, 'stopped' organ-pipes); whether it has finger-holes or not; and whether the sharp edge of the *embouchure* is notched or modified in some other way, etc. There are even some cylindrical flutes in which the energising air jet is not transmitted by the player's lips but his nostril. The known permutations and com-binations of the secondary features make for a most complicated system of classification, but fortunately this need not concern us in the present study. For an admirably concise survey the reader who may be inter-ested is referred to Chapter VII of Anthony Baines's *Woodwind Instruments and their History*. The instruments which form our main consideration here all belong to the tubular variety with a free air-reed, and open at both ends (for although the tube is in fact plugged at one end, in practice the mouth-hole restores the doubly open condition).

Modern Flutes

Present-day flutes used in orchestral, military, and recital music are almost invariably constructed in three sections: the 'head' in which is cut the mouth-hole; the 'body' containing the six holes controlled by the first three fingers of either hand which provide the diatonic 'primary' scale of the instrument, and a variable number of additional holes for semitones governed by keys;[3] and finally the 'foot' which lengthens the tube sufficiently to afford two more semitones. The holes for these are controlled by interlocking keys which at rest stand open, and which can be closed, one or both, by the right little finger. A hole and a 'closed' key to provide the first semitone above the 'six-finger' note is usually placed on the foot also. The joints between the sections are made by sockets and tenons, the former being bored out from the head and foot respectively, and the latter turned down from the thickness of the body wall. To make a truly air-tight union the tenons are lapped with thin cork sheet or greased thread. The head tenon is usually made fairly long so that the joint, while remaining firm, may be pulled out to some extent to adjust the overall length of the instrument, and so act as a tuning slide. In wooden flutes with necessarily rather thick tenons this has a minor disadvantage in that it introduces unavoidably a sudden expansion of the bore which may have a bad effect on the tuning. With metal instruments the same basic construction is used, though often there are no actual tenons, and the sockets are no more than short lengths of tube which telescope over the ends of the body. Obviously the discrepancy introduced by pulling out the head joint is in this case no more than twice the thickness of the body-tube itself, and many makers of wooden flutes take advantage of this by lining the head with a very thin metal tube which extends slightly inside the body (see Fig. 1). The pros and cons of lining a wooden head completely with metal are discussed elsewhere.

Within the accepted three-part construction, two main types of bore are recognised today—the so-called cylindrical and the conical, though in fact neither term gives a completely accurate description. In the cylindrical, which is the ultimate refinement of that introduced c. 1847 by Theobald Boehm of Munich as a result of his own labours and the support of the physicist C. von Schafhäutl, the body and foot have no taper, but the head narrows from the socket to the cork in a curve that has been described as parabolic. The conical bore is more or less a reversal of this, the head being a true cylinder and the rest of the tube having a regular taper. Since the contraction of this bore begins right at the top of the body, the tenon cannot accommodate a telescopic tuning slide, so this is commonly introduced in the head itself below the mouth-hole (see Fig. 2).

Today the cylindrical Boehm instrument is undoubtedly predominant among professional flautists. On its introduction, however, it met with

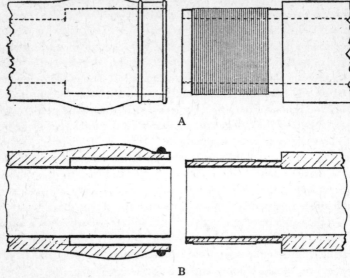

Fig. 1
    A. Simple socket and tenon joint (thread lapping)
    B. Section of modern socket with metal lining.
       Cork-lapped tenon

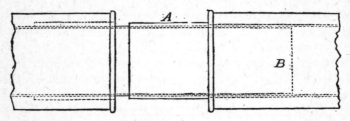

Fig. 2   Tuning slide formed in Head
    A. Outer metal tube attached to lower section
    B. Extended lining tube of upper section

considerable opposition, mainly, we may suppose, on account of its
necessarily revised fingering system, though very shortly its manifest
advantages led to its wide adoption—except in Boehm's own country
where once again the prophet was without honour. An account of
Boehm's work with both the old conical bore and his new cylinder will
be found in Chapter 7.

In Germany in the early 19th century many influential players used a type of flute directly descended from the typical 18th-century instrument with its small finger-holes, and by long practice had attained great technical mastery. They held its very characteristic tone in great affection—indeed even Wagner is said to have preferred it all his life—and to be fair we must admit that probably the first exponents of the cylinder flute did produce a much more 'open' sound. As in all such cases there was also no doubt some element of prejudice, but, be that as it may, we still find in modern Germany some preference for the cone-bored flute, especially among amateur players. German makers today produce magnificent examples equipped with all the technical facilities of modern mechanism, including an adaptation of the ring device perfected by Boehm about 1832, and axles instead of simple levers for the foot-keys. Such instruments are frequently spoken of as the 'Reform-Flute' but this title is properly, I believe, a brand-name introduced by Schwedler.[4] The reader will find that today 'reform-flutes' vary somewhat in detail, and from maker to maker, but on the whole we can say that they stand in relation to the cylinder Boehm much as do the advanced simple system clarinets (say the Oehler, or *Vienna Akademie* models) to the familiar Klosé–Boehm instrument. In particular they satisfy the orchestral player's needs as to dynamic range, which with the older simple instruments was frequently a problem.

The field in which the traditional cone-flute finds fullest use today is that of military duty music, and the civilian flute—or more properly 'Flute and Drum'—band. These bodies regularly use a simple five- or six-keyed instrument without a separate foot joint, robustly built for outdoor use, and usually requiring more forceful blowing than the orchestral flute—a revival in a way of the 'loud music' idea of the later Middle Ages. As with some medieval instruments too, band-flutes are built in various pitches so as to form a homogeneous choir of voices. All are transposing instruments, the 'six-finger' note being invariably written as D. Traditionally, however, they are *named* after the actual sound of this D and not the adjacent C as in orchestral practice. This custom sometimes causes confusion and many musicians and theoretical writers have called for its abolition. So far, however, the flute bandsman has remained adamant. At the present day the highest development of the flute band is to be found in Northern Ireland and here the groups range from boys' bands of quite moderate size all playing B♭ flutes in unison, or with occasional thirds, to twenty-six musicians harmonising in perhaps six or seven parts and supported by four percussion players. The sound of these bands heard in the right perspective, though to some ears perhaps a little lacking in 'foundation tone', has a limpid crystalline quality which can be both affecting and exciting to a degree. It is indicative of the standards the players set themselves that in recent years some of the best known bands have found the simple instrument inadequate and have gone over to more advanced models. The first move in this direction took place over forty years ago when the celebrated Argyll Temperance Flute Band had themselves re-equipped with Rudall Carte's 'Guards'' model cylinder flute, an instrument of all-round excellence which we shall look at more fully later on. In the largest flute bands the organisation is on much the same lines as that of the brass band[5] and a full complement of instruments for twenty-six players would consist of

1 E♭ piccolo	3 E♭ flutes
1 solo B♭ flute	3 B♭ bass flutes
2 1st B♭ flutes	2 F bass flutes
3 2nd B♭ flutes	1 E♭ bass flute
3 3rd B♭ flutes	4 Percussion
3 F flutes (scored as 1st, 2nd, and 3rd)	

It will be readily understood that such a force lends itself to complex and sometimes adventurous scoring (usually by the bands' own conductors), and that competition playing is taken very seriously indeed.

Reference to the flute in a military context leads us to look next at the one example of a completely unmodified cylindrical bore that the reader may encounter today. This occurs in the true *fife*, still used in some Continental establishments as a time-marking and signal instrument. In Britain the fife has been superseded in these duties for nearly a century by the six-keyed B♭ band flute, though the name has survived in the 'Fifes and Drums' of Britain's famous foot regiments. Fig. 3 shows a typical call taken from British Army Regulations.

The typical fife is extremely simple in construction, consisting of a plain wooden tube, some thirteen inches long all in one piece, with a

Fig. 3   Duty call for flute and drum, *c.* 1900

cylindrical bore, a mouth-hole, and six finger-holes. Modern examples usually have a protective metal ring or ferrule at each end, but otherwise the instrument is entirely without refinements, even an ornamental cap at the head end. In this form it presents all the characteristics of its parent type, the keyless cylindrical flute of the late Middle Ages and the Renaissance, and indeed, but for a very slight increase in the diameter of the bore relative to the length, we could say that this is the very instrument that made so brave a show on the Field of Cloth of Gold. In the early 16th century the true fife was often known as the *Schweitzerpfeiff* (Swiss Pipe) from its association with the Swiss *lansquenets* who played such an important part in European military history, and from that time on it has remained (in combination with side-drums) *the* marching instrument of foot soldiers. At the period mentioned the larger transverse flutes were coming under the influence of a developing Art music, and in the course of improvement, especially as regards the lower register, their relative bore diameter was slowly enlarging. The *Schweitzerpfeiff*, however, retained its extremely narrow bore and shrill sound and the historian Praetorius writing in 1618–19 tells us that in his time its fingering differed slightly from that of the other flutes. In the late 18th century the fife did acquire some minor improvements. The bore remained as it had always been, but many examples are known in which the outside profile of the tube is irregularly fusiform with the greatest diameter at the mouth-hole which thus becomes somewhat deeper. The significance of this is discussed elsewhere. Occasionally too, a key for d♯, opened by the right little finger, was provided. On the keyless instruments chromatic notes outside the basic scale could be sounded only by the expedient of 'fork-fingering' (see Chapters on Acoustics and Technique) but the first semitone could not be so produced. A growing concern with musicality in military circles at the time is also revealed by the fact that sometimes a fifer was equipped with two instruments pitched in C and B♭ so that he might be the better assimilated into the formal military band which was then gaining some degree of organisation.

Other Quasi-cylindrical Flutes

We have already mentioned the hostile reception accorded to the Boehm flute on its introduction in Germany, and we have seen that later on, in spite of this, improvers of the cone-flute borrowed extensively from its key-work—and in this connection we must bear in mind that the Boehm *system*, configuration of bore, disposition and size of tone-holes, etc., is one thing, while the Boehm *mechanism* with its covered holes and linked keys is another. In England conservative reaction to the Boehm flute took a different and, as it turned out, a most fruitful turn. The first half of the 19th century in this country was marked by a generation of flautists whose names are still a legend, and foremost among them was Charles Nicholson the younger. Playing on a cone-flute with a somewhat modified bore and relatively large finger-holes, his brilliance and power were the admiration of all and the despair of many. Granted that this was a period when the English concert audience admired mainly the 'popular air with brilliant variations' type of instrumental solo, it was this very demand that called forth the virtuoso player and gave him opportunities that are now lacking in an age when we think our musical taste better. It is on record that the desire to emulate Nicholson's powerful tone, especially in the lower register, was one factor which led to Boehm's researches, and viewed from the present distance of over a century the subsequent events may appear just a little ironical. In a country where powerful tone was so much admired it would seem obvious that the new cylinder flute should commend itself and many players tried it out in high hopes, only to find the different fingering system too great an obstacle.

Some abandoned the new instrument forthwith, but others, convinced of the value of the cylinder bore, attempted to ally this with the old fingering. The result was a whole crop of curious instruments, many single examples which are only of interest to the student collector, but others of such lasting worth as to have been taken up by leading manufacturers. A few of these special models are still used quite extensively in English speaking countries, especially among amateur players, and can be obtained from the makers. The most important are those associated with the names of Richard Carte, Radcliff, and Pratten, all well-known players in their day, and we shall consider them in more detail later.

Wood versus Metal: Thinned Heads, etc.

The relative merits of wood and metal for flutes are matters on which it is difficult and unwise to be dogmatic. Certainly the latter seems at this time to be the world favourite, and probably a metal flute is the less fatiguing to blow over a prolonged period. Tonally, however, the choice is a matter for the individual player and belongs to that indefinable realm of 'taste'. Some flautists can produce an equally solid—or ethereal—tone on either a wooden or a metal instrument. Others maintain that only with one or the other material can they produce the particular tone quality they desire. Further, and quite apart from whatever tonal properties they may find inherent in either material for the flute body, there are many players to whom the comparatively easy blowing of a metal or a thinned wooden head is a boon. But again, there are others who are happier with the greater 'resistance' of a full thickness head of wood, or even of ivory. Thus there are many combinations to suit the individual player, and the student may well see metal heads on wooden flutes of either bore; thinned wooden heads on bodies either thinned or of normal wall thickness; or normal heads allied to thin metal bodies. In Germany a heavy ivory head attached to a wooden 'reform-flute' was at one time a popular arrangement, one which in its very solidity of appearance suggests a grave and sonorous tone.

The demand for heads with thin walls either of metal or of wood led to some interesting details of construction since, for a flute of any given length, the depth of the mouth-hole is a parameter, and it follows that the thickness of the wall at the point where the hole is placed must be maintained. The most common way of securing this with metal flutes today is one which Boehm employed over a century ago. The actual mouth-hole is formed by a metal ring or collar—often called a 'chimney' —of suitable shape and depth which is soldered to the head tube. To this ring, in turn, is soldered a perforated lip-plate curved to correspond with the outer surface of a head of normal thickness. A similar method of construction has been used for finger-holes also, but we shall defer discussing this till a later chapter. In some metal flutes, mostly English ones built after the middle of the 19th century, the lip-plate took the form of a complete cylinder or barrel which gave some opportunity for ornamental treatment, though it certainly did add some unnecessary weight to the head, and this, with a very light metal body, some players found uncomfortable. Somewhat earlier a similar result was achieved by mounting a solid cylinder of wood or ivory on the head tube and boring the mouth-hole right through both. This, too, had the disadvantage of weight (see Plates 7G and 8D, F, and H). The lightest and probably the most popular method of building up the mouth-hole is to rivet a small piece of ebonite, suitably curved, to the wall of the tube. This need be no bigger than is necessary to lie comfortably against the player's lip, and, providing that the depth of the actual hole is maintained, the surface can be shaped to individual preference. Not infrequently raised cusps are formed on either side of the actual hole—the *Reform-mundstüke* introduced by certain German makers about the end of the century—and these some players find helpful in controlling the air stream.[6]

One other form of flute which the student or collector may still occasionally come across is the double-tube metal variety. As far as I am aware, this construction has never been used for the more advanced instruments, but cone-flutes with eight or ten keys so built are not uncommon. Briefly, one thin tube forms an outer skin of normal dimensions while another represents the bore, and the tone-holes consist of smaller tubes penetrating both and soldered into place. Such a structure would appear 'fiddling' to build but at one time it was credited with great virtues. The body of air trapped between the two tubes, it was claimed, would act as a heat insulator and once the bore had been fully warmed up by the player's breath the pitch of the instrument would remain very constant. In fact the efficiency of the air insulator is in some doubt with so much conducting metal joining the inner and outer tubes. Nevertheless one enterprising instrument maker carried the scheme even further and produced the so-called 'Thermos Clarinet' in which the player could give his instrument a preliminary 'warm up' by breathing both down the bore and between the two tubes.

Screw-corks, etc.

The reader may have noticed that in the foregoing paragraphs— following the habit of most players—we have referred quite indiscriminately to the end stopper of a flute as the 'cork'. In his *magnum opus* Rockstro speaks most disparagingly of this substance and states that the stopper should always be made of some more stable material, preferably ebonite, with only the thinnest lapping of cork to render the plug air-tight. However, the fact remains that very many of the best makers have never used anything for their stoppers but fine grained cork, sometimes faced with a metal disc.

When we come to consider the basic acoustics of the flute we shall see that according to strict mathematics there should be a different position of the cork for every sounding length of the body tube, i.e. for each hole when opened. This is manifestly impracticable and so a compromise position is adopted whereby relative errors in tuning within the scale are minimised. Formerly, however, when pitch standards were less certain than today, the flautist had frequently to adjust his instrument overall either by means of the tuning slide, or by the use of alternative middle joints of different lengths (*corps de réchange*). In these circumstances the

cork had often to be shifted a considerable distance. To effect this
quickly and positively various screw arrangements were employed, and
something of the sort may be found on many modern flutes. The efficiency of the screw-cork depends a great deal on its design and the
accuracy of its manufacture. Fig. 4A shows a good pattern as recommended by Rockstro, while 4B is a poor example of a more common type
taken from an anonymous flute, c. 1820, in the author's collection. In
Fig. 4B it will be seen that the stem of the screw is extended beyond
the thread and passes clear through the end-cap. On older flutes this
extension was frequently graduated to correspond with marks on the
tuning slide, or on the alternative joints, so that the cork might
be quickly set to the required position. Occasionally ingenious mechanisms have been devised linking the stopper with the tuning slide so
that both are correctly adjusted automatically. One at least of these
will be worth examining in detail in a later chapter; for this descriptive
section it is sufficient merely to notice it in passing.

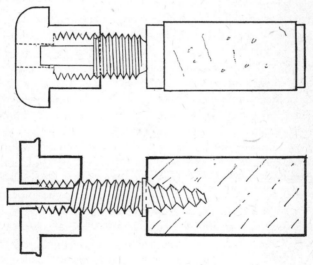

Fig. 4 Screw stoppers
   A. As recommended by Rockstro (cork
      lapped)
   B. Common solid cork type. The weakness of
      this design is that, unless care is taken, the
      coarse screw (usually of ivory) tends to tear
      out of the cork.

Extended Compass

From time to time flautists, especially solo or recital players, have felt
the need for an extended compass to the C flute, and instrument makers
have answered the call with greater or less success. In instrumental
collections the student may well come across cone-flutes with an extended foot joint furnishing as many as six or seven additional semitones.
The excessive length of the foot was sometimes dealt with by folding
the joint back on itself (Plate 7J. These instruments are not very
common however, and experiment has shown that the extra notes are
usually somewhat uncertain. Even at its best the mechanism must have
been difficult to keep in adjustment. Modern 'reform-flutes' usually
carry a foot joint extended to b♮, and this is the limit that Boehm would
permit himself when designing his cylinder flute. At the present time
a greater *range* of flute tone is secured by the use of larger or smaller
instruments, with additional players in the orchestra if necessary. The
more specialised history of these instruments we shall consider in
Chapter 10.

The smallest flute that we may call 'standard' in the orchestra today
is the *piccolo* (Ital. *ottavino*, Ger. *kleine flöte*) sounding one octave
above the concert instrument. This can be found in all the models
described above but it is usually constructed without a foot joint, the
lowest key, which is placed on the body, being the e″♭ for the right
little finger. Accordingly, the lowest note on the normal piccolo is d″,
though some composers have written parts for it down to the c″. In
small combinations where there is but one flautist he is normally
expected to 'double' on the piccolo, and most professional players
possess an instrument. In large orchestras the piccolo is regularly played
by the third member of the flute team who therefore has the opportunity
to become something of a specialist, and this is to the good, for it is not
by any means an easy instrument to handle well. All three men will,
however, switch over in such works as call for three piccolos, when the
'third flute' will usually act as 'first piccolo'.

The tone of the piccolo, unless very carefully controlled, has a distinct
tendency to be shrill, though it does impart a brilliance and glitter in
the ensemble that no other instrument can match. In quiet passages
it is somewhat difficult to sound evenly throughout its compass and,
although Boehm fingering is nowadays the orchestral standard, the
conical bore is often retained as this seems to foster an overall smoothness. On the Continent and in America today the orchestral player

would not consider using a piccolo that did not match his flute exactly as to fingering, and as far as possible as to embouchure. In England, however, there has for long been a curious conservatism in the matter, and as late as the 1920s it was not uncommon to see a first-rate symphony player turn from a Boehm flute to a simple system piccolo with no apparent difficulty on either count.

In flute band circles the orchestral piccolo is represented by a similar instrument pitched a semitone higher and there termed the 'E♭ Piccolo'. Its construction follows the lines of the other flutes in this group and requires no special comment. The same instrument is still sometimes found in military bands where it forms the octave to the D♭ instrument (orchestral terminology) which was formerly the principal flute in these organisations. The reason for this choice of pitch for band work was that it tended to keep flute parts in sharp keys which best suited the traditional eight-keyed flute.[7] Printed band-sets are still published which include parts for the piccolo in D♭. Between the orchestral piccolo and the concert flute we find two more instruments of intermediate size. These are the B♭ and F flutes which we have already listed in connection with the flute band. They appear almost exclusively as simple system cone-flutes, and call for no special notice here.

Larger Flutes

To complete this short survey we must notice some half-dozen instruments of deeper tone than the concert flute. In some respects these correspond with the larger members of the transverse flute family as known in the 16th and 17th centuries, though they can hardly be regarded as direct descendants. They have been called into being, it would seem, rather to meet newly felt needs than by any hang-over from the days of the 'whole consort'.

First, then, comes the *flûte d'amour* in A, hardly called for in the orchestra, but sometimes used by recital players on account of its warm grave tone which is especially effective in solo music. This instrument is nowadays built simply as a larger concert flute with all normal facilities. It is some four inches longer than the C flute and bigger in bore, and the tone-holes are proportionately larger and more widely spaced, but with modern mechanism, covered holes, etc., it presents no inconvenience. This was far from the case, however, with the older six- or eight-keyed A flutes where the finger stretch was sometimes almost unmanageable.

Next in order of pitch comes the A♭ (so-called B♭ *bass*) band flute, and although it lacks the two semitones of the foot joint which makes it slightly shorter overall than the A♮ instrument, it introduces the inevitable problem of all the larger wind instruments—that of man's normal physique. With open holes to be covered by the unaided fingers the distance from the mouth-hole to No. 1 (left forefinger) is such as to push the left hand almost awkwardly far across the body. The practical solution has been to bend the head back upon itself sufficiently to bring the two holes comfortably near to each other. Further, in most good up-to-date models an open key or two is added to ease the stretch between second and third fingers of each hand (see Plate 10M).

The orchestral flute in G, often called *bass* but more properly *alto* (Fr. *contralto en sol*), is a most valuable instrument which has long been a favourite with recitalists—Boehm himself was particularly fond of it—and for which composers are now writing more and more important orchestral parts. Its relatively wide bore necessary for the full production of the lower notes tends to reduce the strength of higher harmonics in its tone spectrum and gives the upper register a languid sonority which is very appealing. Although at modern 'flat' pitch the alto flute is nearly 34 inches long, the mechanism permits the fingers to lie in a comfortable position relative to the mouth-hole, and the need for a reflected head has been avoided.

The two basses, nominally in F and E♭, of the band group come next. They are seldom found except as metal instruments on one or other of the more advanced systems (i.e. the 'Guards' ' model already mentioned on p. 6) and as such their mechanism allows the finger plates to be put in any comfortable situation. The excessive length between the mouth-hole and the top tone-hole is disposed of by making one complete coil in the head towards the socket end. This is the method favoured also in the latest and most satisfactory versions of the true orchestral bass flute pitched exactly one octave below the concert flute. A truly magnificent instrument which is only now gaining full appreciation, the C bass, has been built in a number of shapes.

The above instruments, larger or smaller, constitute the transverse flute family as in use today. In addition, if the student cares to delve in museums or musical collections, he may find a number of curiosities, *flauti di voce*, walking-stick flutes, etc., and some of the more interesting we shall discuss in a later chapter. To close the present one here is a tabular summary for quick reference.

Orchestral and Band Flutes in Current Use

Name and Pitch (orchestral terminology in brackets)	'Six-finger note'	Lowest note in cases where a foot joint is provided
E♭ piccolo (D♭)	e″♭	
Orchestral piccolo (C)	d″	
B♭ flute ('fife') (A♭)	b′♭	
F flute (E♭)	f′	
E♭ flute (D♭)	e′♭	d′♭*
Concert flute (C)	d′	c′ or b′
Flûte d'amour (A)	b	a
B♭ bass flute (A♭)	b♭	
Orchestral bass (alto) flute (G)	a	g
F bass flute (E♭)	f	
E♭ bass flute (D♭)	e♭	
Orchestral bass flute (C)	d	c

* With a foot joint this is the D♭ flute of the older military bands.

NOTES

[1] Donington, R., *The Instruments of Music*, London, Methuen and Co., 1949.

[2] The tonal qualities of 'flute' pipes are most difficult to describe in words, but are instinctively recognised by the organ builder, much of whose art lies in adjusting structural details and proportions to elicit the desired characteristics. The reader is referred to the monumental volume *The Organ* by Hopkins and Rimbault, 3rd edn., London, 1877. Reissued 1965 by Frits Knuf, Hilversum, Netherlands.

[3] Occasionally the body of the simpler flutes is made in two sections for convenience in boring, and to economise in wood.

[4] Maximilian Schwedler, a Leipzig flautist, went into partnership with the instrument maker Karl Kruspe and c. 1900 produced the 'reform-flute'. See Schwedler, *Flöte und Flötenspiel*, Leipzig, 1923. The modern firm of Mönnig—members of the family are established in Markneukirchen and in America—use the term 'reform' for their particular type of cusped mouth-hole, much esteemed by German flautists.

[5] See Baines, Anthony, *Woodwind Instruments and Their History*, London, Faber and Faber, 1956, p. 61.

[6] The idea was not at the time entirely new. Tebaldo Monzani mentioned such a device in a patent specification of 1812.

[7] Baines, *op. cit.* p. 60.

CHAPTER 2

Acoustics

THE STORY of the transverse flute, like those of most orchestral woodwinds, has from the beginning borne the mark of empiricism, and the notable achievements of the best flute-makers have, until quite modern times, been based on trial and error methods. Until quite recently, too, the behaviour of woodwinds has been accounted for fairly satisfactorily according to the concepts of classical acoustic theory with, perhaps, the reservation that some of them do show certain anomalies which are not so readily explained. Today the classical concepts are subject to review and probably some revision, but they still form the most useful starting point for a condensed account such as this. They were certainly the basis of the researches which in the first half of the 19th century led to the complete reorganisation of the flute, as we shall see when we come to look more closely at the work of Theobald Boehm.

In considering the acoustic properties of the flute in a general way we need not go very deeply into physics, but there are one or two elementary facts that we must bear in mind. The first is that the experience that we call 'hearing' is produced by the mechanical stimulation of the complicated and very beautiful mechanism of the ear. Sounds may be roughly divided into 'musical', i.e. periodic—those which are smooth, regular, pleasant, and of definite pitch—and 'unmusical' or 'noises' which are rough, irregular, unpleasant, and of no definite pitch. Such a division cannot, however, be absolute, and nearly all known sounds contain some element of each category. The distinction is a relative one—the most agreeable musical sound nearly always has some associated noises which the mind is able more or less successfully to ignore, and in most noises some musical characteristics can be detected.

Our second point is that the ultimate source of a musical sound is always what the scientist terms a 'system' in a state of vibration. It may be a stretched string, as in the harp or the violin; a column of air, as in a wind instrument or an organ-pipe; or it may be a wooden bar, as in the xylophone; or a bent metal rod—the tuning fork. The properties essential in the material of a vibrating system are elasticity and inertia, and air possesses these just as do the solid bodies mentioned. The only difference between the vibrations of a solid body and of an air column is one of kind. In the solid body vibration involves some degree of periodic physical deformation—as we can actually see in the case of a long harp string, for the vibration is *transverse*, while in the air column it is *longitudinal*, i.e. it consists of periodic cycles of compression and rarefaction among the component particles. In either case the sound reaches the ear by longitudinal waves of alternate compression and rarefaction. In the case of the harp, the cross vibrations create longitudinal motion in the air surrounding the instrument itself, termed the *medium*.[1]

The frequency with which the cycles of disturbance in the medium— which we call *sound waves*—follow each other determines the *pitch* of the sound heard; whether it be a high or a low one. We may also look at this matter in another way. The distance between similar points or phases in any two successive sound waves, say crest to crest, or trough to trough, is called a *wavelength*. High sounds have short wavelengths, deeper ones have longer. Thus wavelength is also a measure of pitch. The wavelength being halved, the frequency is doubled, and vice versa. If we relate frequency to a time scale we have a simple means of defining the pitch of a sound in absolute terms. Thus in 1939 it was agreed internationally that 440 cycles of vibration at 20 degrees Centigrade should be accepted as the standard note a'. The temperature at the time of measurement should always be included in a truly definitive statement, since frequency does tend to rise somewhat with heat, as the reader may well have experienced in the concert hall. The speed with which sound waves are propagated in any medium (in our case the air) is just under 1,125 feet per second at 20°C. It will be obvious that this speed is the product of the frequency and the wavelength. The longer the wavelength the lesser the frequency, i.e. each is inversely proportional to the other and their product approaches 1,125. Thus a note of frequency 440 is produced by waves $2\frac{3}{4}$ feet long which is the distance between successive centres of maximum compression (or rarefaction). In common usage the temperature is more often than not neglected. It is much more usual to hear an orchestral player refer to 'a—440'. Prior to the international agreement a standard of a' = 435 c.p.s., called *Diapason Normal*, was nominally in force in France and Germany and instruments built to that pitch are still common. The would-be purchaser of a second-hand wind instrument is accordingly warned to be on his guard.

c

From the point of view of physics, then, all wind instruments appear as highly complex vibratory systems, but all have certain easily recognised common features. First, there is always some form of *generator* or *exciter* which initiates and maintains the sound. Next, there is a *resonator*, commonly taken to be the body-tube of the instrument, though more accurately it is the air column contained therein whose size and shape are defined by the tube wall. Together these form a coupled dynamic system, and the vibrations of the two are related in a very intimate and often complex way. The resonator is, however, the dominant partner which determines and stabilises the pitch. That this may be so, the mass of the air column is made fairly large and its coupling with the generator fairly 'tight', i.e. there must be no leaks between them. Should this acoustic coupling momentarily fail, as may happen for instance when a mouthpiece socket fits badly, the generator will take charge and emit its own natural note. This is the cause of the dreadful squeaks and quacks which occasionally embarrass even the best of reed players. The generator, in fact, whatever form it may take, acts as a sort of valve which constantly maintains the vibrational energy of the resonator by converting a steady flow of slightly compressed air from the player's lungs into a series of pulses whose frequency is determined *by* the resonator.

Let us now examine the actual behaviour of an air column when it is vibrating. The familiar case of a stretched string will give us a useful starting point. When a cord such as a harp or violin string is twanged we can clearly see that it vibrates in an elliptical loop with no movement at the fixed ends but maximum displacement in the middle. If, however, we prevent any movement in the middle by gently touching the string with a finger it will divide itself into two segments, end to finger and finger to end, and the note we hear will rise an octave. Again, if we touch the string at one-third of its length it will divide into three segments and we shall hear a still higher note, the twelfth, and so on. When a string vibrates in this way the points of no motion are termed *nodes* and those of maximum displacement *antinodes* or *loops*. Because of the general similarity of all elastic vibratory systems we can draw parallels and conveniently apply the same terminology to any of them. Hence, in an air column a point where there is least displacement of air particles (but conversely most pressure variation) is called a node, and one where there is most displacement an antinode. Suppose our air column is contained in a doubly-open cylindrical tube, usually called an 'open pipe'. At each end it communicates with the ambient air, so there can be little or no rise of pressure there. On the other hand, displacement at these points is virtually unrestricted. The two ends therefore become displacement antinodes when the column is energised, and in the first or simplest mode of vibration there will be a node between them. But, like the violin string damped by the finger, in certain conditions an air column can vibrate in higher modes and sound a higher note. What happens then? Clearly the end conditions cannot change; the terminal antinodes persist and symmetrical groups of nodes and antinodes develop between them. These facts can be both deduced from purely mathematical considerations and proved by practical experiment. By a mathematical process rather too complicated to be quoted here it can also be shown that in a gently tapered tube such as we find in musical instruments very similar conditions occur. Doubly-open air columns have a lowest or *fundamental* vibration frequency whose sound has a wavelength of twice the length of the tube, and this is where the direct connection between the length of a tube and the sound generated comes in. For example, a tube effectively open at both ends and approxi-

mately 8 feet long yields the note we commonly call C or ♪ .

This fact, incidentally, gives us a useful method of indicating the particular octave to which any note belongs, i.e. the 'four foot' or the 'sixteen foot' octave, etc.

For the sake of completeness we should note here that air columns contained in pipes effectively open at one end only have a fundamental frequency corresponding to a wavelength of *four times* the length of the

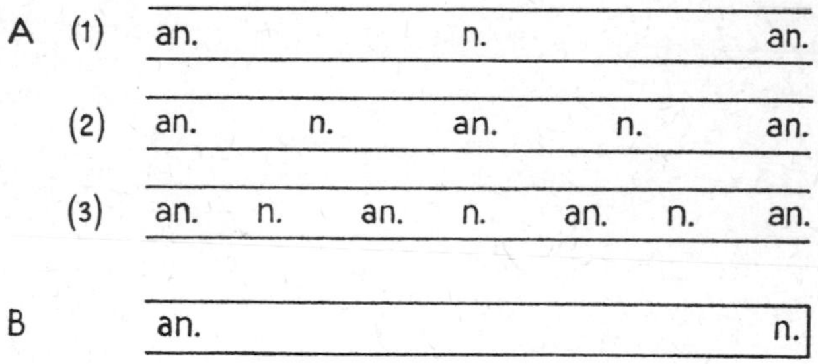

Fig. 5
    A. Air column in an open pipe vibrating in (1) Fundamental mode, (2) 2nd or Octave mode, (3) 3rd mode
    B. Air Column in stopped pipe. 1st mode

tube. Such tubes are found in some musical instruments, notably the clarinet and 'stopped' organ-pipes, but they are not used in *transverse* flutes.

When an air column vibrates in its higher modes it generates sounds whose wavelengths are integral fractions of the fundamental ($\frac{1}{2}$, $\frac{1}{3}$, $\frac{1}{4}$, $\frac{1}{5}$, etc.). These form what is called the *Harmonic Series*, and its components are termed *harmonics* or *partial tones* by analogy with the tones produced when a stretched string vibrates as a whole, or in *aliquot* parts.[2] To illustrate the Harmonic Series in musical notation Fig. 6A presents the

Fig. 6 A. First 16 notes theoretically available on an
8′ open tube, No. 1 being the fundamental

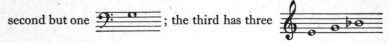

Fig. 6 B. First seven available harmonics of an 8′
stopped pipe

first sixteen sounds theoretically obtainable from an 8-foot open pipe, No. 1 being the fundamental. We can see at a glance that this is a very curious series. The first octave contains no intermediate notes; the second but one  ; the third has three

but in the fourth there are eight running approximately scale-wise. Moreover, Nos. 7, 11, and 13 are considerably out of tune according to the diatonic scale now universally used in Western music. The Harmonic Series does not, of course, end with the fourth octave but continues, at least in theory, into the fifth and higher octaves by semitone and progressively smaller intervals. But here we must take note of that word *theory* and be a little careful. In tubes used for musical purposes the ratio of diameter to length (what the organ builder calls 'scale') is of considerable importance, and although the entire series of harmonics is nominally available with any tube, in actual practice the range of 'scale' that is useful is rather limited. It is quite possible for a tube to be so wide or so narrow that no musical sound can be extracted from it. Further, within the useful range, a tube narrow in relation to its length will more readily yield its higher harmonics, while a wider one is more generous at the lower end of its series. We have already noticed this in our descriptive chapter in connection with the characteristically shrill fife and the more sombre coloured alto and bass flutes (see pp. 7–14).

Looking again at Fig. 6B shows the Harmonic Series of an 8-foot *stopped* pipe and we notice that the first interval is the twelfth not the octave, and that only odd-numbered partials are present. Clearly neither of these series can meet the needs of Art music at all fully and means of extending the possibilities of resonating tubes have had to be found. The gaps in the lower octaves have had to be filled in, and the simplest way of doing this lies in opening a number of side-holes in the tube, more or less remote from the exciter. Incidentally, the traditional position of the exciter, at or near one end of the resonator tube, is purely a matter of convenience in constructing a practical instrument. An air column can be energised at any point along its length.

The practical effect of opening side-holes in a resonating pipe has been known and exploited empirically by musical instrument makers from the earliest times, but it is only during the present century that methods of *quantitative* investigation have been developed. Indeed, even Helmholtz's classic researches into the *qualities* of sounds only date back to the 1860s. It has sometimes been said that the opening of a side-hole is equivalent to cutting the tube short at that point, but this is in fact to over-simplify the situation. The size of the hole is of first importance and the actual 'cut-off' condition is approached only when the diameter of the hole equals that of the tube itself. A small hole placed higher up can sound the same note as a larger one in a lower position on the tube, albeit with some difference in *quality* as we shall see later on. Fig. 7 illustrates the effect upon pitch of progressively increasing the diameter of a side-hole without shifting its position.

The result of boring a series of holes in a resonating tube is equivalent to reducing its *effective* length by stages which will depend both on the size and position of these holes. As each hole is opened in sequence a new fundamental tone is produced, and by adjusting the size and

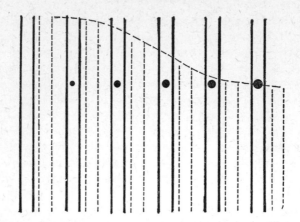

Fig. 7   Illustrating the effect of progressively enlarging a side-hole. The effective sounding length
indicated in broken lines in each case (*adapted from
Benade*)

position of the holes these new fundamentals can be made to conform
to a musical scale.

The compass called for by present-day music is, however, very
extended, sometimes requiring as many as thirty notes from one individual instrument. How are these to be obtained? Fortunately there is no
need to have as many holes as notes. We have seen that the air column in
a doubly-open tube will sound the octave when it passes into its second
mode of vibration. To fill the gap between the fundamental and this
octave diatonically will evidently require no more than six holes. Since
both the dimensions and positions of the holes can to some extent be
varied it becomes possible, in a moderate sized tube, to bring all of them
directly under the control of the fingers. The simple pipe thus becomes
a practical if primitive instrument of music. The fundamental tone
proper to the whole length of the tube followed by those generated
when one, two, three, four, five, and six holes are uncovered gives the
first seven notes of the octave. The eighth is obtained by again closing
all holes and blowing in such a manner that the air column assumes its
second vibrational mode. The player calls this 'over-blowing'. If now
the opening of the holes be repeated while maintaining the second mode
a further six notes become available and the instrument is said to be
sounding its *second register*. By a modification of this process, making
use of one or other of the higher modes, the compass of our simple

instrument can be further increased to yield a third register. The actual mechanics by which the air column is coerced into assuming its second or third mode are primarily concerned with the generator and we shall consider them under that head, but before passing on there is a little more to say about side-holes.

In this chapter so far we have built up from first principles a concept of a practical wind instrument with a diatonic compass of two octaves plus. This was the state of development reached by the cylindrical one-piece flutes of the 16th and 17th centuries. But Art music, even in those comparatively early times, demanded the so-called chromatic scale of *twelve* degrees to the octave (whatever the system of *temperament* adopted to adjust these degrees among themselves so as to sound agreeable). With the straightforward sequential fingering we have so far postulated this would not have been possible, and any instrument so used would have been confined to playing in the key in which it was built. Although the idea of 'key' and key-relationships has dominated Western music for many centuries and has only been relaxed in quite modern times, the use of accidentals is an essential part of that system. How, then, were they to be obtained with such simple instruments? The early player had two methods open to him; one by partially closing or 'shading' a hole with the finger and so more or less flattening its sound; the other by 'fork-fingering', in which one hole is opened while the one or two immediately below it are kept closed. In such conditions the mass of air in the tube below the hole exerts a sort of 'loading' effect on the remainder of the column, and so slows its vibrations to some extent. Clearly neither of these expedients was very efficient or convenient to the player, although, having nothing better, many became expert in their use. With the advent of simple *closed* keys near the beginning of the 18th century, it became feasible to bore suitable holes for every note in the octave and to place more than one under the control of any convenient finger. Thereafter fork-fingering was no longer an essential, but became a most useful alternative technique which, with improved mechanism, is much employed today. We shall see in our chapter on Theobald Boehm's work that, differently employed, fork-fingering is indeed the basis of modern flute mechanics, and even shading has to some extent been re-introduced for specific purposes (see Chapter 8, p. 145).

Of course we must not assume that just because closed keys could offer a solution to the semitone problem on the flute they were immediately and extensively adopted. On the contrary, for a very considerable time the single d♯ key (right little finger) remained the sole addition, and this is of particular interest for we have no evidence as to when it actually came into use. The most that we can say is that while it was unknown early in the 17th century, it had appeared well before the century was out; and when it did appear it was associated with the three- or four-piece conical flute. The transition from the keyless one-piece cylindrical flute to the one-keyed cone-flute is much lacking in documentation (see Chapter 4). Although some of the forked notes were unavoidably of veiled quality and dubious intonation—notoriously the f♮ sounded by raising the right middle finger only, because of the lack of sufficient tube-length below the hole for adequate 'loading'—the one-keyed flute seems to have been accepted with resignation for a very long time. Bach, Handel, Mozart, and Haydn would have known no other *traverso* and it is not till well on in the 18th century that there is evidence of the sustained effort towards improvement which made the four-keyed instrument the standard flute of Beethoven's day. Even so the flute was undoubtedly the pioneer among woodwinds in the acceptance of chromatic keys. Oboes, for instance, were still often made without them as late as *c.* 1820, and we may perhaps wonder why one particular instrument should take so marked a lead. Instruction books of the early 1800s suggest that at first the three 'additional' keys were used mainly for shakes and ornaments, and that the old fingering was still regarded as basic. The fact seems to be, as James McGillivray has pointed out, that the late 18th- early 19th-century two-keyed oboe with its narrow bore, small holes, and extended bottom joint, was acoustically a more efficient device than the contemporary transverse flute, and was more easily 'humoured' by the player according to the requirements of tonality.[3] It has repeatedly been said that crude construction and uncertain stopping militated against a general acceptance of closed keys among woodwind players for some long time. If this is true it would seem that the chromatic intonation of the one-keyed flute, at least with average players, was so bad that any improvement was better than none, and mechanical failure an acceptable calculated risk.

We now turn to the matter of the generator. In the divers musical wind instruments used today the generator takes many forms, but among the orchestral woodwinds we are concerned with no more than three. These are the so-called 'air-reed' peculiar to the flute; the double-cane reed of the oboes and bassoons; and the single or 'beating' reed of the clarinet family. The air-reed as already mentioned in our descriptive chapter, is actually a thin jet of air shaped by the player's lips and

blown across the upper end of a resonating tube, or across a special
mouth-hole which is the acoustic equivalent. The jet impinges on the
sharp edge of the tube or hole, away from the player, and in these
circumstances it vibrates according to cyclic changes in the velocity of
the air at the upper end of the resonator. Rushing in and out of the bore
more or less at right angles to the plane of the jet the resonating air
column drives it upwards and downwards at a frequency that is dictated

Fig. 8   Generation of edge-tones (*after Carrière*)

by the dimensions of the bore. As long as the jet continues it will maintain the vibrational energy of the air column. Thus, in contrast to the
cane-reeds which depend on cyclic variations of *pressure*, the air-reed
is a *velocity* operated device.

To understand a little more fully how this all comes about we must
go back to a well-known acoustic phenomenon, the *edge-tone*. It has
long been recognised that a flat jet of air projected through a slit tends
to break up into curls or vortices, but without any orderly sequence. If,
however, the jet be directed against a more or less sharp edge the
vortices are marshalled into regular cyclic order, and the jet plus edge
system becomes a form of tone generator. The frequency of an edge-
tone depends on two factors: (*a*) the velocity of the jet and (*b*) the distance from edge to slit, and the two are related in a rather complex
manner. If the velocity is kept constant and the distance gradually
increased the pitch of the sound heard falls steadily till a critical point
is reached where there is a sudden upward jump. A further increase of
the distance again causes a progressive fall in pitch until a second
upward jump occurs. Later a third jump will occur and then the tone
finally breaks up into an irregular and undefined noise. If we keep the
distance constant and gradually increase the velocity of the jet (or the
pressure behind it) a similar series of changes in frequency will occur.[4]
Now if we can bring together an edge-tone generator and a suitable
resonator we shall produce a *coupled* vibratory system, and this is exactly
what we find in an organ flue-pipe. In the sections shown in Fig. 9 the
space between the lower lip and the languid or block (in metal and
wood pipes respectively) is the slit through which the jet is projected,
and the chamfered upper lip provides the edge. The whole structure is
indeed simply a 'whistle'—a fact immortalised by that old Puritan who
first dubbed the church organ a 'box o' whistles'. The air column in the
pipe above is the resonator, and, since its mass is large compared with
that of the air forming the jet, it will be the dominant partner. The whole
system when energised will vibrate with a frequency near one of the
natural modes of the air column, favouring the one nearest to the
natural frequency at the time of the edge-tone. If these two frequencies
do not exactly match the air column will to some extent coerce the jet,
but if they do match the entire system will operate at its maximum
efficiency. This is why the organ-pipe voicer goes to so much trouble to
get the height of the mouth—the 'cut-up' as he calls it—just right. Now
let us suppose that our coupled system is vibrating efficiently at its
fundamental frequency and, keeping the cut-up constant, we gradually

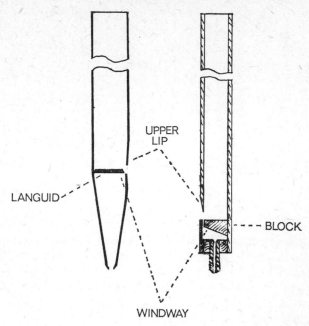

UPPER
LIP

LANGUID

BLOCK

WINDWAY

Fig. 9   Sections of organ flue-pipes. *Left:* metal.
Right: wood

increase the air pressure. The pitch of the edge-tone will strive to go up
with the pressure but the resonator will respond very little until the
frequency of its second mode is approached by the edge-tone. Then the
note of the pipe will jump to the second partial—in the case of an open
pipe, the octave. This is the condition the older organ builders sought
for when voicing their 'harmonic' stops, and as many ranks of pipes
in an organ are usually 'winded' on a common supply and at a common
pressure, they varied the other operative factor, the cut-up.[5] With a
further increase in pressure the process will be repeated and the note
of an open pipe will jump to the third partial, the twelfth.

To be quite fair it must be admitted that the above account is slightly
over-simplified. The jumps in pipe frequency do occur suddenly just
as has been said, but in certain circumstances the partial tone may
appear a little before the fundamental ceases and for a space both tones
are heard. The next Figure may help to clarify this point. Here the heavy
lines represent graphically the frequencies of the system, and the dotted
line that of the edge-tone as it would be if divorced from the resonator.

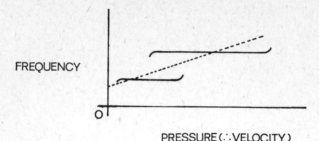

FREQUENCY

PRESSURE (∴ VELOCITY)

Fig. 10 Behaviour of flue-pipe with increasing wind pressure

It will be noticed that the frequency lines have a slight upward trend at each end. This indicates that the fundamental does get slightly sharp just before the jump, and that the partial tone is slightly flat on its first appearance and slightly sharp just before the next jump. These are the points where the edge-tone, though always the weaker partner, has the most influence on the frequencies of the resonator, and by subtle adjustments of wind pressure advantage can be taken of them to blow a pipe slightly sharp or flat.

In actual structure the recorders, flageolets, tin whistles, and other flutes *sensu lato* of the 'confined air-reed plus open pipe' group (see p. 2) resemble the organ-pipe very closely, the only important difference being that with them the resonator is of variable length because of the finger-holes. It follows that for each note in the fundamental scale there should ideally be a different cut-up. Obviously this is not practicable so the dimensions of the mouth, particularly the height, have to be a compromise. No doubt this accounts for a degree of instability in the behaviour of these instruments which takes some skill and experience to overcome. The reader may perhaps point out that the bore of modern recorders and flageolets is characteristically tapered, while the great majority of organ flue-pipes are cylindrical. Acoustically this makes little difference except to disturb somewhat the symmetrical disposition of the nodes when sounding a higher partial.

To pass from the simple case of the organ-pipe or recorder to the rather more complex one of the transverse flute is no great step, but it does take us from relatively unexpressive instruments to one of the most sensitive and artistically rewarding of all. The reasons for this we shall now examine.

In the first place we have precisely the same acoustical elements to consider. We have a resonating air column whose dimensions and shape are determined by a cylindro-conical open pipe, the effective length of which is variable by means of side-holes. We have also an edge-tone generator, but in this part of the system we now find additional factors which give the transverse flute an immense advantage. The player's lips now form the slit through which the jet is projected; the sharp rim of the mouth-hole represents the 'edge' which marshals the vortices; the distance from the chink between the lips to the far side of the mouth-hole corresponds to the cut-up; and these elements are variable at will. With a 'whistle'-type generator the one factor that the player can control directly is the velocity of the jet—i.e. air pressure; this is his principal means of coaxing the resonator into assuming its higher modes. With the transverse flute the player can not only adjust the velocity, but he can vary the cut-up by turning the instrument on its axis towards or away from the mouth. He can change the angle at which the jet strikes the edge of the mouth-hole by more or less advancing the upper lip over the lower; and he can even alter the shape of the jet by control of the lip muscles. We must not suppose, however, that these facilities are at all easy to master. On the contrary, the minute degrees of adjustment are only learnt after long practice—the *art* of embouchure; but once learnt they become a matter of habit and instinct. Once the flautist is really master of his instrument the extreme lightness and mobility of the air-reed give the flute an agility that is almost unmatched by any other woodwind. In addition, the virtually unrestricted *embouchure* of the transverse flute permits of great dynamic range, and even allows the player to force the antinode at the mouth-hole fractionally out of position and so blow any particular note appreciably sharp or flat. All these considerations add greatly to the expressive possibilities of the instrument, and with the approach of the 'Classical' period they made the orchestral demise of the recorder almost inevitable.

Now, having considered the traditional and empirical use of side-holes in woodwinds we may look briefly at what is known today about their actual behaviour physically, and their effect on tone quality. Our knowledge of these matters is largely the result of research done during the last forty years and, indeed, at the time of writing all the various parts of the flute are undergoing quantitative re-investigation with the aid of modern research techniques.[6] Today we possess formulae which relate all the different factors that govern the note sounded by a given hole—i.e. its diameter; its position in the body of the instrument; the length, diameter, and wall thickness of the main tube; and whether or not other holes are open at the same time. In addition there are the effects of temperature, viscosity, and humidity in the air itself to be brought in. Such a group of inter-related quantities can only be fully expressed by the extensive use of calculus, and this is outside the scope or intention of such a book as this. We shall therefore limit ourselves to general statements which can be illustrated by no more than a few simple algebraic symbols.

First, the necessary formulae can be expressed in equations which can be solved for all sorts of practical conditions in the form of graphs from which an instrument maker's working drawing could be constructed. Thus it is now possible to design a woodwind resonator from first principles to any given specification as far as compass and tuning go and, quite recently, to some extent as regards tonal quality. The process is, however, a long one, and it is perhaps doubtful if it would be of much service to the musical instrument industry today with its vast accumulation of laboriously acquired practical 'know-how'.

Second, most modern work has been based on a concept enunciated in 1919 by the late Professor Webster of Clark University—that of 'acoustic impedance'. Impedance can most conveniently be regarded as a sort of reluctance inherent in all tubes (and in this context a side-hole is thought of as simply a very short wide tube) to permit free oscillation of the air particles contained therein. (The word is borrowed from the properties of electrical conductors carrying alternating currents, and indeed modern electrical knowledge has furnished many other analogies which have helped to elucidate acoustic problems.) This reluctance is due to the air not being *perfectly* elastic in the sense that no electrical conductor is perfect—hence the property of electrical impedance. Imperfectly elastic media have an objection to changes of pressure when produced suddenly (*adiabatically*) as opposed to slow changes (*isothermally*). Sound waves are caused by changes in pressure much too rapid to be considered in the *slow* category.

Many years ago Lord Rayleigh defined the 'conductivity' (*c*) of a side-hole as the ratio of its area to its depth, but observed that in measuring the latter a little more—actually about one-third of the diameter—must be allowed because the interference with free air motion extends somewhat beyond the limits of the hole. The same thing occurs at the ends of any pipe and in dealing with these a similar allowance must be made, termed 'end correction', whose absolute measure will depend on the relative dimensions of the pipe. Rayleigh's definition can be expressed quite simply as

$$c = \frac{\text{area}}{\text{depth} + \text{correction factor}}.$$

Now, because of the effects of temperature, viscosity, humidity, etc., the impedance of a tube is not the exact inverse of its conductivity, and as already mentioned, representative formulae become very complicated. If, however, we take several stages in the calculation for granted (which we may do since at any given instant of time the above factors can be regarded as a constant)

$$I = \frac{fda}{c}$$

can be accepted as a simple generalisation where:

I = impedance
d = density of the air
a = velocity of sound
f = frequency
c = conductivity as defined by Rayleigh.

In practice it is often convenient to think of the inverse of impedance for which the rather obvious term 'admittance' has been coined.

$$A \text{ (admittance)} = \frac{c}{fda}$$

may then be called the 'admittance equation'.

Let us consider the tube of a woodwind instrument with one note-hole open. This can be regarded as a simple pipe of known dimensions with a side-hole in a known position. The air 'admitted' to the surrounding atmosphere from inside the pipe comes partly from the section above the hole and partly from that below it, so that we can say that the admittance of the hole equals the sum of the admittances of the two sections. Because d and a may be regarded as constants for any given set of conditions and all the dimensions of both sections of the pipe are known, it is possible to calculate their impedances or admittances (A_1 and A_2). The admittance of the hole $A_3 = A_1 + A_2$. Applying the admittance equation again, substituting the known dimensions of the hole, the result will give the pitch of the note it will sound. Conversely, if the pitch of the note wanted is known, the equation will give its position if the size is known; or the size if the position is known.

Third, the above principle can be extended as far as required. If the

tube of a musical instrument is imagined as made up of a series of
sections each cut off by a note-hole at either end, the admittance
equation can be applied as often as necessary to determine the note that
will be sounded by any given hole when other holes below it are also
open. Moreover, a theory of fingering can be evolved which will cover
not only the successive opening of holes as in running up a scale, but
will show quantitatively the effect of opening intermediate holes. Thus
we can fully explain the empirical technique of 'fork-fingering' and
'half stopping' holes. The process gives very precise results, as shown
by the late E. G. Richardson in the 1920s, but it is laborious to apply
since each hole must first be treated separately and then their mutual
effects reconciled.[7]

Irregularities in the Bore of Woodwinds

In examining a series of flutes made between, say, the late 18th
century and the early 20th, it will be seen that in very many of the older
instruments the bore, while maintaining its general geometrical form
of cylinder + inverted cone, is subjected to abrupt step-like contractions.
In later examples this feature disappears and the whole tendency is
towards a completely smooth bore (subject to an exception which we
shall notice shortly). This may well be explained simply as an improvement stemming from better manufacturing techniques in a developing
machine age, but the interrupted bore is to be seen so often that it must
be recognised as a one-time accepted and possibly intentional characteristic. Its practical effect was well understood by the empirical instrument makers and today it has been examined scientifically. In 1953
F. C. Karal published an investigation into the effects of abrupt
changes in the cross-section of circular tubes. He summed up as follows:
'The constriction inductance . . . can be interpreted physically as an
increase in the equivalent length of the tube.' Since, as Richardson
states,[8] the formulae pertaining to cylindrical tubes apply with but little
modification to gently tapering cones also, similar effects may be expected in all types of woodwinds. It will probably not be far wrong to say
that the general effect of 'steps' in some antique flutes is equivalent to
an overall lengthening of the tube.

Another fact now well known is that, in the case of a basically cylindrical pipe, a widening of the bore near an antinode will raise the pitch
of the note sounding, and, conversely, will lower it if near to a node.
Now, an irregularity in the bore which is near a node when the fundamental is sounding may be approached by an antinode when the air

column breaks up to give an harmonic. Thus it is possible for harmonics to be out of tune with their prime tones. Further, as Bouasse of Paris pointed out in 1929, in a cylindro-conical pipe the ratios of the fundamental frequency to those of the higher modes is slightly *more* than the simple 1 : 2 : 3, etc., of the theoretical cylinder.[9] It follows that in the flute the second register is naturally a little sharp to the first, and the third a little more so. Of course Bouasse's observation had been recognised in practical terms by flautists for over two centuries, and steps had been taken accordingly. The situation is explained by Richardson in respect of the modern Boehm flute, where all the contraction of the bore lies between the top side-hole and the mouth-hole, more or less as follows: the mouth-hole being open to the air will always be an antinode. When all the holes are closed the open end of the flute will also be an antinode, and the fundamental sound will be that proper to a cylindrical tube of length equal to that from mouth-hole to open end *lowered* slightly by the contraction near the mouth-hole. In the higher vibrational modes the sounds heard will also be lowered slightly by the contraction near the mouth-hole *but not to the same extent* since some of their antinodes occur at points in the truly cylindrical part of the tube where there is no contraction. The flattening effect of the contraction at the mouth-hole is progressively less as we move into higher modes. The second harmonic will therefore be a little more than the octave above the fundamental, the third a little more than the true twelfth, etc. In the case of the old 'cone-flute' we may apply similar reasoning. Here there is no contraction in the region of the mouth-hole, but there is at the open end, the other antinode of the fundamental. The fundamental sound will therefore again be rather lower than from a pure cylinder of equal length. In the higher modes the intermediate antinodes will fall at points in the tube where, in spite of the general taper, there is *less* contraction than at the open end, so we may again expect less overall flattening or conversely relative sharpness in the higher registers.[10]

How, then, are we to reconcile the three registers of the flute and get reasonable intonation throughout the compass? The answer lies in the small section of the bore between the mouth-hole and the stopper. This small chamber seems to be an essential feature of all more or less sophisticated transverse flutes but its historical origin appears to be untraceable. Perhaps it may be attributed to that hypothetical period when man first began to close the end of natural tubes with artificial stoppers. Such plugs would presumably be pushed in till the most

D

satisfactory results were obtained, and it would then be observed that there remained a space between the face of the plug and the blow-hole. This idea is of course based on hindsight, but it is interesting to note that even in primitive instruments where the natural knot of a reed stem forms the stopper, there is usually some evidence of this chamber. We have already mentioned the need to apply end correction in our calculations concerning side-holes and the open ends of tubes. The mouth-hole, though it has a special function as part of the generator system, is no more exempt from this requirement than any other hole that communicates with the ambient air, and the position of its antinode lies in fact slightly beyond the surface of the head.[11] The true 'speaking length' of any note is from the centre of the mouth-hole to the centre of the note-hole plus appropriate end correction at *both* ends. The body of air in the small chamber that lies beyond the mouth-hole has a similar 'loading' effect to that in the main tube below an open side-hole. In other words it displaces the mouth-hole antinode a little even beyond its 'end corrected' position and so exerts a slight flattening effect on the fundamental. (If we adopt the electrical analogy mentioned on p. 42 below it is in effect a shunt capacity.) Of course ideally, just as with the cut-up of the recorder, there should be a different position of the cork for every note in the fundamental scale, but this being impracticable, a compromise position has to be adopted (see Chapter 1, p. 10). In the two next vibrational modes the air column divides into segments one-half and one-third respectively of the fundamental length, but the dimensions of the chamber cannot change, so its flattening effect becomes markedly greater in these conditions. The practical difficulty is to find the best compromise position for the cork in all circumstances. In some excellently made flutes it is found that although the first and second registers are brought into agreement fairly easily, the third remains stubbornly out. Another compromise is then called for, and the player may find that his best course is to bring the third octave into tune by adjusting the cork, thus rather over-correcting the second which is, however, more readily brought back to pitch by a change of embouchure. It is generally recommended that the cork be placed its own diameter beyond the mouth-hole and fine adjusted so as to bring the d', d", and d''' as nearly into agreement as possible without consciously blowing either 'up' or 'down'. With a well designed and constructed flute any discrepancies within the octaves due to the fixed position of the stopper should now be minimal and readily corrected.

Before leaving the matter of irregularities in the bore we must just touch on two more features which the reader may find in older flutes. The first is the frequent undercutting of the finger-holes which makes them bell-mouthed where they meet the bore. This was usually done with a sort of conical milling cutter or *fraise* (see Chapter 12, Materials and Manufacture). Fraising was initially applied, no doubt, as a practical means of adjusting the tuning of a hole once it had been drilled in its approximate position, and recent investigation has shown that its acoustic effect is generally to increase the admittance of a hole when it is open, and to increase the effective cross-section of the bore when the hole is closed. While not much seen in modern flutes with large holes, fraising is used a good deal in clarinets and oboes and, according to Benade,[12] has benefits to confer in several directions. It has considerable effect on the 'filtering' properties of side-holes which we shall look at in a later section.

The second feature is also concerned with the effective cross-section of the bore. If we measure carefully the bores of older flutes produced by some of the most esteemed makers, we shall find that in many, whatever the average taper of the bore may be, there are specific places where a small local expansion can be detected. We have already noticed on p. 32 the effect of a local expansion in a cylindrical bore—sharpening or flattening according to whether it is near an antinode or a node—and this 'chambering' of the bore, as it is called, represents a rule-of-thumb method of improving certain notes whose holes are, for some reason or other, not ideally placed. It must be remembered that with the wide compass expected in the concert flute some holes must necessarily serve a double or even triple purpose, so that compromise positioning may well be called for. To quote Rockstro: 'Some of the flutes made by the old firm of Rudall and Rose were marvels of ingenuity in this respect'—praise indeed from one who was so often censorious.

Complex Tones and Tonal Spectra

It has been recognised from very early in the history of acoustics that nearly all the sounds that we regard as musical—those which are most appealing or satisfying to us—incorporate frequencies higher than the fundamental. The first satisfactory explanation of the origin of these *partials* or *overtones*, whose presence can often be detected by the unaided ear, was due to Sauveur who, in the course of his investigations of stretched strings, showed that complete and segmental vibrations can occur simultaneously. The same phenomenon can be shown to take place in vibrating air columns.

In 1843 G. S. Ohm, best remembered for his basic law regarding electrical circuits, also formulated a Law of Acoustics which is of the greatest importance. He stated that the ear perceives as pure tones only Simple Harmonic vibrations (harmonic in the mathematical sense here) and that the quality of a complex musical sound depends only on the order, number, and intensity of simple tones which are its components. In the 1860s Ohm's dictum was fully investigated by Helmholtz who, by means of tuned resonators applied to the ear, was able to identify the separate components of complex musical sounds. He was, however, unable to measure their relative intensities,[13] and it was not till the advent of the telephone receiver and the phonograph in the '70s that the first quantitative work came in sight. The extreme complexity of the whole matter then became evident, and it remained for Dayton Miller with his 'phonodeik' of c. 1909, and still later workers with electrical methods, to start getting things formulated. Nowadays, through development of these electrical techniques, we have methods by which the displacement/time relations of air vibrations can be visually displayed on a cathode ray tube, or as a graph, and these analysed by various means. All the standard orchestral voices have by now been subjected to tonal analysis and their characteristics and variations plotted.[14]

For some illustration of these points let us look at the following figures showing wave forms of the sort that are nowadays obtained with the cathode ray oscilloscope. Fig. 11 is the wave form of a pure tone such as that generated by a tuning fork. We notice at once that it is a smooth, symmetrical curve. (Indeed it is the sort of curve that a mathematician would recognise as the resultant of combining sine and co-sine functions for the motion of a particle in a state of simple harmonic or 'pendular' vibration. This fact need not concern us here, however.) Fig. 12 is drawn from one of Dayton Miller's early photographic records made with his phonodeik. It represents the note b″, 995 vibrations per second, as played on the E string of a violin. If we take one complete cycle of vibration from this—points x to y—we see that the curve is not smooth; it has 'humps and hollows' not symmetrically distributed, which immediately suggests that it does not represent a pure tone. Fig. 13 is the result of submitting the same curve to analysis in an harmonic analyser[15]. It shows that there are three components: (1) the fundamental; (2) a second or octave component making two complete cycles in unit time; and (3) a third component making three cycles in unit time. Each of these is, as we see from its shape, a pure tone in itself as postu-

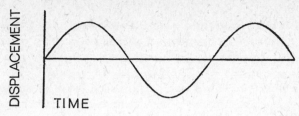

Fig. 11   Wave form of a pure tone

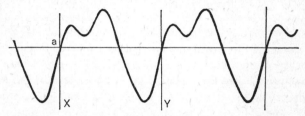

Fig. 12   Wave form of a violin tone (2 cycles)

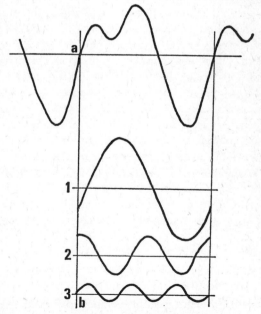

Fig. 13   Harmonic analysis of curve shown in Fig.
12 demonstrating the presence of three principal
components

37

lated by Ohm. Thus this particular violin b″ was a complex tone containing elements of the fundamental, the octave, and the twelfth, and the relative intensities of these partials to each other were as the amplitudes of their individual curves.

Experimenters who have much experience of such wave forms can often recognise the principal components present by the characteristic effects they have on the total wave forms. Tonal analysis by the above method is, however, a slow and laborious process though it remains a monument to the imagination and experimental genius of Dayton Miller. Today other more direct and speedier methods are employed, notably that of 'search-tones', and for a concise description of this we cannot do better than quote the late Professor Bernard Hague in a paper delivered before the Royal Musical Association in 1947. He said: 'The principle of the method can be explained by a simple example. Suppose an instrument to be emitting a pure tone of fixed pitch and given amplitude, and that we have at our disposal a second pure tone of constant amplitude but continuously variable frequency. As the frequency of this "search-tone" is slowly raised from zero, the two sounds will be heard independently until the variable tone approaches the pitch of the fixed tone, when a low-pitched, first-order difference-tone will be observed. This disappears when the fixed and variable sources of sound come into unison, reappears as the variable tone becomes slightly sharp and disappears again as the pitch difference increases. If the sound emitted by the instrument is not pure but contains overtones, difference-tones will appear when the pitch of the search-tone approaches and passes through the frequencies corresponding to each of the partials in turn. The intensity of the difference-tone is in each case proportional to the magnitude of the partial concerned, since that of the search-tone is constant. The experiment is most easily carried out by electrical means, all the sounds being converted into equivalent electric currents which can be amplified and detected by thermionic devices similar to those with which we are all familiar in our wireless sets.'

It is customary today to refer to the products of tonal analysis as *Tonal Spectra* by analogy with the line spectra obtained when examining light with the spectrograph. A very useful type of comparative diagram can be made from tonal spectra by plotting each component identified in a complex tone at its appropriate frequency along a base line measured off in cycles per second, while the relative intensities are represented vertically. A linear scale of frequency is adopted as this

makes it easier to recognise whether the partials are harmonic or not. It
is, however, convenient to use a logarithmic scale for the intensities,
since the type of microphone used in modern investigations measures
the pressure of the sound waves impinging on it, and this convention
allows weaker partials to be more readily displayed. As an example let
us take Fig. 14 which shows the tonal spectrum for three notes distributed over the compass of a typical modern oboe. It reveals three
remarkable facts:

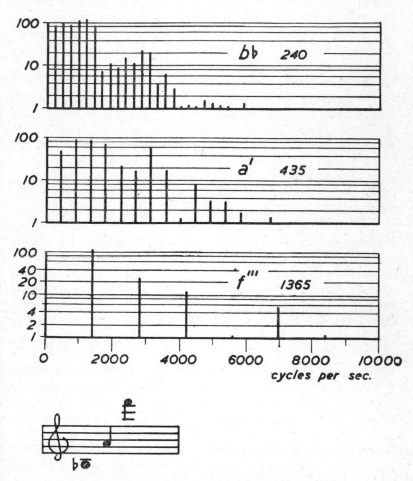

Fig. 14   Tonal spectrum of Oboe (*by permission of the
executors of the late Professor Bernard Hague*)

(1) There are no important overtones of more than 7,000 cycles per second in any part of the compass.

(2) The low and middle registers are rich in overtones up to about the sixteenth harmonic, but the upper is relatively poor.

(3) In the lower register the first five overtones are about equal in strength with the fundamental. The fundamental becomes relatively more prominent in the harmonic array as we ascend. This accounts for the fact that in the orchestral ensemble the different woodwinds are easily identifiable in their lower and middle registers but more difficult for the ear to separate in high passages. In addition, an extended series of such spectra shows that tonal characteristics of instruments are far from consistent throughout their compass and, indeed, even a moderately acute ear can often distinguish differences between one note and the next in the course of a scale.

Now what can tonal spectra tell us about the flute in particular? Fig. 15 shows analyses of the notes d' and d''' as played *mezzo forte* on a cylindrical Boehm flute and on an old conical bore instrument. Comparison of the two spectra is most revealing. In the first place we see that in the d' (288 cycles), the 'six-finger' note of the Boehm instrument, there is little of the fundamental, more of the octave, a prominent twelfth, and the fifteenth or super-octave about equal to the octave. The cone-flute shows a dominant fundamental, a fairly prominent octave, and a rather weak twelfth. In the d''' both instruments show a dominant first frequency of 1,152 cycles per second, but the cylinder flute has two more fairly powerful overtones, while the conical has only one, and that not at all strong. Both types of flute tone are much less complex than that of, for instance, the oboe as we might expect from simply listening to the two instruments in the orchestra. The tone of the Boehm flute is still less pure, however, than that of the conical instrument, a point stressed by the opponents of the new flute long before the days of tonal analysis. Which of the two is the more *interesting* sound is another matter. Both are instantly recognisable as 'flute' and neither could be mistaken for any other instrument except perhaps the French horn, some of whose higher tones approach those of the flute in simplicity of structure.[16] This point we shall take up again in a later paragraph, but before doing so we must turn back for a moment and look at two more functions of the side-holes in a woodwind tube which so far we have regarded as concerned only with the *pitch* of the note sounded.

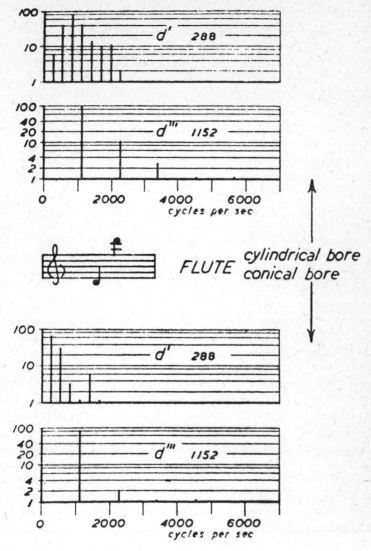

Fig. 15 Comparative spectra of cylindrical and conical flutes (*after Hague*)

Tonal Filtering Effects

The power of discrimination possessed by the ear is one of the marvels of nature which we are only now beginning to understand. From the dawn of human intelligence man has had to 'believe his ears' and he has been aware of many peculiarities in the behaviour of sounds which he has simply had to accept. Among these are the differences in texture between adjacent notes in the scale of an instrument to which we have just referred. How do we now explain these differences in the light of recent research?

Accepting that the tones of nearly all musical instruments are of a complex nature it would seem that there must be some mechanism operating which affects the relative strength of the component partials of adjacent tones to different degrees. What may this be? And where does it come in? In woodwind instruments there are many such factors and possibly not all of them have yet been identified. Certainly one is to be found in the so-called 'annular' or 'skin' effect. It was at one time thought to be sufficient to liken the motion of the air body in a tone-hole —or, for that matter, in any tube—to that of a simple piston in a cylinder. It is now known that such a body of air does not in fact oscillate as a uniform whole, but is much more active near the walls than in the centre. This has a complete analogy in the behaviour of alternating currents which in large conductors tend to crowd into the outer layers. In both the electrical and the acoustical sense this tends to increase the impedance, and the effect is known to increase markedly with the speed of vibration. Thus the skin effect is not the same for all the different frequencies that may be present in a complex tone and may result in a 'tone filtering' process. This phenomenon no doubt accounts in a large measure for the different quality of the same note when sounded from holes of different sizes differently placed in the body of a woodwind (see p. 21 above). To minimise this change in tonal quality is a constant concern with instrument makers, for there are often compelling reasons for placing a tone-hole somewhat away from its theoretical position.[17]

Again, let us look once more at the simple form of the admittance equation we used on p. 31:

$$A = \frac{c}{fda}.$$

We accepted there that for any given tone-hole at any given instant of time the terms d = density of the air, a = the velocity of sound, and

c = Rayleigh's correction factor could all be regarded as constants. But in a complex tone several frequencies are present at once, and for each of them there will be a different value for the term f. It follows that the admittance A of the hole may not be the same for all the components of the note sounding. Thus, again, we may expect a tone modifying effect.

Yet another factor affecting the quality of complex tones as heard from a wind instrument lies in the behaviour of the tube wall itself. This has been fully investigated in respect of brass instruments during the last twenty years or so[18] but there is no doubt that it is to some extent present in all resonating tubes. Briefly, we know that the body-tube of a wind instrument, whatever its material, cannot be *absolutely* rigid and unyielding. Indeed, the stiffer we try to make it the more likely it is to develop mechanical resonances of its own. A proportion of the energy applied to the generator is used up in making the walls of the body vibrate in their own natural frequencies. If any of these frequencies correspond with those already present in a complex tone there may be great amplification, a larger proportion of the total applied energy will go into them, and the sound heard may be greatly modified. In the case of woodwinds where the body-tube is far removed from a simple cylinder or cone by reason of the side-holes the factors governing its natural vibration frequencies become extremely complicated, but research which is still in progress suggests that such tubes may indeed be sensitive to the materials of which they are made. For centuries the playing musician has asserted that the material of his instrument affects his tone profoundly, while the physicist has strenuously denied this. It now begins to look as if there is some scientific basis for the player's view, though it is deeply buried and will call for much more investigation.[19]

Venting

On p. 35 we made passing reference to the fact that in modern woodwinds the note-holes have to serve multiple duties. Not only do they determine the length of the air column in two or more modes of vibration, but in the higher modes they may also be called upon to act as *vents*. In the case of the flute particularly is this important. It will be remembered that when the flautist by adjustment of his embouchure and blowing pressure coaxes his air column to sound its octave, twelfth, or super-octave, groups of antinodes and nodes form in appropriate positions along its length. This is not always easy to bring about and the opening of a side-hole where an antinode is required will assist greatly by not allowing the internal air pressure at that point to rise above that outside the tube. Conversely it will inhibit completely the formation of a node at that point. Part of the traditional technique of flute playing therefore has always been to 'vent' notes in the top register by opening appropriate secondary holes. But just as for the best sound there is an optimum ratio between the diameters of a *tone-hole* and the bore, so there is for a *vent-hole*, and these two optima may not agree. For a given size of bore an efficient vent-hole must be neither too large nor too small, so in boring a hole to serve both functions the flute-maker has again to make a compromise. His best solution to the difficulty may involve slightly displacing a *tone*-hole from its theoretical position and adjusting its size, or re-tuning it by 'undercutting' or 'chambering' the bore. This problem was particularly acute with the older cone-bored simple flutes with small holes, but it is also present in modern cylinder instruments. In the former case the need to make the holes small enough to be easily covered by the fingers and yet be in tune resulted in their being placed far too high to be ideal vents, and various hybrid fingerings became necessary in the third octave. Theobald Boehm gave great attention to this matter when designing his new instrument.

Apart from the value of vent-holes in *easing* the production of the highest register (and a strong player *can* in fact produce three octaves on his flute without recourse to them) they have another function which was, I believe, first commented on by R. S. Rockstro in 1889. On pages 60–61 and 178–79 of his *Treatise on The Flute* he states that the twelfths and fifteenths used in the third register are, unless vented, uncertain, and of unpleasant quality due to the audible presence of what he called 'lower attendant sounds.' We must remember that Rockstro's observations were made before the days of tonal analysis, but it appears that these objectionable sounds may have been persistent fundamentals or octave harmonics which would have been inhibited by venting at the appropriate point (see p. 27 above). Furthermore, as Rockstro also pointed out, a well placed vent-hole by its influence on the distribution of nodes and antinodes may do much to improve the tuning of the difficult third octave.

Formants

In our consideration of the tonal spectra of woodwinds we have already noticed the differences in quality which the ear can distinguish between adjacent notes in a scale, and which have been confirmed by tonal analysis. We must accept that this tonal inconsistency does exist, yet in spite of this our ears also tell us that each instrument gives us a sense of homogeneity over its entire compass and possesses an overall individuality of timbre to which it owes its accepted place in organised music. How does this come about? The matter may be purely subjective, and perhaps it is due to the listener becoming conditioned to accept any quality of sound within certain previously experienced limits as characteristic of the instrument. It seems, however, to go much deeper. We suspect, in fact, that running through the entire compass there is some further factor which is not explained by the classical acoustic concepts that have so far served us. The *Theory of Formants* seems to supply an explanation.

It appears that throughout at least the most distinctive part of its range each instrument shows a fixed group of prominent frequencies which are always present in the tonal spectrum whatever the nominal note sounded may be. This phenomenon was observed as long ago as 1837 during Sir Charles Wheatstone's investigation of vowel sounds, and it led to his 'fixed pitch' theory of vowels, later to be established by Helmholtz. Briefly, the Wheatstone–Helmholtz concept was that every vowel, no matter on what note it may be uttered, is determined by certain fixed frequencies that are invariably present.[20] To a great extent experiment has confirmed this theory, and very sensitive methods devised by Dayton Miller revealed the presence of these characteristic frequencies even in whispered vowels quite un-phonated. Further, it has been shown that certain vowels contain more than one outstanding permanent frequency. This can be explained by the existence of *selective resonances* in the air cavities of the head. In 1897 these distinguishing frequencies were named 'formants' by the physicist Hermann-Goldap. Now we have already seen that the body-tubes of wind instruments possess complicated natural resonances; a thick-walled tube with side-holes has certain frequency filtering properties as do the bells of brass instruments; the bells of certain woodwinds possess permanent cavity resonances which we can measure. Further, the tone quality a given air column will yield is profoundly influenced by the type of generator by which it is energised.[21] Facts of this sort taken together seem to offer some analogy with the human voice apparatus. Assuming this analogy Hermann-Goldap analysed the tones of a number of orchestral instruments and satisfied himself that each showed a characteristic array of frequencies always present throughout the compass.

He therefore announced that orchestral instruments, like the voice, possessed formants, and in them he claimed to have identified the source of *timbre*. To the acousticians of his time Hermann-Goldap's theory appeared quite revolutionary and, in spite of some early confirmation in Dayton Miller's work and by Stumpf in 1926,[22] it has proved rather slow of acceptance. Today the theory is more generally accepted, though some few authorities are still sceptical. It will be wise, I think, to admit that it still requires further work, and indeed some of the originator's own findings show this clearly. For example, two instruments of very different character which he investigated, an oboe and a clarinet, both showed the same formant range, the only difference being that in the oboe it proved to be more powerful than the fundamental tone, while in the clarinet the fundamental was predominant. The conclusion is that the mere presence of a formant may not be the sole determinant of timbre. In woodwind spectra the formants are very clearly distinguishable (less so in the flute than in the reeds, it must be admitted), but in the brass, with the notable exception of the horn, they are not so easy to recognise, being often masked by the large range of other closely packed harmonics.

Beyond its application to single instruments the idea of formants can be extended to an infinite degree and opens up vast fields of speculation. Just as some simple tones will 'beat' together to produce a 'difference tone', so, we conceive, may the components of a formant range. Perhaps we may find that the formants of two different instruments playing together will unite to give a new formant characteristic of the combination. Consider, too, that instruments playing in unison may yet perhaps have formants whose components are dissonant. Multiply these simple cases by the number of individual instruments which now appear together in the symphony orchestra, and the complexity of the resultant sound almost baffles the imagination. Yet it is probably in this very complexity—in what Bonavia-Hunt has called 'the clash of myriads of formants'—that we find the brilliance of the full orchestra or the grandeur of the organ chorus; brilliance and grandeur that no single instrument possesses.[23]

To end this chapter it is necessary to add a few words about the future of acoustical research in connection with wind instruments. In the foregoing paragraphs the general behaviour of the flute as it is known today, its inconsistencies and apparent anomalies, have been described. Much of our knowledge of these matters is based on methods of physical experiment that were not available to practical acousticians even as late as the first quarter of the present century. These have revealed the influence of some factors not envisaged in the concepts of classical acoustics. In a small book such as this it is neither possible nor, I think, desirable to do more than draw the reader's attention to such factors, but there is no doubt that future work in instrumental acoustics will be directed to quantitative investigation of them. Such work is indeed already under way in the hands of A. H. Benade of Case Institute of Technology, Cleveland, Ohio, and other scholars. Their method of approach is to formulate mathematical equations representing the ideal characteristics of musical tubes, and then to modify their equations by quantities representing the known departures from the ideal that are found in practical playing instruments. This line of research will in due time lead to new methods of experimental verification, and perhaps ultimately to formulae that would make it possible to synthesise musical instruments from first principles. This is, of course, an exercise for mathematicians of high attainment, but those readers who are familiar with the operations of calculus will take great pleasure in those papers which have already been published since 1959 (see note 6, p. 48). In illustration of this approach, and the clarity of thinking it calls for, we may well end by quoting the heading summary of Benade's first paper 'On Woodwind Instrument Bores'. 'The properties of horns that are suitable for use in woodwinds are deduced from first principles. The cylindrical pipe and complete cone are shown to be the only shapes which satisfy the requirements exactly. The behavior of nearly perfect cylinders and almost complete cones is described, the influence of closed finger holes on the effective bore of an instrument is discussed, and the effect of the mouthpiece cavity is analysed. Damping of the normal modes by the walls of the bore is shown to play a dominant role in the playing behavior and tone color of woodwinds, and various consequences are deduced.'

NOTES

[1] The *medium* may in fact be solid, liquid, or gas. The last is the most familiar only because we live all our normal lives, as it were, at the bottom of a sea of gas. There are plenty of examples of sound conduction in solid media, however, in our every-day experience.

[2] This phenomenon was observed by Aristotle; was discussed by Marin Mersenne in his *Harmonie Universelle*, Paris, Baudry, 1636; and was fully investigated by Sauveur of Paris in 1701.

Joseph Sauveur (1653–1710) was born a deaf-mute but learned to speak at the age of seven. In later life he became a most distinguished acoustician and wrote several original and important works on his subject. It was he who, from his observations of vibrating strings, coined the term *Partial Tones*.

From the series of fractions quoted in the text it will be seen that it is possible for some partial tones to be mathematically incommensurate and therefore mutually 'out of tune'. They can, in fact, be 'inharmonic'. The noun *Harmonic* is quite commonly used as a synonym for *Partial Tone* or *Overtone*, and the British Standards Institution *Glossary of Acoustical Terms and Definitions* (1936) recognises this. French acousticians, however, make the definite distinction that a harmonic is a pure tone while a partial is complex and may contain its own array of overtones. (See A. Wood, *Students Physics*, Vol. II, London, Blackie, 1943.)

There are also differences in accepted usage between physicists and musicians. To the former the nth harmonic implies a frequency equal to n times the fundamental, whereas in music it means a frequency of $(n + 1)$ times the fundamental.

[3] McGillivray, A. J., in the *Galpin Society Journal*, Vol. X, 1957, p. 92.

[4] For an excellent description and illustrations of experiments to demonstrate these points the reader is referred to E. G. Richardson, *The Acoustics of Orchestral Instruments*, London, Edward Arnold and Co., 1929, pp. 34 *et seq.*

The reader will appreciate that the accounts of organ flue-pipes given in both Richardson's and Wood's books are confined to their general behaviour, and have only been drawn upon here sufficiently to make a basis for the discussion of 'air-reed' orchestral instruments. A full investigation of 'labial' organ pipes as they are today after centuries of empirical development reveals many factors that affect their total behaviour, and some of these have not yet been completely formulated.

Pipe voicers have long been aware of these factors and have manipulated them by 'rule-of-thumb', but even with modern acoustical knowledge their work still remains less an exact science than a fine art practised by the specially gifted individual.

[5] The peculiar limpid quality of so-called harmonic stops is greatly appreciated by connoisseurs of organ tone. It is obtained by voicing the pipes so as to suppress the fundamental completely and stress the octave harmonic. Formerly this effect was secured by keeping the mouth extremely low in relation to the wind pressure, and adjustment for certainty in speech was extremely tricky. A more secure method of obtaining similar results, now almost universally used, was introduced by A. Cavaillé-Coll, the celebrated Paris organ builder, in the mid-19th century. He made a small perforation in his pipes at the mid point, thus positively preventing the formation of a node there. The effect is parallel to the use of 'speaker' or 'register' keys in reed instruments. See Philip Bate, *The Oboe*, London, Ernest Benn Ltd., 1956 and 1962, pp. 119 *et seq.*

The reader's attention is here drawn to a point that, for the sake of simplicity, has not been stressed in the general text. In making comparisons between organ flue-pipes and the tin whistle or vertical flutes we may note that although the length of air column in the latter is variable, the diameter of the tube cannot be. Hence in playing a scale on the whistle the length/diameter ratio may vary from note to note, and result in a progressive change in tone quality. In a stop of pipes both length and diameter decrease proportionately as we go upwards. If an organ builder wishes to make a stop to imitate an orchestral wind instrument he will remember this point and will progressively vary the voicing of his pipes.

[6] Benade, A. H., 'On Woodwind Instrument Bores', *Journal of the Acoustical Society of America*, Vol. 31, No. 2, Feb. 1959, pp. 137–46; 'On the Mathematical Theory of Woodwind Finger Holes', *op. cit.*, Vol. 32, No. 12, Dec. 1960, pp. 1591–1608; A. H. Benade and J. W. French, 'Analysis of the Flute Head Joint', *op. cit.*, Vol. 37, No. 4, April 1965, pp. 679–91.

[7] Richardson, E. G., *op. cit.*, Appendix, pp. 147 *et seq.*

Irons, E. J., 'On the fingering of Conical Wind Instruments', *Phil. Mag.*, Vol. 11, 1931, pp. 535 *et seq.*

As long ago as 1775 Lambert published a theory of fingering for the conical flute in the Memoirs of the Academy of Berlin; again see Irons.

[8] Richardson, E. G., *op. cit.*, p. 62.

[9] Bouasse, H., *Tuyaux et Resonateurs*, Paris, Librairie Delagrave, 1929, Chapter 10.

[10] The reader who cares to experiment with older flutes is advised that he may in fact get very inconsistent results. There appears, for instance, to have been little agreement between makers as to the degree or regularity of taper to be employed, and the preferred sizes of finger-holes relative to bore vary a great deal. Bessaraboff, in his *Ancient European Musical Instruments*, Harvard University Press, 1941, points out that nominally cylindrical heads are often slightly tapered in the bore, which he attributes to the need to allow for 'draft' in the use of reamers. The writer's own experience in wood turning does not bear this out. Many cone-flutes are also slightly opened out at the extreme end of the foot joint. All these are factors which may have some influence on the total performance of an instrument.

[11] This particular end correction is very difficult to assess correctly as it is constantly modified by the changing position of the player's lips. Indeed, deliberately varying this factor is one of the accepted techniques by which the flautist controls the intonation of his instrument. Moreover the player's actual mouth cavity has an effect here. When he is blowing his instrument the air-body in the flautists's mouth—and, to extend the point, in his lungs as well—is loosely coupled to that in the tube of his instrument, so that resonances between the two may be set up. But the shape and volume of the mouth cavity are continuously variable, so the complexity of the relationship becomes extreme.

[12] Benade, A. H., note 6, above, reference 2, p. 1603.

[13] Helmholtz, H. L. F., *The Sensations of Tone*, translated by Alexander J. Ellis, 2nd edn., London, Longmans, Green and Co., Chapter IV.

[14] Wegel, R. L., and Moore, C. R., 'An electrical frequency analyser', *Transactions American Institute of Electrical Engineers*, Vol. 42, 1924, pp. 457–65.

Grützmacher, M., 'Eine neue Methode der Klanganalyse', *Elektrische Nachtrichten-technik*, Vol. 4, 1927, pp. 533–45.

Salinger, H., 'Zur Theorie der Frequenzanalyse mittels Suchtons', *Elekt. Nach.*, Vol. 6, 1929, pp. 293–302.

Meyer, E., and Buchmann, G., 'Die Klangspektren der Musikinstrumente', *Sitzungberichte der Preuss. Akad. der Wissenschaft*, 1931, pp. 735–78.

Fletcher, H., 'Loudness, pitch, and the timbre of musical tones and their relation to the intensity, the frequency and the overtone structure', *Journal of the Acoustical Society of America*, Vol. 6, 1934, pp. 59–69.

Damman, A., 'Analyse des sons musicaux', *Comptes Rendus*, Vol. 208, 1929, pp. 1283–5.

[15] The need for a convenient method of determining the relative values of the components of complex curves led, about the turn of this century, to the design of several most ingenious mechanical harmonic analysers. With these machines the passage of a stylus over a trace of one wavelength of the subject curve drawn to a specific scale caused different dials to indicate directly the proportions of some of the higher harmonics present. For an explanation of the mechanics involved and the limitations of the method see Dayton C. Miller, *The Science of Musical Sounds*, 2nd edn., New York, The Macmillan Co., 1926.

E

[16] For example, according to the same set of analyses already quoted in the text the d′ of the French horn crooked in F has only three components—a powerful definitive frequency of 288 cycles and two much less powerful at 576 and approximately 861 cycles, a spectrum very similar to many in the range of the flute.

[17] An extreme case is illustrated by the c″♯ hole on the Boehm cylinder flute. The arguments for its finally accepted size and placing as set out by Boehm himself, with comments by Dayton C. Miller, will be found on pages 29–31 of *The Flute and Flute-playing*, Miller's invaluable translation of *Die Flöte und das Flötenspiel*, second English edn., London, Rudall, Carte and Co., 1922.

[18] Jeans, Sir James, *Science and Music*, London, Macmillan and Co., 1937, p. 144.

Knauss, H. P., and Yeager, W. J., 'Vibrations of the Walls of a Cornet', *Journal of the Acoustical Society of America*, Vol. 13, 1941, pp. 160–62.

[19] Benade, A. H., note 6 above, reference i, p. 144.

[20] As an illustration, if I, a baritone, sing the vowel *ah* on every note in the range of my voice, measurements show that there is always present a constant frequency of around 824 cycles per second. Now let somebody else, say a soprano, sing the same vowel on her complete range of notes. We shall find again the outstanding 824 cycles. This is because when we sing *ah* the lips, tongue, and soft palate take up a definite position and the mouth and other air cavities become a resonating chamber which responds chiefly to a frequency of 824.

See Also Mackworth-Young, G., *What Happens in Singing*, London, Newman Neame, 1953, pp. 20, 25, and 98–9.

[21] If, by way of an experiment, the reader cares to fix a clarinet mouthpiece to the body of a trumpet or a trombone he may be a little surprised at the tone this hybrid will produce. It will be essentially clarinet tone with very little suggestion (except as regards pitch which is of course a function of tube length) of characteristic brass quality.

[22] Hermann-Goldap, E., 'Uber die Klangfarbe einige Orchesterinstrumente', *Ann. der Phys.*, Vol. 23, 1907, pp. 979–85.

Stumpf, C., 'Splachlaute und Instrumentalklänge', *Zeitschrift für Physik*, Vol. 38, 1926, pp. 745–58.

[23] Bonavia-Hunt, N. A., 'What is the Formant?', *Musical Opinion and the Organ World*, Dec. 1948, p. 151, and Jan. 1949, p. 209.

CHAPTER 3

Origins: The Flutes of Primitive Peoples: The Transverse Flute in Antiquity

IT IS a rather surprising fact that in spite of its familiarity today, less is known of the transverse flute in its ultimate origins than of most other wind instruments. In the stories of most orchestral instruments there are points at which we can say 'here the modern form began clearly to emerge'—but in the case of the flute this is not so. As we have seen in Chapter 1, flutes are in use today which range from the very simple to the highly mechanised, and although the latter are in general dominant in the orchestral field, the simple instruments are not excluded from it. They are regularly employed in other forms of highly sophisticated music. It is true that in the course of its history the transverse flute has undergone two major reforms, one of which we can date with tolerable accuracy, and the other absolutely, but neither can be regarded as the starting point of a definitive instrument. It follows, then, that in preparing even a condensed history of the flute the writer must start as far back as any available information permits, and he must realise that although the fundamental principles involved have been recognised since prehistoric times, practical evidence of the earliest stages is meagre indeed. Moreover, the situation is complicated by the fact that the transverse flute—to many non-specialists the only flute they recognise—is in fact only one sub-species of the great genus *Flute* which musico-ethnologists have defined.[1] The first diagnostic feature throughout this genus is the presence of the so-called 'air-reed', regardless of how it is modified or controlled, and of the form of the resonating body. The word *flute*, therefore, must be used with some care and regard for context.

It is a generally accepted principle of ethnological research that we may gain some idea of the life of prehistoric peoples by observing the behaviour of primitive races who still live in remote parts of the world in what we believe to be prehistoric conditions, as shown by their artifacts, dwellings, and so on. Thus, for instance, we sometimes hear of the 'stone-age' people of central New Guinea. No doubt this principle is in its essence sound, but it must nevertheless be applied with

considerable caution. We have no means of knowing for certain that the
modern primitive and the prehistoric communities we wish to compare
actually thought along the same lines, or indeed, if they represent the
same stage of mental development. Similarity in their artifacts may have
been dictated by the mere availability of similar raw materials. The
behaviour of a modern primitive community is not necessarily a sure
guide since it may possibly be conditioned by the very circumstances
that make it amenable to observation. Though retaining what we
regard as primitive characteristics, a community may have been
influenced by continued contact with more advanced people, and may
well have absorbed something from the latter into their own original
culture. Flutes in particular, from their shape, have for many races
a phallic connotation and are involved in fertility rites or magic
ceremonies which may not be shown to the stranger. It is not at all
easy in such circumstances to interpret our observations with true
objectivity.[2] We must also remember that today we find a continued use
of quite unsophisticated 'home-made' folk instruments in the remoter
parts of some European countries whose general level of culture is as
high as any, and whose metropolitan centres provide up-to-date symphony orchestras of international repute.

Primitives

A serious difficulty in determining the relative age of really ancient
musical instruments lies in the fact that many were, no doubt, made of
perishable materials, and where interment is involved only shell, bone,
or metal has as a rule survived. In an effort to define alternative criteria
of the age of musical instruments the late Professor Curt Sachs in 1929,
and Erich von Hornbostel in 1933,[3] adopted what they termed a
'geographical' method of assessment that did not involve supposed
levels of culture and workmanship as then generally accepted. The
theory of this method is rather too complicated to be quoted at length
here, but Sachs outlined it very clearly in a later book to which the
reader is strongly recommended.[4] Since this publication a considerable
literature on various aspects of the subject has accumulated, but there
is still little that is comprehensive. It is mainly on Sachs, therefore, that
we shall draw in this chapter, and we begin by noticing one of his most
remarkable conclusions: viz. that of all the flutes, the transverse type and
the plain tube blown across the open end are both of later origin than
the 'whistles', though both are obviously of simpler construction.
Sachs quotes what we may call 'generic' flutes without side-holes from

paleolithic excavations; similar instruments with side-holes from *neolithic* sites; but transverse flutes only from *late neolithic* sources.[5]

At this point the reader may well remark that although we have made some progress towards *dating* the earliest known flutes we still have not accounted for their actual origin—how they first came into being—and it must be confessed that we just do not know. It has been suggested that perhaps an attempt to suck or blow the marrow from a broken bone gave rise to a sound that some prehistoric man interpreted as the voice of the bone itself, or perhaps the wind blowing across the broken ends of a grove of reeds generated sounds that attracted his attention. All this is conjecture, and utterly unsupported, but as to the latter idea the writer well remembers a curious experience. Many years ago, while walking over a cliff top golf links in eastern Scotland he heard a strange, not unmusical, wailing. On investigation this rather eerie sound proved to be due to the wind blowing through holes in the stout bamboo poles that carried some of the putting-green flags. A local golfer told him that these self-actuating whistles had been intentionally designed to give an audible direction signal in some cases where the green was out of direct sight of the tee. A man-made device this certainly, but was it perhaps remotely allied to the ultimate origin of the flute? Who can tell?

Antiquity

Between prehistoric man and the earliest civilisations with something of a recorded history we encounter the first great gap in our knowledge of musical instruments though this, to be sure, represents a break in a cultural sense rather than a definite time interval. We must remember that the terms Paleolithic, Neolithic, Bronze Age, etc., signify phases in man's technological development and not particular divisions of an absolute time scale. Nor did these phases necessarily give place to their successors at the same time in all parts of the world. Thus, the Stone Age drew to a close in the Middle East with the discovery of metals about 4,000 years B.C., but in Britain Stone Age culture persisted for at least another two millennia. Further, we have some evidence to show that certain prehistoric peoples had a way of life that was by no means primitive. Our difficulty lies in linking the prehistoric with the remote historic, and it was during this interregnum that a new concept emerged —that of music as art or for entertainment, and with it the seeds of a professional class of musicians. From this point on we can begin to divide instruments into two categories, folk or popular instruments, and those cultivated by professional players, though, of course, the two need

not be mutually exclusive. Also, with written evidence to draw on, we
have to distinguish if we can between factual accounts, legends which
may or may not be founded on fact, and frank mythology. Concerning
the flute we have to deal with mythology in a big way. [6]

The history of the higher civilisations as it concerns us here appears
to begin in Mesopotamia, the once fertile plain between the Rivers
Tigris and Euphrates which is today divided between the states of
Syria and Iraq. Here the earliest recorded rulers were the Sumerians,
a people of uncertain race who seem to have entered the area from
further east between 5,000 and 4,000 years B.C. After some two thousand
years of occupation, more or less contemporary with the 'Old Kingdom'
in Egypt, the Sumerians gave place to the Babylonians who were a
semitic race. About 1750 B.C. the Kassites, a non-semitic race, invaded
the area again from the east. These were succeeded in turn by Assyrians,
a second wave of Babylonians (the Dynasty of King Nebuchadnezzar
and the period of the Babylonian exile of the Jews), and the Medes and
Persians. Finally, from 331 B.C. the land fell under the domination of
the Greeks as they pushed their empire eastward and into Egypt. The
writing of the Sumerians was cuneiform and recent success in decipher-
ing this script has given us a good deal of information about their
musical instruments. We know the Sumerian names for a number of
these, and illustrations on seals, sculptures, and mosaics have shown us
their forms, but scholars have had much trouble in correlating names
with pictures. Actual examples of instruments from ancient Mesopotamia are very rare, and the few we have come mainly from excavations
in the royal cemetery at Ur, reputed birthplace of Abraham. Among all
these sources we find no mention of anything that may be identified as
a *transverse* flute, although a simple vertical tube does appear.

Egypt

During the earlier periods of their history there was evidently intimate contact between the great civilisations of Mesopotamia and Egypt,
and in musical matters the relationship is very clear. At some time before
2700 B.C., however, the link seems to have been severed. The Kassite
invasion from Central Asia ended the first Babylonian period, and the
nomadic Hyksos destroyed the Egyptian Middle Kingdom. There
followed a period of darkness about which we know very little, but with
the emergence of the New Kingdom, whose warlike rulers in their turn
took the initiative and penetrated eastwards, fresh influences become
evident. Rather surprisingly the characteristics of Egyptian music now

appear as strongly Asiatic, as if the invaders had absorbed the culture
and habits of the lands they conquered instead of imposing their own.

In respect of Egypt there are two factors which are of great importance to the archaeologist, one the climate, the other the psychology
of the people. The extreme aridity of much of the country has favoured
the preservation of organic materials so that more or less complete
musical instruments have survived in some quantity. As to psychology,
for long periods the religious concepts of the Egyptians were dominated
by the idea of a heaven in which the redeemed would live an idealised
version of his earthly existence. The belief that representations of
happy domestic scenes, feasting, singing, dancing, etc., could by magic
influence assure the same felicity in the after life gave birth to a wealth
of tomb paintings and sculptures in which musical instruments often
figure. Moreover, the tomb painters had a charming habit of filling in
spaces in their compositions with short pithy captions from which we
know the authentic names of nearly all Egyptian instruments. From
New Kingdom Egypt we have datable flutes both in captioned illustrations, and in actual substance, but they are still not side-blown *transverse* flutes. For the first evidence concerning these we have to wait
nearly another two thousand years, and to look not in Africa but in
Europe.

The ancient Egyptian flutes, though not ancestors of our modern
orchestral instrument, are of great interest and importance, for they
represent the earliest illustrations of a type which exists today all over
the Islamic world under the common title of *nāy* (Persian origin) or in
parts of North Africa as *quasāsba* (Arabic). A slate slab from Hieracono-
polis dating from the fourth millennium B.C. carries the oldest known
picture of the instrument, after which illustrations are common. These
flutes usually take the form of a simple straight tube cut from a cane
about a yard long, approximately half an inch in diameter, and pierced
with from four to six holes towards the lower end. Although they are
smaller than many ceremonial flutes used by primitive peoples today,
the length of these instruments nevertheless dictated the position in
which they were held for playing—slanting obliquely downwards
across the body. In this position the player could blow across the upper
end of the tube and control his *embouchure* with ease, thus commanding
far greater musical possibilities than are yielded by any sort of whistle
mouthpiece (Fig. 16). To quote Sachs, 'no instrument had a more
incorporeal sound, a sweeter *sostenuto*, a more heartfelt *vibrato*'. These
virtues depend, of course, on the comparatively narrow bore of the cane

used for the tube. Larger canes such as we find in many primitive flutes today imperatively demand the use of some sort of channelled mouth-piece since the unconfined breath of the player is too weak to blow across so wide a tube. The inevitably lower musical potential of these devices is one of the principal characteristics which led Sachs to assign whistle flutes to a lower, and probably older, cultural stratum than the simple cross-cut tube.

Fig. 16   Ancient Egyptian flute-player. From a damaged stele, *c.* 1350 B.C.

Israel

Of all the ancient peoples of the Near East, Israel, with her many vicissitudes, contacts with other civilisations, and survival to the present day, might be expected to yield information about the music of the past. In some respects this is so, for it is among the present-day Jewish people that we find in use the one instrument that has remained exactly as it was in the time of Moses—the ritual horn *Shophar*; and we have also detailed descriptions of the metal trumpet *Hasosra*. This very word *description*, however, epitomises the enquirer's problem in dealing with the musical life of Israel. As Mosaic teaching was opposed to the por-trayal of men or objects of any kind, scholars are deprived of the help of contemporary painting or sculpture, and philological sources are almost all that are available. The bulk of our information, then, is drawn from the Bible and the Talmud. We can hardly imagine more different circumstances and material than those offered by Sumeria or Egypt.

The ancient history of the Jews can be conveniently divided into the *Nomadic Period* which lasted till about 1000 B.C., and the *Period of the Kings* extending up to the dawn of Christianity. In the Pentateuch we find comparatively little mention of music, though, as Sachs has been at pains to point out, this does not mean that it was unusual or disdained. On the contrary, the references we have show that music was a common and universal expression of the people in both joy and sorrow. At that period they only differed from some of their contemporaries in not recognising a specific musician class. The first mention of musical instruments in the Bible occurs in Genesis 4:21, where Jubal, son of Lamech, is described as 'the father of all such as handle the harp and organ', and we can at once discard the second name as a translator's convenient substitution. The Hebrew text has the words *kinnor* and *ugâb*, the latter an extremely rare term which occurs again only in Job 21:12 and 30, and the 150th Psalm. Curiously enough both these references belong to the most recent sections of the Old Testament, while the first is among the earliest. The true interpretation of *ugâb* is in great doubt though there is perhaps some justification for supposing it to have been a flute of the type that was certainly in use among shepherds in Mesopotamia, Egypt, and ancient Arabia. Some translators have interpreted the word as pan-pipes but this can hardly be supported since the first evidences of that instrument occur only some two thousand years later than the epoch described in Genesis. There are also linguistic reasons for rejecting pan-pipes.[7] *Kinnor*, the other instrument connected with Jubal, is also that made famous by King David, and has for ages been erroneously called 'King David's Harp'. If, however, we go back to the first translators of the Hebrew text, and to the Vulgate of *c.* A.D. 400, we find what is almost certainly the correct interpretation, i.e. a *lyre* of the sort that the Greeks called *kithara*.

When we turn to the Period of the Kings we find a very different state of affairs in Israel. There was now a monarchical form of Government similar to that of neighbouring states; there was a Court which received embassies from them; and the people generally were exposed to foreign cultures. In these circumstances professional musicians were recognised and officially encouraged, especially in the time of King David to serve the Temple. In the Old Testament books covering this period we find the names of several instruments that are new to us— but again none that can be specifically termed a flute. It is true that modern translators of the Bible have used 'flute' for the Hebrew word *hālîl* (derived from a verb *hālál* meaning 'pierced'), but there is no justifying evidence from parallel civilisations of the time. On the other hand the Talmudian tractates contain a wealth of commentary on the Jewish use of *reed-pipes*, both twinned and single, as known all over the ancient world. For example, the tractate *Ktubot* IV:4 tells us that in Israel even the poorest men hired at least two *hālilîm* to play at the funerals of their wives; and much later we read in St Matthew that when Christ entered the house of Jairus he found the funeral pipers playing by the body of the supposedly dead daughter. These reed-pipes the Romans later called the 'Phoenician Pipe', and it seems probable that the Jews absorbed them from that nation.[8] Finally, we note that in the *Septuaginta hālîl* is translated exclusively as *aulós* and in the Vulgate as *tibia*; respectively Greek and Latin terms associated with the reed-pipe.

Greece, Rome, Etruria

In such a condensed survey as this we may reasonably consider Greece and Rome together, since in their times southern Europe in general formed one musical area enjoying overall the same heritage and influences. Basic instrumental types were the same throughout the area even if their names varied according to language or local usage.

The arts in which the Greeks excelled were those of sculpture and architecture, and, although naturally they derived technical principles from earlier civilisations, their genius was such as to create a classical canon which directed the progress of Western art for two thousand years and even influenced the Buddhist Orient. With such achievements in the visual arts it seems a little strange that music in Ancient Greece did not undergo a parallel development, but such appears to be the case. Certainly the Greeks worked out the mathematics of music to a very advanced degree and their philosophers discussed its psychological effects, but the *practice* of music seems in the first place to have been imported. The Phrygian and Lydian *modes* which became part of Greek musical organisation are interval sequences strongly reminiscent of some common in Asia Minor; and concerning instruments the geographer Strabo remarks: 'One writer says "striking the Asiatic cithara"; another calls auloi "Berecyntian" and "Phrygian"; and some instruments have been called by barbarian names.' Admittedly, when the Greek musical system had been codified its terminology was clearly derived from instrumental allusions,[9] but the instruments themselves remained simple, almost primitive, by comparison with other appurtenances of Greek life. The words 'kitharody' and 'aulody', meaning the accompaniment of song on the *kithara* or *aulós*, are common in Greek texts and indicate that among the Hellenes instrumental music was generally held as subordinate to, and taking its inspiration from, the spoken word. Plato, though probably representing ultra-conservative opinion, went so far as to condemn pure instrumental performance as pointless 'show-off' and to regard it as in the worst of taste. Ancient Greek literature abounds in references to music, as do her sculptures and particularly her vase paintings. Here we repeatedly find representations of musical scenes and instruments, somewhat formalised perhaps, but none the less informative for that. On the whole strings predominate among these illustrations, as we might perhaps expect since the invention of string music was traditionally attributed to Apollo. The *lyre* in particular symbolised for the Greeks the so-called Apollonian side of their ethos, harmony, moderation, and mental balance. Pipes, on the other hand, stood for the Dionysian aspect, ecstasy, and even inebriation. This, too, is readily understood when we consider that the most prominent Greek wind instrument was the *aulós*, a reed-pipe of somewhat Oriental appearance whose shrill voice could be as stimulating as any Highland bagpipe. It was no 'soft complaining flute' that excited the warlike passions of the Greek Heroes and encouraged the young men to prodigies on the athletic field.[10]

It has over the years become the custom to interpret *aulós* as 'flute', which is both wrong and misleading, and which has given rise to much confusion among scholars in other disciplines than music. This has resulted in such errors as the restoration of broken antique statuary in attitudes dictated by the cross-blown flute,[11] when no undamaged examples earlier than about 200 B.C. are known. During pre-Christian times Greek and Roman artists depicted many vertically blown pipes, but there is no evidence that any of these were in fact flutes even in the Egyptian tradition. Indeed, the mouth-band *phorbeiá* or *capistrum*[12]—so often illustrated by these men—is clearly incompatible with the sensitive *embouchure* demanded by such instruments. How this error first crept in is not known; but we should not blame the older scholars over much, for it certainly originated at a time when the science of organology hardly existed, and long before we possessed all the data on which the modern classification of instruments is based. No doubt its origin could be traced, but at the present time this would surely be an unprofitable piece of research. One suggestion may perhaps be made; that the word *flute*, presumably derived from the Latin *flatus* = a blast or breathing, might reasonably be applied to any *blown* instrument, much as in parts of America today popular usage terms any tapered brass instrument a 'horn'. On the other hand, we must observe that throughout antiquity trumpets and horns seem always to have had their own distinctive proper names. Today, I think, we must just accept the situation and be on our guard when referring to the older historians. Fortunately the descriptive value of much of their work is very little affected.[13]

It has already been said that in pre-Christian times neither Greek nor Roman artists are known to have depicted any flute, but by the second century A.D. Rome seems to have become acquainted with the instrument, though from what source we cannot tell. Stamped on a coin of the Syrian town of Caesarea and dating from the year 169, there appears a true flute, and, moreover, this is a *transverse* flute. Since this coin originated in an Eastern colonial area of the Roman Empire we might perhaps suspect an Eastern influence in its design, but this is no more than speculation. For a long time this specimen remained unique, but a few years ago a second illustration came to light, this time from an Etruscan source. We have not so far touched on Etruria in this chapter, mainly because compared with the other civilisations of the ancient world she seems to have remained rather backward in music. The major achievements of the Etruscans lay in the field of metal working; they were the great bronze-founders of the Mediterranean area in pre-Celtic times and both Greeks and Romans attributed to them the invention of the trumpet. Today sufficient tomb paintings and reliefs of Etruscan origin are known to give us a good idea of their musical resources, and though they did have both reed-pipes and lyres, these were considerably less developed than contemporary Greek examples. Yet, recent excavations in the *Sepolcro dei Volumni* near Perugia have revealed one of the most important of all musical remains. In an Etruscan tomb dating from the second century B.C. an urn has been found on which is carved in relief the head and shoulders of a musician playing a transverse flute. The instrument is held to the right as is the modern flute; both hands are stopping the finger-holes; and a mouth-hole about one-quarter along the tube is clearly visible. Thus, from this rather unlikely source we have the oldest known portrayal of the true transverse flute.

———

In the course of this chapter we have several times noticed the entry into Mesopotamia, the eastern Mediterranean area, and Egypt, of cultural influences from some undefined source farther to the east. It is, of course, not impossible for identical artistic principles to have been discovered independently in different parts of the world, but the repeated stress on Eastern provenance for several different musical phenomena certainly suggests the existence of a cultural focus somewhere in western Central Asia. The principle of the reed-pipe so common in the Near East seems traceable to some such source, as does the vertical flute recorded from the New Kingdom in Egypt. That the influence of this supposed cultural focus should extend only westwards seems unlikely on the face of it, and it may therefore be useful to enquire briefly if there is any evidence of an extension farther eastward also. It is a fairly common cliché to say that all civilisation began in the Far East and travelled westwards; that 'the Chinese had it while Europeans were still savages', etc., and no one doubts that the products of China came into Near East and Western markets by the 'silk road' from very early times indeed, but this does not necessarily imply that cultural influences depended also on what was fundamentally a commercial route of communication, or that this was a one-way road.

In his excellent book *Woodwind Instruments and their History* A. C. Baines has said: 'The ancient civilisations—Egypt, Sumeria, China— each entered history already provided with three- or four-holed open ended flutes'; the question which remains unanswered is whether these flutes might not have had some common ancestor external to all three nations—and in this connection we must also include India. For the fullest examination of all the evidence we have at present we turn again to Curt Sachs. Beginning with China, he tells us that the oldest literary sources mention four flutes; in the twelfth or eleventh centuries B.C. the *kuan* and the *hsiao*; in the ninth the *ch'ih*; and in the eighth century B.C. the *yueh*. Two other names derived from later sources are *yo* and *ti*. All these names, Sachs warns us, must be interpreted with care, since they have to a great extent changed their precise meanings during the last three thousand years. An ode composed during the ninth century B.C. says that the *ch'ih* was a bamboo flute customarily played in unison with a globular pottery flute or *ocarina*, and medieval writings describe it as stopped (at the upper end) and with a blow-hole 'like a sour jujube', from which we can only conclude that it was a transverse flute—the oldest recorded. As with many another product of classical Chinese art the *ch'ih* has a modern Japanese derivative in the *fuyé* (Fig. 17). At the present day the principal Chinese flute is the *ti tse*, a slightly different instrument (Fig. 18) though also made of bamboo bound at intervals with silk thread and usually lacquered. Its special characteristic is the provision, between the mouth-hole and the highest finger-hole, of an extra opening covered by a thin vegetable membrane which imparts a

reedy quality to the sound (see also *Flauto di Voce*, p. 195). This
instrument is also known in modern Japan.[14]

When we look to ancient India a rather different picture presents
itself. Although not the first that we know of, the oldest Indian culture
that has left useful evidence is the so-called 'Indus Civilisation',
roughly contemporary with the culture of Sumeria and evidently
related to it. Excavations have shown the life of the Indus people to
have been remarkably advanced in many respects but unfortunately

Fig. 17   Japanese *Fuyé*

Fig. 18   Chinese *ti tse* and player. Notice hole covered
with translucent vegetable skin

few musical remains have come to light. Flutes in particular make a very late appearance in this part of the world and when they do, somewhat to our surprise perhaps, it is the *transverse* instrument that is outstanding. Vertical flutes and pan-pipes appear to have had no importance, while whistle flutes were evidently contemned as mere shepherds' instruments. Under the Sanskrit title *vāmsī* the transverse flute is first depicted in temple reliefs at Sanchi, central India, which date no earlier than from the first century A.D.—a period when we know that Greek influence was powerful in the north-west of the country. In view of the apparent absence of the instrument from metropolitan Greece at this time, however, and its very rare occurrence in Etruria and colonial Rome, we can hardly suppose that the Indian flute found its parentage in these countries. Between the first and fourth centuries A.D. the famous reliefs of Amaravati were carved, and here we find the flute repeatedly illustrated—often in a convention which depicts it suspended in space as if only to be touched by divine hands, and emphasising its aristocratic character as part of the so-called *celestial music*. The great god Krishna himself played it, we are told, and in the Kathakali style of narrative dance there is a series of singularly beautiful flute-playing gestures (*mudras*) associated with him. These may well be familiar to readers through the dance recitals which celebrated Indian artists have brought to the West in recent years.

In contrast to the flutes, stringed instruments, particularly the archetype which Sachs has generically named *Lute*, seem to have appeared fairly early in ancient India, and these can be traced to an Iranian source of some eight hundred years B.C. Was this also perhaps the source from which the Indian flutes came? Curiously enough, in ancient India, as in Egypt, we know of no musical instrument for which we can prove a native origin, and the Middle Ages were to come in before such a growth can be positively identified.

To revert now to China—does the known history of archetypal stringed instruments in that area shed any light on the provenance of the flutes? Under the *Han* dynasty (206 B.C.–A.D. 220) ancient China reached the peak of her power, and her western borders extended as far as the Caspian Sea. This direct contact with areas occupied by Western cultures greatly enhanced two-way traffic, and, among other things, Western musical instruments travelled eastwards. From this time on strings became much more important in China, notably *lutes* of a west Asiatic type. The direction of travel between central Asia and China is clearly established in respect of the strings, and, although China had her flutes some centuries earlier, there seems to be little doubt that the prototypes of these instruments entered by the same path.

Though some links in the chain of evidence may still require strengthening, what we have is sufficient to convince many leading scholars that the flutes, both Western and Far Eastern, once had a common origin in Central Asia. Speaking of the Chinese, Baines has said, '—their flute *ti* came, like our flute, from Central Asia', and Curt Sachs went even further. He wrote: 'The old path from West and Central Asia to the Far East, that is more clearly traced by the lute than by any other object, seems to have been extended, as early as the neolithic age, to a further westeastern path leading from the Pacific coast of China to the Pacific coast of America. There has been much discussion about whether, how and where the American civilisation was influenced by ancient China.' This fascinating subject will no doubt occupy future scholars for many years, but it does not appear to bear directly upon our main subject in the present book and here we must leave it untouched.[15]

NOTES

[1] Donington, R., *The Instruments of Music*, London, Methuen and Co., 1949.

Galpin, F. W., *European Musical Instruments*, London, Williams and Norgate, 1937.

Veenstra, A., 'The Classification of the Flute', *Galpin Society Journal*, Vol. XVII, 1964.

Bessaraboff, N., *Ancient European Musical Instruments*, Harvard University Press, 1941, Introductory section.

Here is probably the most satisfactory detailed classification we have to date, though even this meticulous writer admits to difficulties due to ambiguous terminology. See also Curt Sachs, *The History of Musical Instruments*, New York, W. W. Norton and Co. Inc., 1940, pp. 454–67, 'Terminology'. It is to be noted that Sachs, in speaking of ancient or exotic double reed instruments, uses the generic term 'oboe'. This is in line with the custom of most German scholars today. The present writer prefers to reserve 'oboe' for a more limited use and has found 'reed-pipes' sufficient in the context of this book, although it is of course a less precise term, and might include single beating reeds and free reeds.

[2] Sachs, *op. cit.* p. 45, quotes Ernest Hemingway in *A Farewell to Arms* regarding a present-day belief in the Abruzzi. 'When the young men serenaded, only the flute was forbidden. Why, I asked. Because it was bad for the girls to hear the flute at night.'

[3] Hornbostel, E. M. von, *Africa*, Vol. VI, 1933, 'Ethnology of African Sound-Instruments'.

[4] Sachs, *op. cit.* p. 62.

[5] *Ibid.* pp. 62–3. See also *The Galpin Society Journal*, No. v, 1952, pp. 28–38, for an account of the 'Malham' pipe, an advanced example which has been fully investigated and which shows considerable musical possibilities. This pipe is

attributed with some certainty to the Iron Age in Great Britain, say between 200 B.C. and A.D. 200.

[6] In Chapter I of his *Story of the Flute*, 2nd edn., London, William Reeves; New York, Charles Scribner's Sons, 1928, H. M. Fitzgibbon has summarised all the more important classical legends concerning the flute while drawing his readers' attention to the old wide usage of the word.

[7] Sachs, *op. cit.* p. 106.

[8] Bate, Philip, *The Trumpet and Trombone*, London, Ernest Benn Ltd., 1966, p. 92.

[9] Sachs, *op. cit.* p. 129.

[10] *Ibid.* p. 139. Sachs here gives an admirable account of Greek reed-pipes and the details of their construction that enabled them to be adapted to various modes.

[11] *Ibid.* p. 141. Also Rockstro, R. S., *The Flute*, Rudall, Carte and Co., 1890, p. 135. The latter allusion is, of course, to the *plagiaulós* with which a transverse *playing position* was obtained by inserting the reed in a side-hole instead of in the end of the tube. The top of the tube was then plugged. Acoustically there is no difference in the behaviour of the two types of *aulói*. See also Baines, A. C., *Woodwind Instruments and their History*, London, Faber and Faber, 1957, p. 222.

[12] The use of a leathern mouthband, *phorbeiá*, to support the cheeks as well as to locate the two reeds in playing the Greek double *aulós* has been cited as evidence of the great wind pressure used. On the other hand, there are classical illustrations of double pipes played *without* such support and occasionally we find poets praising the *sweet* tone of the *aulós*. Sachs points out that by a curious freak, the leather mouthband still survives in Java where a double reed-pipe was known before the year A.D. 1000.

[13] See note 6 above. Sachs, *op. cit.* p. 138, speaks with amused affection of his old schoolmaster who, when supervising Greek 'construes' and encountering *aulós*, never failed to remark on the sensitive ears of his heroes who could be inflamed to ecstasy or combat by this gentlest of *flutes*. The good mentor seems to have found the ears of his modern students glutted with the riches of Wagner, who, nevertheless, is recorded as always preferring the more sombre German old style flute to the brilliance of the newer Boehm model.

[14] The different tunings of these instruments, and the disposition of their finger-holes by which they are adapted to the scales of various Eastern musical systems, do not immediately concern us here. Readers who may be interested are referred particularly to E. M. von Hornbostel, 'Die Massnorm als kulturge-schichtliches Forschungsmittel', *Festschrift für P. Wilhelm Schmidt*, Vienna, 1928. Here the measurements of various Eastern wind instruments and their bearing on philosophical considerations, not always musical in the first place, are fully discussed. Sachs, *op. cit.* pp. 180–82, summarises well.

[15] Sachs, *ibid.* Chapter 9, summarises the evidence we have today and points out that a large corpus of instrumental types found exclusively in an area comprising China, the territory between China and India, the Malay Archipelago, and the Pacific Islands have representatives among the Indians of Central and South America.

F

CHAPTER 4

The Transverse Flute to 1700

THE BODY of evidence that we have looked at in the previous chapter, incomplete though it is in many respects, is sufficient to support the belief that the transverse flute as a musical entity had its origin somewhere in western Central Asia, and that in quite ancient times it migrated both to the East and to the West, where it acquired the particular characteristics called for respectively by widely divergent Oriental and Western musical philosophies. From this point on our interest is mainly confined to the European manifestation as the parent of our modern orchestral instrument. We know that early in the Christian era the instrument existed—if not abundantly—both in Syria and in the Italian peninsula, and we must now consider how it came to penetrate throughout western Europe.

Between the end of the Roman period and the mid-Renaissance our knowledge of wind instruments in Europe is derived almost entirely from literature, pictures, and sculpture. To quote from Adam Carse, 'the occurrence of the names of wind instruments in the records and literature of the Middle Ages or contemporary pictorial or carved representations of such, does little more than establish the existence of certain types at more or less vague periods'. Such sources assure us of the continuity of basic principles (e.g. the double reed), but they provide little or no technical information. It is not until the early 16th century, whence both actual instruments and specialised writings about them survive, that we can begin to speak in some detail.

Towards the middle of the 4th century the Roman theatre, owing to its moral laxity, fell under the ban of the Church, and for nearly eleven hundred years secular drama in Europe suffered a total eclipse. In the theatre music had for long found its principal home, but now its cultivation passed exclusively into the care of the monastic houses. In the ritual of the early Church vocal music alone was allowed, for instrumental playing was tainted by its association with the stage. Indeed, instrumental music might have disappeared entirely but for the fact that, after the suppression of the theatre, many musicians took to a wandering existence, playing and singing as opportunity and livelihood offered. To them we owe the fact that knowledge of instruments and their techniques was preserved, to be developed later by minstrels of different periods and social standing—the knightly troubadours and their jongleurs, the solid and respectable Brotherhoods of Town Musicians, and the exclusive Guilds of Trumpeters. As regards the Church, after some three hundred years a change of opinion occurred, and by the middle of the 7th century instrumental music had again become acceptable. Of all instruments, the organ, once the accompaniment to gladiatorial displays, was regarded as fit to support choral worship.

In music, contrary to the other arts, the direct debt of western Europe to ancient Greece and Rome is less than is sometimes supposed.[1] Most musical instruments in their basic forms entered Europe from the East, by way of Byzantium, from the north-east along the Baltic coast, or through the Islamic Empire of North Africa. Arabian civilisations are much older than is often realised—for example Sheba, contemporary with the reign of Solomon in Israel, was an Arab state—so a line of communication with western Europe via Islam may have existed for a very long time. As F. W. Galpin pointed out over fifty years ago, *commercial* traffic between Islam and Christian Europe was in being long before the first of the Holy Wars, so some at least of the supposed innovations often credited to the returning Crusaders—*inter alia* the trumpet—may in fact have been known, if not widely exploited, in the West much earlier. Although, according to Suetonius, Nero possessed some skill on the *flute* as well as on the water-organ, lyre, and bagpipe, we do not know what sort of flute this was, or, indeed, if it was a flute *sensu stricto* at all.[2] The meagreness of our information to date concerning the flute in any part of the Roman Empire suggests that the instrument never attained much importance in that civilisation, and although the two oldest illustrations we possess of transverse flutes originated in colonial Rome and in Etruria respectively, there is no evidence that they advanced from the Italian peninsula into the rest of Europe. On the other hand, a line of migration from Asia via Byzantium as far as Germany can be traced without difficulty. In the later Middle Ages Germany became, as it were, a secondary centre of distribution, and from there the transverse flute spread throughout the rest of Europe. The consequent appellation 'German Flute' can be traced in a number of countries, notably Spain and southern France, where in the 13th century (according to Galpin)[3] it became popular with the Minnesingers. In general, however, really wide distribution west of the Rhine did not occur until about a century later. In Germany itself the flute seems to have gained an aristocratic status quite early, and to have been accepted as a chamber instrument in company with the Minnesinger fiddle. Sachs suggests that England, too, adopted the 'German' label at this early period, but this, I think, may be in some doubt. In art works of undisputed English origin the instrument does not appear till the 16th century, and the first written reference at present known dates only to 1492. In that year there occurs in the *Privy Purse Expenses* of King Henry VII an item of £3 10s. paid to one Guillim for 'flotes with a case'.[4] The great musical inventory of Henry VIII compiled in 1547[5] to which we shall refer again in Chapter 9, divides the flute kind into 'fflutes' (without any prefix) and 'recorders', and in 1575 Queen Elizabeth I was welcomed to Kenilworth with decorations which included a trophy of musical instruments comprising 'luts, viols, shallms, cornets, flutes, recorders and harpes'. Again we note no prefix, and this in an eyewitness account by one who was not, as far as we can tell, a musician. In 1683 Henry Purcell was appointed 'keeper, maker, repairer, mender and tuner of all and every His Majesty's Musical Wind Instruments, that is to say, virginalls, organs, flutes, recorders. . . .' We may perhaps smile a little at the Court clerkship which placed the virginals in a commission regarding wind instruments, but the point of the document for us here is clear—flutes *and* recorders. These are but a few of the references to the flute which occur in English records of the 16th and 17th centuries,[6] but they do surely show us the terminology that was customary in the country. It is not until nearly the beginning of the 18th century that we find the term 'German Flute' coming into use in England, and when it does it seems to be coeval with the first great reform of the instrument (see p. 79) and with the decline of the specifically English word 'recorder'.[7]

The path of the transverse flute into Germany is pin-pointed at various stages in a most striking way. According to Sachs it is mentioned as *plágios* in a Greek treatise of about A.D. 800 and it is actually depicted in Greek miniatures in the Bibliothèque Nationale, Paris (10th century) and in the British Museum (11th century). From the same centuries there are ivory caskets respectively in the Museo Nazionale, Florence, and the Victoria and Albert Museum, both of which depict transverse flutes in carving; but probably the most significant representation that remains from this period is on an Hungarian aquamanile of *c.* 1100 now in the National Museum, Budapest.[8] About this period, too, through another branch of Byzantine influence we find the instrument depicted in the ancient cathedral at Kieff. At

the present day the path is still marked by the prominence of transverse
flutes in the folk music of Romania, Yugoslavia, Hungary, Bohemia,
Austria, and Switzerland.

What we may for convenience call the second phase of spread—from
central Germany south and west—is illustrated for us from many
sources. Among the most notable are a miniature in the *Hortus Delicia-
rum*, a celebrated encyclopaedia compiled by the Alsatian abbess
Herrad von Landsberg near the end of the 12th century—in which,
incidentally, the Middle High German name *swegel* is used; the very
beautiful Book of Hours of Jeanne d'Evreux, of *c.* 1320, belonging to
the Metropolitan Museum of Art, New York; the manuscript of the
'Romance of Alexander', illuminated by Jehan de Grise in Flanders in
1244, now one of the treasures of the Bodleian Library, Oxford; and
the *Cantigas de Santa Maria*, a most important manuscript prepared
by Alfonso the Wise of Spain (1221–84), preserved in the Library of
the Escorial. Some recent scholars have tended to regard this latter
work not so much as evidence of contemporary musical practice in
Spain but more as a compendium from many sources, and some of the
illustrations may indeed be of early 14th-century date, i.e. considerably
later than the body of the text. These doubts notwithstanding, the
Cantigas remains one of the most valuable of pre-Renaissance musical
documents.[9]

Literary references indicating the spread of the flute in Europe during
the Middle Ages are equally abundant. In a French document of the
13th century a *flauste traversaine* is mentioned, and about a hundred
years later the poets Deschamps and Guillaume de Machault wrote of
the *fleuthe traversaine* and *flauste*. In particular Machault associated
flaustes traversaines and *flaustes dont droit joues quand tu flaustes*, which
has been translated colloquially as 'cross flutes and flutes that you play
straight when you pipe', a most significant phrase which reminds us
that both types of flute were known in medieval Europe, and were
probably of equal importance to judge by the number of contemporary
illustrations. Our difficulty is that, while we have been able to trace
the arrival of the transverse type, we are still in the dark about the
provenance of the more complicated fipple-flute which was to become
for some long time the preferred instrument in Art music.[10]

There is no doubt that the courtly vertical flutes—*flûtes douces*—known
to Machault and his contemporaries were of the recorder kind, for the
plain cross-cut tube (descendant of the Sumerian flutes and the Egyptian ancestral *nāy*) seems to have left little trace in western Europe,

and then only as a rustic instrument. Among the decorations of the
'Queen Mary's Psalter', of early 14th-century English workmanship
(British Museum MS. 2B VII), there is a figure holding a long, slightly
curved pipe in the characteristic diagonal *nāy* position, which Galpin
identified as a goatherd playing such an open ended flute.[11] The illustration is unique in coming from a Western source, and by this seems
to underline either the rarity of the instrument, or its insignificance in
the eyes of the people who could afford illuminated missals in the late
Middle Ages. On the other hand, the instrument is well known today
as the Irano-Balkan flute *kaval* which well deserves Sachs's eulogies
(see p. 55) in spite of its very difficult technique on which many writers
have commented.[12] The earliest English illustration of the fipple-flute
at present known is found in the 12th-century 'Hunterian Psalter' in
Glasgow University Library. Canon Galpin called this instrument
simply a 'recorder' and although the figure holding it is a subsidiary
one in a picture dominated by King David tuning a harp, he is drawn
with great liveliness and humour. His expression of concern as he
apparently struggles with the fingering is delightful. Recently Harrison
and Rimmer have identified this example as a *bone* fipple-flute and have
taken it, in contrast to all but one of the other instruments depicted, to
be a rustic type. This is presumably the result of comparison with an
actual specimen found at White Castle, Monmouthshire, and attributed
to the second half of the 13th century.[13]

An interesting point in connection with early representations of
fipple-flutes is the frequency with which they are depicted as twinned
pairs. Two examples will be enough to illustrate the matter, and from
many we may take two that are of English origin. The British Museum
MS. 10 E iv shows a gymnast balancing on his hands on the points of
two swords, while two musicians accompany the act on double recorder
and pipe-and-tabor (see below). It seems that in the early 14th century
the acrobat employed musicians to work up excitement in the audience
at the climax of his show just as in the present-day circus. Our second
example is an early 16th-century carving of a double recorder player in
Cirencester Church, Gloucestershire, in which the 'whistle' part of
each tube is clearly to be seen. Both these are illustrated in Galpin's
Old English Instruments of Music. Frequently these twinned flutes appear
to be separate, and are shown held in a ∧ position as we so often see
the Greek double *aulós*, or contemporary folk pipes such as the Russian
brelka. Does this perhaps suggest an Eastern origin for the instrument?
On the other hand, almost as often the two tubes lie side by side—

possibly joined together, or even bored out of a single piece of wood, as is a double recorder of 15th- or early 16th-century date, found beneath the soil in the court of All Souls College, Oxford. This particular instrument has another feature which is frequently seen in Eastern pipes—the two tubes are of different length, and, according to a modern facsimile, sounded a fifth apart.[14]

To fill in the picture of the flute family as a whole in Europe during the period under review it is necessary just to mention several special types of whistle flute, although they do not bear directly on the main subject of this book. Most of these do not seem to have found a place in the Art music of their times, though, as we have already suggested, it is not impossible for an instrument to pass from the 'folk' to the 'art' category.[15]

From troubadour times right up to the present day the *Three-holed Flute* in various guises, accompanied by a small drum, has played a major part in the lighter music of Europe. Essentially it is a whistle flute with a very narrow cylindrical bore, usually in diameter about one-fortieth of the sounding length. These proportions favour the production of the higher harmonics (see p. 21) and thus three holes, two on top and one beneath, all placed near the foot of the tube, serve to provide a diatonic scale of two octaves or more. The scale begins with the octaves of the four fundamentals and then continues without a break by the four twelfths and the four double octaves, all elicited by skilful adjustment of the blowing. Some players can produce yet higher harmonics, and by fork-fingerings and half-stopping some chromatic notes can be added. The instrument is usually fingered by the left hand, leaving the right free to mark the rhythm on a small drum suspended from the left forearm or shoulder. In France this flute, as the *galoubet*, is still the main accompaniment to folk dancing, especially in Provence. In Spain a relatively larger bore is favoured and in some cases *three* holes are placed on top in addition to the thumb-hole below; and in Catalonia, where pipe-and-drum bands are organised on a municipal scale, this *fluviol* is even equipped with one or two keys. The Basque citics show a further sophistication of the basic instrument by the addition of a short mouth-pipe at the top, a metal ring at the foot for the supporting little finger, and an inset metal lip to the 'whistle'. Two sizes are in use among Basque players; the soprano or *chistu* in G being pitched a fifth below the French *galoubet*, and the bass or *silbote* another fifth lower. The music of these apparently simple pipes, when well played, is extraordinarily expressive and exciting. In England the three-holed flute, except in the hands of a few folk-dance enthusiasts, has been obsolete for some seventy years, but in the 1860s every district in Oxfordshire and the surrounding counties had its piper who played for village dancing. Officially his instruments were simply known as 'pipe-and-tabor'—there is an account written in 1609 of one Hall of Herefordshire who was then still playing at the age of ninety-seven, 'giving men light hearts by thy pipe and women light heels by thy tabor'—but other appellations were known, among them the charmingly onomatopœic 'whittle-and-dub'.[16] As a curiosity, examples of the smallest of all three-holed flutes, the Picco pipe, may sometimes be seen in musical collections. This instrument, only some four inches long, was brought into prominence by a blind Sardinian piper named Picco who appeared as a virtuoso in London in 1856. By using the palm or second finger of the right hand to half or fully stop the foot of the tube he is reputed to have commanded a compass of three full octaves. Picco's appearances started a passing vogue for his instrument, which, though little more than a toy, was reproduced in considerable numbers and with good workmanship.

Small high-pitched whistle flutes are often simply termed *flageolets*, a surviving diminutive of the medieval *flagiol* = flute, but there are distinctions to be observed within the group. These instruments range from tiny pipes reputedly used to encourage singing birds, to the 'flageolette' a foot or so long, beloved of Samuel Pepys, and they appeared in both single and double form. In *Samuel Pepys, Lover of Musique*, Sir Frederick Bridge wrote that the Secretary of the Admiralty 'lived with his beloved "flageolette" in his pocket that he might pipe on it whilst waiting for his dinner or riding on the coach'. With modern fashions for men we might think this rather inconvenient, but doubtless the full-skirted coats of the Restoration were a different matter in respect of pockets. We do not know precisely the details of Pepys's own instrument, though from his aquaintance with Thomas Greeting we may surmise that it was of the sort illustrated in that virtuoso's book *The Pleasant Companion, or New Lessons and Instructions for the Flageolet*, and by Mersenne.[17] In Mersenne's figure the general appearance of the flageolet is similar to that of the contemporary recorders, but the arrangement of the finger-holes is very different. According to the chart supplied, the 6th or highest hole was stopped by the left thumb, the 4th and 5th by the left first and second fingers respectively, the right first finger controlled the 3rd hole, the right thumb the 2nd, and the right second finger the lowest. The instrument was supported by the

right third finger below the open end and the left third finger higher up.
Dr. Burney stated that this type of flageolet was invented by one Juvigny
of Paris about 1581 but there is good reason to suppose that it was
known considerably earlier, and both Virdung and Agricola show small
whistle flutes with varying arrangements of the holes. There is little
doubt, however, that the variety with *two* thumb-holes below originated
in France, and for this reason, as Carse pointed out, the name *French
flageolet* is properly reserved for it. Side by side with the later recorders,
the French flageolet seems to have maintained something of a separate
existence in the 18th century, and in the 19th it acquired chromatic
key-work following the lead of the transverse flute. It seems in the main
to have been confined to the lighter side of music for most of its
existence, as the name 'quadrille flageolet' introduced in the mid-1800s
suggests, but, according to Carse, it does find a place in some serious
18th-century scores before the transverse piccolo became fully
established as the highest of the orchestral woodwind.

Finally in this section we must notice a small group of instruments
which originated in this country in the last years of the 18th century,
and have become generally known as the 'English flageolet'. Since the
bore of these flutes was tapered, and the majority of them had a single
thumb-hole, they must be regarded fundamentally as recorders, though
different makers modified them in different ways. Between 1800 and
about 1815 numerous patents were granted for these instruments under
such titles as 'flageolet or English flute' and 'trio flageolet', and, as the
last tells us, they were made single, double, and even in triple form.
Although they can be regarded as no more than elegant drawing-room
instruments for the amateur, they show great ingenuity and workmanship of a very high order, and as specimens in many a musical collection
they have a singular charm.[18]

In tracing the continuity of some of the non-orchestral fipple-flutes
we have passed somewhat beyond the time boundary intended for our
main subject in this section, and we must return.

With the dawn of the 16th century we pass from indirect to direct
evidence in instrumental matters, and at the same time enter on an
era of surprising richness. As Dr. Alexander Buchner has pointed out,[19]
no period either before or since the Renaissance has produced so great
a variety of instrumental types. Many of these are today obsolete, in

spite, or perhaps because, of the high development of our present music. Probably they had already reached the limit of their structural possibilities and were not susceptible to further improvement with the technologies of their time. Among the woodwind, two families then flourishing —the cornetts and the mirlitons—have passed quite out of use in Europe and have no modern representatives at all, if we except such mere toys as the 'kazoo'. Of other families certain features have survived, though in much smaller instrumental groups, or in specialised instruments which are seldom admitted into the orchestra.

During the 16th and first half of the 17th centuries at least six treatises on music and its instruments were published in Europe, and four of these are of the greatest importance. They are *Musica Getutscht* by Sebastian Virdung (1511); *Musica Instrumentalis deudsch* by one Sohr, who after a not uncommon custom of his time, adopted the pseudonym of Martin Agricola (1528, 1532, 1542, and 1545); *Syntagma Musicum* by Michael Praetorius, a prolific German composer, Music Director to the Duke of Braunschweig-Wolfenbüttel—Vol. II of the work subtitled *De Organographia* (1618 and 1619) contains dimensioned drawings of all the instruments then in use; and *Harmonie Universelle* by Father Marin Mersenne of the Order of Minorites. This was published in 1636 although much of the material is known to have been compiled as much as ten years earlier. All four of these writers mention the transverse flute, both as to construction and musical use, and by comparing them we can form a detailed picture of its progress over more than a century. For the moment it will be convenient, I think, to take only the descriptive side, and to defer considering musical usage till later (p. 169).

In Virdung only one transverse flute is mentioned—a military type which he calls *zwerchpfeiff*. It is in fact what we should now distinguish as a *fife*, and the bore is narrow in relation to the length as we should expect in a shrill, penetrating, instrument. Unfortunately the woodcut given is crude, and possibly ill-drawn, for the holes appear quite curiously close together. Agricola's illustration shows a group of four flutes, apparently rather better proportioned than Virdung's. The two middle members (*altus* and *tenor*) are shown as practically the same length and they share a fingering chart. From this latter it seems that only *three* sizes were generally recognised, and that these were pitched a perfect fifth apart. The compass quoted is just over two octaves, and it is clear that fork-fingering was already in use. The instruments in this case are termed *Schweitzerpfeiffen*, i.e. Swiss-pipes. From Praetorius we get more specific information. He makes a clear distinction between the *Querflöt* (Ital. *traversa* or *fiffaro*) and the small *Schweitzerpfeiff* or *Feldpfeiff*, for which he notes a slightly different fingering. There are only three actual sizes of *Querflöten* shown in Praetorius, but the mid-size again served as both alto and tenor. The compass he allows is but two octaves plus four 'falset' notes which were to be expected only of specially skilled players. From the drawings given and the fingering charts it has been possible to calculate the sizes of the Praetorian group in modern terms as follows:

Instrument	Natural compass	Falset notes	Length—mouth-hole to foot
Discant	a′–a‴	b‴–e⁗	14 inches
Alto or tenor	d′–d‴	e‴–a‴	22 inches
Bass	g–g″	a″–d‴	32 inches

It is in the middle member, the alto/tenor, that we recognise the parent of the standard D flute of the 18th and succeeding centuries. Praetorius also mentions an instrument which he calls *Dulceflute* and says it is 'also called a cross flute . . . except that it has eight holes like a recorder'.[20] The illustration furnished suggests that this instrument had a whistle head, and was in fact a recorder built to be held crosswise. We hear nothing more about this from any contemporary writer, but it does remind us that the idea was revived in the 19th century by several makers who supplied alternative whistle heads for the normal transverse flute of the time (see p. 198). From Praetorius's woodcut we see also that his bass transverse flute was constructed in two sections, a fore-shadowing of what was to become the standard practice from the latter part of the century on. We may suppose that this division of a tube nearly a yard long was made as a matter of convenience in boring, a suggestion that is borne out by an example in the Vienna Collection. This instrument, a keyless flute of the 17th century, is divided into *three* sections: a normal head joint, a second joint with no holes, and a third joint which carries all six finger-holes. There appears to be no musical advantage in dividing the tube in this particular way, and the instrument is, as far as I am aware, unique.

Mersenne is rather less informative, citing only two transverse flutes, those in D and G which he calls *Flûtes d'Allemands* (see also p. 67). According to calculations the shorter of these measured about 23½ inches from the face of the stopper to the open end, which, bore and other factors being equal, would imply a slightly lower pitch than Praetorius's. Mersenne's fingering table gives a diatonic scale of D for this instrument, with a compass of two octaves using fundamentals and first harmonics with an extension up to a''' by means of twelfths and double-octave harmonics.

So much then for printed records themselves from the 16th and 17th centuries. Much more important is the fact that we can refer to them side by side with a considerable store of actual instruments, for this is the earliest period of European music from which more than a few isolated specimens have survived. The major collections today are those of the Vienna Kunsthistorisches Museum and the Conservatoire royal de musique, Brussels, who between them possess some 130 wind instruments of the time. Next in importance are the collections of the Biblioteca Capitale, Verona, and the Berlin Hochschüle, while smaller accumulations are housed in Frankfurt, Nürnberg, Salzburg, Prague, Amsterdam, and Paris. Specimens of local interest—from town bands and the like—are to be found in many Continental museums, but unfortunately few such early wind instruments are as yet to be seen in Great Britain except the White Castle pipe (National Museum of Wales, Cardiff); the very fine cornetts in the Christ Church library, Oxford, and in the Norwich Museum; and the double recorder in All Souls College, Oxford. Private collections here are rich for their size, but not many contain material earlier than 18th-century.[21]

It is fortunate for the musical scholar that in many countries museum curators have allowed accurate copies of some of their unique specimens to be made and placed in other representative collections. Such replicas, though expensive, are also being used by devoted students in attempts to re-create authentic performances of old music. Three copies of cylindrical keyless flutes of the Agricola–Praetorius era, in the Verona Collection, were shown at the Royal Military Exhibition in London in 1890 and attracted much interest. They measured:

(1) Length from cork 32·4", Bore 0·9"
(2) Length from cork 34·5", Bore 1·02"
(3) Length from cork 38·4", Bore 1·02"

and sounded f♯, f♮, and e♭ respectively as their lowest notes. Together with an original B♭ flute by C. Rafi of Lyons (1515–53) these formed a most important group as shown in Plate II of Day's famous catalogue.[22] Three, it will be noticed, were of deeper pitch than any of the Praetorian group, and the two longest showed the two-piece construction. The

great length of the E♭ instrument must have made its handling
awkward indeed (Day's contributor regarded it as impossible to a man
of normal stature without assistance) but the bass flute in Urs Graf's
quartet (Plate 1) must have been at least as long if we assume the player
to have been no more than five feet six inches tall. A feature of great
interest is that the holes for each third finger are doubled and offset
from the centre line. Again Urs Graf's drawing shows the practical
value of this placing, and the duplication suggests that at the time right-
or left-handed playing was *ad lib*. The earlier recorders, shawms, and
even true oboes, often show this feature, the custom having been to stop
up the unwanted hole with wax. There are also many pictures known of
left-handed flute players, and, indeed, there was nothing inherent in
the instrument to fix the right-handed position until the advent of
chromatic keys on the body-tube in the last quarter of the 18th century
(see also Plate 2A).

During the sixty years or so following the issue of Mersenne's treatise
a number of musical writers mention the transverse flute in various
contexts, but none give us any further contemporary technical information until the extreme end of the century.[23] When such does appear
c. 1690 it is evident that in the interim the instrument has undergone
a complete reorganisation. The keyless cylindrical flute, known since
medieval times, has disappeared entirely (except as the military fife)
and has been replaced by a much more advanced instrument built in
three (later four) sections united by tenon and socket joints. The head
of the new flute is cylindrical in bore, but the body is tapered, and the
separate foot carries a key providing the one semitone in the natural
scale which could not, on the older instrument, be even approximated
by special fingering. From now on the diagnostic features of the transverse flute become:

(1) The cylindro-conical bore, similar to that of contemporary
    recorders.
(2) The closed key furnishing the first semitone of the scale.
(3) Three- or four-part construction.
(4) A natural scale of D; for the *mean* or alto/tenor of the older group
    was clearly the most convenient size for a general purpose
    instrument.

The actual years in which the new flute made its appearance and who
was responsible for it are matters of some doubt, but the majority of
modern scholars agree in attributing it to one, perhaps several jointly,

of a very remarkable group of *artiste-ouvriers* who served the French
Court during the opulent days of Louis XIV (1643–1715), and who are
known to have reformed several of the early woodwind. These men as
instrument makers *and* players were both influenced by, and exerted
an influence on, the changing musical aesthetics of their time and
therefore demand consideration from both standpoints. Here we shall
confine ourselves to the purely physical part of their work and, at the
risk of some repetition, defer aesthetic matters to a later chapter. Most
of these men, among whom several generations of the Hotteterre family
seem to have held a leading position, were members of the *Grande
Ecurie* (see p. 165) and as such enjoyed opportunities for experiment
which were probably beyond the reach of the common run of instrument makers.[24]

What then do we now believe that the Hotteterres and their colleagues
may have done for the flute? We know a considerable amount about the
family relations, etc., of these men, but unfortunately their actual work
is less well documented. They were by family tradition makers and
players of the small bagpipes or *musettes* which, over the greater part
of Europe, were the staple instrument at 'dances, weddings, and other
diversions' (Mersenne) and which in more refined form had become
highly fashionable in Court circles. Their skill and experience in the
boring and fine turning of small wooden tubes is therefore beyond
question, but how they as a group became concerned with the remodel-
ling of almost all the important woodwinds of their time is less certain.
From surviving specimens of known provenance we can, however, say
that their experiments and innovations covered both the double reeds
and the flute in its two forms. Of the former we need say little here
except that in their hands the medieval one-piece shawm disappeared
and re-emerged as the three-section true oboe, with a modified bore,
elegant external ornament, a more refined tone, and a much improved
upper register—virtually a new instrument, fit to realise the changing
musical ideas of the time—and a similar metamorphosis affected the old
curtal and gave rise to the first *bassoons* as we now recognise them.

The case of the recorder we must examine in rather more detail.
The typical instrument, as the first of the Hotteterres would have
known it, was a simple one-piece tube with an inverted conical bore,
plugged at the top, and with a lip and wind-way cut out (see Fig. 19A).
Six finger-holes were bored at the front, with a seventh duplicated for
right- or left-handed players, and an eighth at the back controlled by the
uppermost thumb. Hence we have the name *flûte à neuf trous* which we

find in some of the older writings. The thumb-hole could be partially opened—'pinched' is the term often found in instruction books—to assist in the formation of the second octave (see also 'venting', Chapter 2, p. 43 above). Such a tube, we might suppose, would not be particularly difficult for a skilled turner to make in the smaller sizes, but might present considerable problems in the larger. The only available tools for making the bore would be the simple shell bit and reamer, and the deeper these had to go in wood of possibly varying hardness the greater the danger of wandering or tearing the grain. In the larger sizes too, the six primary holes had still to be kept within the reach of the fingers, so they tended to be placed in two groups, the resultant faulty intonation being as far as possible corrected by adjusting their sizes or by drilling obliquely through the wall of the tube so as to gain separation where they met the bore. In cases where the lowest hole had to be placed quite out of reach it was covered by an open-standing key, and this was provided with right- and left-handed touch-pieces. Semitones, or at least approximations to them, could only be obtained by fork fingerings or perhaps by 'shading'.

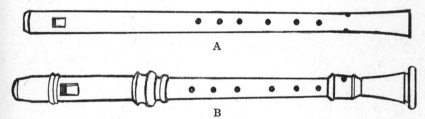

Fig. 19   The discant Recorder. 16th-century and
Baroque forms compared

To men used to the refinement of the 17th-century *musettes*, albeit with much smaller tubes, such instruments must have appeared crude indeed, and the first thing that the Hotteterre group seem to have done was to construct the tube in three comparatively short sections united by tenon and socket joints such as they were accustomed to make between the stocks and drone tubes of their bagpipes. Besides being less uncertain in the boring, this construction gave the immediate advantage of easier access to the inside of the tube, both for finer finishing and for adjusting its proportions at the tuning stage.[25] Admittedly there was still the problem of placing the finger-holes ideally in the larger instruments, but compensation had now become easier. There was no longer any need to duplicate the lowest hole, for the foot joint could be turned to either side as required. The appearance of the recorder—*flûte-à-bec* or *flûte douce*, as it was called in France—was now generally as in Fig. 19B. External ornament in the taste of the time had been added and the result was the 'Baroque' instrument as we now recognise it, and reproduce it for present-day use.

Having compared the features of the early recorder with those of its Baroque successor we can make a like comparison between those of the transverse flutes, and at once we see that a parallel trans-formation has taken place. Moreover, the details of surviving specimens suggest very strongly that the same men were responsible. In the first place we see in the Baroque instrument the three-part construction already applied to the recorder and the new oboe, and which we have not so far traced to any other source. Second, the bore follows the pattern worked out for the recorder—cylindrical head, tapered body, and occasionally a very slight reverse taper in the foot, and the slight overall flattening effect of the taper has enabled the holes to be placed rather closer together than before in an instrument of given pitch. Thirdly, on the oldest reputably dated Baroque flutes the style of external ornament accords closely with that found on oboes and recorders. These are the purely physical features which lead us to attribute the reformed flute to the Hotteterre group of workers, but in addition it seems unlikely on the basis of plain probability that the men who had successfully turned their attention to three of the most used woodwinds should neglect the fourth. Finally, the first distinguished players on the new flute whose names are recorded were all Frenchmen, most of them with Court connections, and some of them members of the Hotteterre family.[26] It is a little sad to have to record that time has shown the one-keyed flute to have been the least successful of the four rebuilds. Somehow the intonation of fork fingerings was less easy to control than with the steadying influence of a pressure-operated genera-tor such as the double reed, although the tender beauty of the tone is beyond question.

The foregoing are the main lines of argument that lead modern students to suppose that the one-keyed cone-flute originated among the French Court musicians, but we have not made much progress towards identifying the actual years during which the work was done. Let us see if we can get a little closer. The first known instruction book for the transverse flute is that of Jacques Hotteterre—sometimes dubbed 'Le Romain' on account of a long sojourn in the Italian capital—and the date of publication is 1707. Rockstro, on the authority of Fétis, states that this work received notice in a list of publications for the year 1699 but doubt exists about the matter, for he also says that the first edition was undated—undoubtedly an error as shown by an example in the Dayton Miller Collection, and by the researches of Ernest Thoinan.[27] The importance of the work, whether it appeared just within the 17th century or not, is shown, however, by the number of times that it was reissued during the next three decades, both in authorised and in pirated editions, as well as in translations. Hotteterre's *Principes de la Flûte Traversière, ou Flûte d'Allemagne* opens with a preface which indicates that the instrument had already become fashionable and was on its way to the phenomenal popularity that it was to enjoy among amateurs in the next hundred years and more. It is, however, the portrait illustration by Bernard Picart that is of most interest to us here for it shows the exact configuration of Hotteterre's own instrument —presumably the type he is credited with introducing at the Opéra *c.* 1697—and a very handsome instrument it is. The head, above the mouth-hole, carries an elaborately turned finial almost two-fifths the length of the rest of the joint. Externally the socket is turned in baluster form, and this ornament is repeated in reverse at the top of the single middle piece. On the foot the key is carried in a slot cut out of an ornamental ring, the heaviest of three, and the section ends with an elongated ovoid. The general profile of this instrument is indicated in Fig. 20B. Three very similar flutes, one in ivory, are shown in the celebrated portrait group attributed to Tournières in the National Gallery, London. For many years this painting was accepted as representing Lulli with some of his musicians—the dominant figure being the flautist Michel de la Barre. About 1943, however, the researches of the late W. F. Blandford and the late Mrs Mabel Dolmetsch led to a revision of opinion and today the group is provisionally referred to as 'La Barre and other Musicians'. Experts at the Gallery date the painting at *c.* 1710[28] (see Plate 3).

Writing many years later (in 1740) de la Barre, who had served in the *Grande Ecurie* between 1702 and 1705, said of Lulli: 'His elevation meant the downfall of all the old instruments except the oboe, thanks to Philidor and Hotteterre—the transverse flute did not come till later.'[29] Now de la Barre's statements are not, we know, completely acceptable as evidence,[30] but there are other good reasons for believing that the new oboe made its debut in 1657, and it is positively listed in a Lulli instrumentation of 1664.[31] We can assume, therefore, with some cer-

G

tainty that the re-modelled flute did not appear before that decade, and probably *c.* 1670 is pretty near the mark.

Actual specimens of the Hotteterre period flute are now excessively rare. Probably the most important example extant is one that formerly graced the Taphouse and Galpin Collections in England, and now

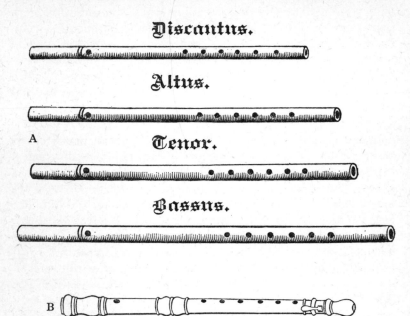

Fig. 20   Transverse Flutes compared. From Agricola,
c. 1528, and Hotteterre, *c.* 1707

figures as No. 38 of the Lesley Lindsey Mason Collection in the Museum of Fine Arts, Boston, U.S.A. This instrument is virtually identical with that shown in Hotteterre's illustration of 1707 and bears the name of Chevalier, a maker not known, as far as I am aware, by any other work. Some authorities have dated this example as late as 1680, but Canon Galpin himself placed it some ten years earlier, and this is provisionally accepted by the Boston experts—just the date in fact that Joseph Marx's oboe researches and de la Barre's general statement suggest. Some further support is found in the statement of J. J. Quantz, a celebrated German player, and flute master to Frederick the Great. Writing in 1752 he averred that the D♯ key was first added to the flute in France, and that it was then 'not yet a hundred years old'; further,

Quantz observed that the key was adopted in Germany 'fifty or sixty years ago'. From this it appears that a one-keyed flute existed in France well before the end of the 17th century. A fine example is preserved as No. 2670 of the Staatliches Institut für Musikforschung, Berlin. This bears the actual mark *Hotteterre*, and a very similar instrument, though with a cylindrical instead of ovoid foot joint, marked *Naust* is in the Paris Conservatoire Collection. Experts have dated both these examples as early 18th rather than 17th century.

Between what we have here called the 'Hotteterre' type and the oldest surviving four-piece flutes we can perhaps discern an intermediate form, originating in the last years of the 17th century and persisting into the 18th. There is a notable example in the Glen Collection, now housed in the Glasgow Art Gallery. This instrument is by Rippert, a distinguished Paris maker known to have been working *c.* 1690, and mentioned in a *Memoire de l'Académie des Sciences* of 1701 where *Sieur Ripert* [sic] is bracketed with *Sieur Jean Hautetaire* [sic] as one of the two most able makers in the city (see Plate 2c). It is interesting to note in passing that the Hotteterre family came originally from the Normandy village of La Couture-Boussey where wood-turning, especially in connection with musical instruments, was a local craft, and whence the modern firms of Buffet, Louis Lot, and Thibouville trace their beginnings.

The Glasgow instrument is in most respects similar to the Boston specimen, except for the head-cap. Instead of the long ball-ended finial it carries an elegant vase-shaped ivory cap, some $1\frac{1}{4}$ inches long, and it is this feature that suggests a distinct sub-type, for it was produced by other makers, notably P. J. Bressan whose working period bridged the 17th and 18th centuries. Bressan was a Frenchman by birth and may well have been in direct touch with the reform work done in that country. He settled in England about 1683 and became a most prolific and esteemed maker, many of whose instruments have survived.[32] At the time of writing thirty-two of his recorders are known, but only three transverse flutes. Two of these are, however, of great importance to the historian. No. 1207 in the Dayton C. Miller Collection (Library of Congress, Washington, U.S.A.) closely resembles the Rippert specimen, the major difference lying in the abolition of the ovoid turning of the foot joint and the substitution of a heavy ivory ring at the end (see Plate 2D). Both types of head-cap, we note, slid on to a long tenon at the top of the joint and it has been pointed out that with this construction a small body of air is trapped between the cap and the cork. If the cap fitted tightly this air might be compressed and so disturb the critical placing of the cork. In the Miller example this difficulty has evidently been encountered, for the inside of the cap has been nicked to provide ventage. In James Talbot's description of a Bressan flute which he examined *post* 1685 he mentions a small 'sound hole' which in the opinion of E. Halfpenny may have served the same purpose.[33] Talbot also writes of the 'cork' as being a wooden plug, and if this unyielding material was in common use we may well imagine that frequent removal of both cap and plug would be necessary, if only for drying out the instrument to avoid splitting.

The second Bressan flute is to be seen in the Victoria and Albert Museum, London. Properly it should be discussed in our next chapter for it belongs to the early years of the 18th century, but it is considered here because it forms through its maker a link with the older types. Constructed in four joints, it belongs to the next phase in the development of the instrument, though it retains the deep head-cap, this time carried out in metal. As a whole this flute is very advanced for its time, and was no doubt regarded as a very rich and superior instrument. The tube is made of ebony, with unusually thin walls, and every section is as it were 'damascened' all over with a filigree of silver. All the tenons are directed downwards towards the foot; each socket is strengthened by a heavy silver mount; and a similar mount protects the end of the foot and is 'spun' over the end of the wood. The key is of the pattern found on the older instruments, but it is mounted in a slotted boss—a feature which foreshadows a much later practice (see Plate 2E).

To conclude this short survey of the Baroque period flutes there are one or two points about their internal structure that we must notice. In the first place, as Baines mentions, although they all conform to the general bore formula of cylinder, cone, cylinder (or occasionally reverse cone), the junctions between these sections seldom merge smoothly into one another and the internal profile is often interrupted by quite abrupt 'steps'.[34] The true oboes show this feature markedly, and in some French examples it is found as late as *c.* 1850. At this advanced period of technology the retention of such a detail must surely have been deliberate, and its acoustical effects recognised, small though they may seem to the unaided ear.[35] In the early stages, however, this may not have been so, and Baines inclines to the belief that the 'steps' found in Hotteterre type recorders and flutes reflect origins in the hands of traditional bagpipe makers accustomed to forming tuning slides in drone pipes, rather than any conscious acoustical experiment (see Fig. 21; but see also 'Acoustics' p. 32).

Second, as we have already said, the division of the whole tube into relatively short sections permitted of easier access to the interior,

Fig. 21   Tuning slide in typical Musette drone

and the benefit of this is shown by the degree of undercutting of the finger-holes that most Baroque instruments show (see also 'Materials and Manufacture', p. 205). Fig. 22 has been drawn from an X-ray

Fig. 22   Section of a Baroque period flute drawn from an X-ray photograph. Note that in this example the bore has wandered slightly near the foot. *See p.* 79

photograph of an Hotteterre type flute, and, in addition to simple coning-out, we see that two of the holes are bored slightly on the oblique. Neither feature is, of course, confined to the Baroque period: both are found to some degree in medieval instruments, and they were to be increasingly employed later. Finally we notice that in the early cone-flutes the mouth-hole is usually small, and, as in the medieval type, is placed high, i.e. further from the top finger-hole than in later instruments of the same nominal pitch. The shape of the mouth-hole seems to have been somewhat variable; probably the common form was circular, but apparently unaltered examples of an oval shape are known. For example the Rippert flute has an oval *embouchure* $\frac{3}{8}'' \times \frac{7}{16}''$ which is also rather larger than average for its time.

NOTES

[1] Bate, Philip, *The Trumpet and Trombone*, London, Ernest Benn Ltd., 1966, pp. 99 *et seq.*

[2] The actual word used by Suetonius is *choraulam*, the accusative case evidently of a Latinised Greek form, *choraula*. This in derivation would presumably imply the *aulós* in the specific role of a pipe associated with Greek dramatic song and dance.

[3] Galpin, F. W., *Old English Instruments of Music*, 3rd edn., London, Methuen and Co., 1932, p. 151.

[4] *Ibid.* p. 152.

[5] From an Inventory of the Guarderobes, etc. British Museum Harleian MSS. 1419. Quoted *in extenso* by Galpin, *op. cit.* pp. 292–300.

[6] For a fuller summary see Galpin, *op. cit.* Chapter VIII. In a valuable survey of musical instruments depicted in Dutch 17th-century paintings— *Galpin Society Journal*, Vol. VI, p. 58—Ian F. Finlay says: 'The use of the transverse flute falls into quite definite categories. In every case it is played by a man or a boy. It occurs mainly in ensembles in upper middle-class homes, although there are a few cases of its use at peasant or popular family gatherings.' This seems to accord with the aristocratic position held by the cross-flute in Germany.

[7] Sachs, Curt, *The History of Musical Instruments*, New York, W. W. Norton and Co. Inc., 1940. On p. 309 he derives the name from an obsolete verb *record*=to warble, but points out that an ensemble of recorders could be unsurpassed in dignity and musical reserve. Galpin also accepted the likelihood of this derivation, but suggested also that possibly the term might have referred to the facility with which the instrument repeats in the second octave. But see a note by Brian Trowell in *Galpin Society Journal*, Vol. X, 1957, p. 83, in which he draws attention to an entry in household accounts of the Earl of Derby, later Henry IV, for 1388. A *fistula nomine Ricordo* was paid for.

Also Eric Partridge, *Origins*, New York, Macmillan Co., 1958. Under *record* he has 'Old French—Early Modern French *recorder* has agent *recordeor*, a remembrancer, a relater, a minstrel (whence the Mus. instrument).'

[8] Illustrated in Kinsky, George, *A History of Music in Pictures*, London, Dent, 1930, 1937, p. 41.

[9] See Harrison and Rimmer, *European Musical Instruments*, London, Studio Vista, 1964, p. 16.

[10] Baines, A. C., in his *Woodwind Instruments and Their History*, London, Faber and Faber, 1957, has an excellent diagram (p. 210) illustrating the rise and fall of various woodwinds in professional and courtly music between the 10th and 19th centuries, and their relative preponderance in different ages.

[11] The instrument appears to have no holes, but the position of the player's fingers applied to the lower end is quite clear. Galpin interpreted this as a method of modifying the note sounded by opening or closing the end of the tube. See also Picco pipe, p. 72 above.

[12] A typical comment from one who has personal experience is that of Baines, *op. cit.* p. 181.

[13] See *Galpin Society Journal*, Vol. XVI, 1963, pp. 85 *et seq.* J. V. S. Megaw presents an able discussion of the pipe itself, its acoustical behaviour, musical capabilities, and relation to known contemporary instruments.

[14] *Ibid.* Vol. II, 'Musical Instruments in Fifteenth Century Netherlands and Italian Art', p. 44. M. Valentin Denis is here translated as saying, 'The use of the *double-recorder* in ordinary musical life before 1500 must be regarded as very doubtful; its representation in art seems a mere reminiscence of antiquity'. Perhaps the very rare Oxford specimen does not invalidate M. Denis's generalisation.

[15] Probably the most remarkable deliberate sophistication of a folk instrument took place at the hands of Schunda of Budapest *c.* 1890 when he remodelled the Hungarian *tárogató*, changing its double reed for one of clarinet type, and equipping the instrument with modern keywork. See Baines, *op. cit.* p. 147, for a felicitous account of the circumstances and their musical *sequelae*. We might possibly claim that the converse transformation has also taken place at times. For example, after the American Civil War, when discarded military band instruments fell into the hands of the Negroes of the Deep South they replaced the improvised ones which these people had hitherto been forced to use. Thus, for a time, cornet, clarinet, and trombone all became the voices of a living folk music—the early jazz. Bate, *op. cit.* pp. 137-8.

[16] These instruments, and the military fife as known in 1588, are illustrated in the *Orchésographie* of Thoinot Arbeau (Jehan Tabourot). This book gives a detailed account of the steps and music of fashionable dances of the 16th century, as well as of military marching routines, etc., and is one of the most valued reference sources to the student of social dance.

[17] There appears to be some uncertainty about the first appearance of Greeting's *The Pleasant Companion*. Galpin (*Old English Instruments of Music*, p. 145) says that it was published in 1661, though he does not quote his authority. The earliest example now traceable is a 'second edition' in the Library of Congress, 1673, which also possesses a 'sixth edition' dated 1683. The British Museum has a copy dated 1682, and the Dayton C. Miller Collection one of 1680.

Adam Carse (*Musical Wind Instruments*, p. 114) states that Pepys bought a copy of Greeting on 16 April 1668, presumably on the authority of an entry in his library list for that date—'Greeting's book – 1s.' Unfortunately this does not positively identify *The Pleasant Companion* as the book in question, though it does seem likely.

No reference to Greeting's book appears in Pepys's library catalogue at the time of his death in 1703, nor is the volume in the Pepysian Library today. It is known, however, that from time to time Pepys disposed of selected books, and this may account for the copy possessed by the late Sir Frederick Bridge which had, he tells us, in two places the monogram SP in a hand which the British Museum accepted as Pepys's own. See *Samuel Pepys, Lover of Musique*, London, Smith, Elder and Co., 1903. Bridge does not give any publication date.

Among the musical references in Pepys's Diary there are two more which are of importance in the present context, and both allude to one Drumbleby, an instrument maker none of whose work, as far as we can now tell, survives. 'Jan. 20th, 1668, To Drumbleby's, the pipe-maker, there to advise about the making of a flageolet to go low and soft; and he do show me a way which do do, and also a fashion of having two pipes of the same note fastened together, so as I can play on one and then echo it upon the other, which is mighty pretty'. So we see that English instrument makers were concerning themselves with the double flageolet at least a hundred and thirty years before Bainbridge and Simpson perfected their pretty toys. A second entry, under 'April 8th, 1668' (compare with the purchase of Greeting's book on 16 April) says, 'to Drumbleby's, and there did talk a great deal about pipes; and did buy a recorder, which I do intend to learn to play on, the sound of it being, of all sounds in the world, most pleasing to me'. These entries, which are followed by several references to learning the scale of the recorder, all come in the later part of the Diary, at a time when Pepys was rising in the world, and could begin to afford himself luxuries. We note the distinction between his former flageolet and his new recorder, and wonder if this indicates an advance in his taste from a somewhat trivial to a more serious instrument. If so, this might account for his not retaining in his library a *flageolet Tutor* though he bought it in the same month.

[18] The ingenuity expended on these *ephemerae* may be judged from a host of patent specifications, of which two granted to William Bainbridge in 1803 and 1807 are typical. In the first he says: 'I make the flagalet or English Flute so as to admit of a regular fingering from D below the lines, up to A above the lines, which was not the case before, as the F sharps and the D on the fourth line were cross-fingered on the old flagalet.'—But we note that he retained the open thumb-hole of the true recorder. The second application seeks to protect the idea of an head-cap provided with a side tube 'by means of which the performer shall and may be enabled to perform on such English flutes of concert

pitch, or of any other large size, by holding the instrument in the same position as the German flute, or in some other similar position as shall be preferred for ease and facility of execution.' Neither idea, we may think, was sufficiently original to merit the protection of a patent—the sideways blowing position was known to the Ancient Greeks (see Chapter 3, note 11)—but among the verbiage some useful information is concealed. For instance, we learn from the above that at the beginning of the 19th century the English flageolet was not necessarily confined to the higher keys, but was sometimes made in unison with the D flute of the period (see further Chapter 11, p. 198).

Though Bainbridge was probably the leading maker of English flageolets in his day, he was not without rivals. In the year of his second patent, Andrew Kauffman, a well-known London flute-maker, also patented an improved 'flageolette' of which he claimed, 'The flageolette constructed according to my improvements is calculated to play in all keys, which was never before attempted', and he attaches a fingering chart to the specification. An interesting sidelight on English history is shed by the patent documents of this period, for they grant the patentee rights to 'make, use, exercise, and vend' the said invention 'within England, Wales, and the Town of Berwick-upon-Tweed'.

¹⁹ Buchner, Alexander, *Extinct Wood Wind Instruments of the 16th Century*, National Museum of Prague, Vol. VII, Historia No. 2, 1952.

²⁰ Praetorius, M., *Syntagma Musicum* translated into English by Harold Blumenfeld (Bärenreiter), New York, etc., 1962, p. 35.

²¹ The private collection of Eric Halfpenny, Ilford, Essex, contains a most important two-piece bass flute of the Praetorian type with the mark of an otherwise unknown maker provisionally identified as Ia. Neni. See *Galpin Society Journal*, Vol. XIII, 1960, p. 38.

A comprehensive list of collections, both public and private, is found in L. G. Langwill's *Index of Musical Wind Instrument Makers*, 2nd edn., 1962. Privately printed.

²² *A Descriptive Catalogue of the Musical Instruments recently exhibited at the Royal Military Exhibition, London, 1890*. Compiled by Capt. C. R. Day, London, Eyre and Spottiswoode, 1891.

²³ The James Talbot Manuscript (Music MS. 1187 of Christ Church Library, Oxford) was compiled some time between 1685 and 1701. See Anthony Baines's article in *Galpin Society Journal*, Vol. I, 1948, p. 10. Detailed measurements are given of a Bressan flute examined by Talbot, though these require some interpretation.

Ottomar Luscinius, *Musurgia seu praxis Musicae*, published in 1536, is largely a translation of Virdung. It contains illustrations of all the musical instruments in use at the beginning of the 16th century.

The *Musurgia Universalis* of Athanasius Kircher, so much admired by Hawkins, was issued in 1650. It is an extensive work, but sheds little light on our present subject.

²⁴ 'Philidor and Hotteterre, who spoiled great quantities of wood and played great quantities of music until finally they succeeded in making the instrument fit for concert use': see Michel de la Barre writing in 1740 of the oboe. See Joseph Marx, 'The Tone of the Baroque Oboe', *Galpin Society Journal*, Vol. IV, 1951, p. 12.

²⁵ Baines, A. C., *op. cit.* p. 276.

²⁶ Descoteaux (1645–1728), Philbert (1670–?), known chiefly as recorder players; de la Barre (1675–1743), Buffardin (1690–1768; became principal flute in the Royal Orchestra in Dresden *c*. 1716 and gave lessons to Quantz in 1719), Hotteterre-le-Romain (?–1768?), Loiellet (?–1728; visited England and

established himself there in 1705. At the time of writing the earliest named specialist on the transverse flute in England, though the instrument itself was recorded in this country by James Talbot pre-1701).

[27] Thoinan, Ernest, *Les Hotteterres et les Chédeville*, Paris, Fischbacher, 1912.

[28] According to the *National Gallery Catalogues (French School)*, London, 1957, possible names suggested for the group include members of the Hotteterre family, the celebrated flautists, the brothers Piesche, and either Marin Marais or Antoine Forqueray as the gambist. These identifications have occupied a number of musical writers since 1907: *viz.* James E. Matthews in *Musical Times*; W.L.C. in *The Musical Standard*, October 1914; L. Fleury in *The Musical Quarterly*, 1923; Julien Tiersot in *Revue de Musicologie*, 1923. None seems to have questioned the nomination of de la Barre as the central standing figure—first proposed by de la Laurencie and presumably based on the fact that we can read on the music sheet which he is turning over 'TRIO DE — DE LA BA —'. Recently, however, while re-examining some old notes in preparation for the present chapter, the writer has felt some doubts. If we compare the face with the accepted portrait of Hotteterre-le-Romain by Picart, which forms the illustration to the *Principes*, there appears to be a strong resemblance about the eyes and the slightly depressed nose. The mouths, of course, we cannot compare. See Plate 4 A and B. Certainly there is little in common between the Picart engraving and any of the other faces in the painting. The compiler of the National Gallery Catalogue suggests that, if we reject the standing figure as de la Barre, he may be the seated figure in the right foreground. We note that he too has his hand on an identifiable part book.

A point of great interest is made by Martin Davies in his catalogue description of the picture. He writes: 'The man on the right is holding a flute with two more holes than usual; these have been deliberately put in by the painter, but it seems that they had no purpose whatever for the playing of the instrument.' This last comment we may now perhaps challenge. See next chapter.

Another splendid painting of the Hotteterre type flute is to be seen in the portrait of F. Semberger by his friend Kupetsky (*c.* 1710), No. 2670 in Sachs's catalogue of the Berlin Musikinstrumentensammlung. Illustrated in Winternitz, *Musical Instruments of the Western World*, London, Thames and Hudson, 1966.

[29] Joseph Marx, *op. cit.* p. 12. The full passage from which this comment, as well as note 24 above, are extracted is quoted in the original French.

[30] Harrison and Rimmer, *op. cit.* p. 34.

[31] *Ibid.* p. 34.

[32] See *Galpin Society Journal*, Vol. XVII, p. 106.

[33] *Ibid.* Vol. I, p. 16.

[34] Baines, A. C., *op. cit.* p. 276. See also Chapter 2, p. 32 above.

[35] In 1953 F. C. Karal published an investigation into the effects of abrupt changes in the cross-section of circular tubes. He sums up as follows: 'The constriction inductance can be interpreted physically as an increase in the equivalent length of the tube.' The converse appears to hold good also. Readers familiar with the more advanced aspects of alternating current engineering will recognise the electrical analogy used. In 1960 also, A. H. Benade compared the conditions in a lumpy duct, such as the tube of a woodwind with the holes closed, to the electrical state of a co-axial cable loaded with shunt capacities where the bulges occur. See F. C. Karal, 'The Analogous Acoustical Impedance for Discontinuities and Constrictions of Circular Cross Sections' in *Journal of the Acoustical Society of America,* Vol. XXV, No. 2, 1953, pp. 327 *et seq.* Also A. H. Benade, *op. cit.*, October 1960.

CHAPTER 5

18th-Century Developments

IF THE 17th century saw the birth of the cone-flute in Europe, the 18th was both the age of its flourishing and the period during which its inherent defects became increasingly irksome. After the appearance of Hotteterre's instruction book in 1707 a whole series of such, good, bad, and indifferent, followed in the course of the next hundred years. Among the more notable are those of Corette (1730?), Schickhard (also 1730), Eisel (1738), Majer (1741), Quantz (1752), Mahaut (1759), Granom (a luxurious publication, but as a 'Tutor' no better than many others, 1766), Heron (probably one of the most informative of the period, 1771), Gunn (1793), and Devienne (1795). In addition there appeared many anonymous works—Corette's was one which was, however, quickly identified—and these rejoice in such attractive titles as *The Modern Music Master*, *The Muses' Delight*, and the more prosaic *Compleat Tutor* which appears many times in different years.[1] These works, as well as the spate of music, both original and arranged for one or two German flutes, which soon appeared, bear witness to the popularity of the instrument among amateurs—whose performance often drew scathing comments from the more sensitive critics.[2] The professionals, however, could hardly claim to be unaware of the defects of the flute, though the majority of them seem to have been content to struggle with the instrument as it was for a surprisingly long time. Dubious intonation and an uneven scale were apparently accepted as calculated hazards. It is only after about 1770 that flautists in general seem to have realised that the basic instrument *could* be further improved, and even then innovations were looked at with much suspicion. Even Tromlitz, who was one of the most active and successful improvers, was to write at the end of the century that keys with more than three sharps or flats were 'difficult and unsuitable' for the flute. Well after 1800 instruction books continued to be based on the one-keyed instrument, with supplements for those who chose to adopt the additional keys which had by then become generally available. Such reluctance to change had, in fact, a respectable basis other than mere conservatism, as we shall see when we come to look at the construction of the many flutes which survive from this period.

Of course instruments in every age have had their outstanding exponents who seem to have overcome every problem, and the flute is no exception. J. J. Quantz and his successor at the Prussian Court, J. B. Wendling,[3] were undoubtedly such men, and the writings of the former give us valuable information. From the time of Praetorius—and long before—a major problem with most wind instruments had been to adjust the basic tuning to pitch standards that were by no means universal, as well as to compensate for the unavoidable rise in pitch due to warming up while playing. Praetorius himself recommended the provision of duplicate flutes, i.e. recorders, one set being tuned half a semitone lower than the other—an expensive solution, but the only possible one with one-piece construction. But mark, he also wrote in the same paragraph: 'But it occurred to me to piece apart the flutes half way between the mouthpiece and the highest finger hole, thus lengthening the upper section of the pipe by the breadth of two fingers. This makes the length of the tube variable and thus its pitch may be accordingly adjusted higher or lower. Although certain reputed instrument makers were of the opinion that this would make some of the tones of the flute false, they actually had no objections to the idea—apart from the fact that some of the highest tones did not respond very well.'[4] This wording suggests that the experiment may actually have been made—and if so we must give Praetorius credit for having anticipated at least one of the Hotteterre modifications, the insertion of a joint that could be pulled out to a limited extent between the head and the body. Even so, 'the breadth of two fingers' suggests something more than a normal tenon.

There can be little doubt that it was this question of basic tuning which led to the *four*-piece construction. By dividing the body between the two sets of finger-holes and inserting another tenon and socket it became possible to use a selection of upper body joints—*corps de réchange*—of different sizes, and so to alter the overall length of the tube. Changing these alternative joints, however, necessitated a proportionate and frequent shift of the cork, so we may suppose that the disappearance at this time of the heavy ornamental head-cap in favour of a much smaller and lighter one was part of the same reorganisation. We do not know exactly when *corps de réchange* were introduced, or by whom, but the consensus of modern opinion suggests about 1720.[5]

From this time on, the provision of numbered alternative upper joints became customary with the makers of high-class flutes, and continued until well after the 'additional' keys had become a commonplace. Writing in 1791, Tromlitz of Leipzig, a noted performer, and latterly flute-maker of whose work there is much more to be said, advocated as many as seven, though I think that few flautists bothered with more than three or four.[6] It must of course be remembered that between 1700 and 1890 pitch in Europe tended to rise, though in a quite disorganised manner, there being no attempt at standardisation between metropolitan centres. Disregarding conventional organ tunings (p. 171), the extremes seem to have been $a' = 376 \cdot 3$ and $a' = 457 \cdot 2$ vibs. per second.[7] Truly the travelling virtuoso must have had a hard life.

From Quantz we learn also that in addition to the matter of basic tuning, the *corps de réchange* could afford a second benefit. A long upper joint, somewhat flat to the pitch, might, he suggests, be useful in the allegro movements of a concerto where the accompaniment was strong. Harder blowing would then be compensated and the soloist remain in accord with the orchestra. Also in the keys of E♭ or A♭ a flatter tuning would allow a greater sonority on the a♭s in each octave. On the other hand, in adagios where a more sombre tone quality should be sought—according to the views of many 18th-century composers, Mozart among them—a sharper joint would compensate for the flattening effect of the type of blowing required. If the sharpest joint were already on, the cork could be pushed in a trifle with much the same effect. Before attacking the final allegro, Quantz warns, the soloist must remember to change back to the original joint and setting of the stopper. There could hardly be a better illustration of the degree of concern that might be expected of a conscientious professional flautist, though few probably carried it so far. Mozart's praise of Wendling (p. 182, note 19) seems, by contrast, to imply as much.

We have said that the use of the alternative joints required each time a corresponding adjustment of the cork, but the matter really goes much further. From the acoustical point of view a change in the overall sounding length of the tube would imply also a re-spacing of the finger-holes if internal tuning were to be kept just, and this was not mechanically practical. Some help could, however, be given by pulling the foot joint in or out at the tenon, though it was obviously a crude procedure. In consequence a sort of telescopic foot joint appeared which had the same effect, but with the advantage that it did not disturb the accustomed spacing between the key and the lowest hole. This foot was made in two parts each lined with very thin metal tubes which slid one within the other, and so caused a minimum of disturbance to the bore (see Fig. 23). Such a foot is mentioned with some disparagement by Quantz in his essay of 1752, but Rockstro took the view that it had some value. Tromlitz esteemed the device and recommended it under the appellation of 'register' in 1791. Possibly the version known to Quantz had only a simple wooden tenon and no metal lining, since he likens it to a needle-case. As an alternative to pulling out the upper joints for fine tuning, Quantz, in his autobiography of 1754, mentions the advantage of having the head divided into two with an additional socket and tenon longer than any of the others. Such an arrangement would of course, when drawn out, leave an annular recess in the bore, and Quantz is known at one time to have employed loose rings of varying thickness as fillers.[8] The difficulty was finally overcome by the introduction of telescopic metal tubes as just described—the 'tuning slide' of today. About this time some makers began to extend the inner of these two tubes to form a lining to the entire head. Quantz objected strongly but other players seem to have found no disadvantages, and the principle is in very general use in some parts of the world at the present time.

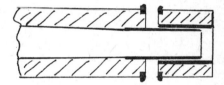

Fig. 23 Section of first type of 'register'. In later forms a construction similar to Fig. 24 was adopted. The taper of the bore as shown is somewhat exaggerated

If the reader cares to look at the fingering chart for the Hotteterre transverse flute (Appendix III, p. 244) he will notice that in addition to a complete chromatic scale from d' to g''', less only the highest F, three special fingerings are shown for the enharmonics f'♯–g'♭, f''♯–g''♭, and c''♯–d''♭. As we might expect, enharmonic distinctions did not escape the meticulous Quantz, and this led to what was probably his only true invention. In 1726, while staying in Paris, he designed a flute on the foot of which he placed *two* closed keys covering holes of slightly different size. These sounded respectively d'♯ and e'♭, according to pitch calculations he made for the purpose, and were also useful for improving

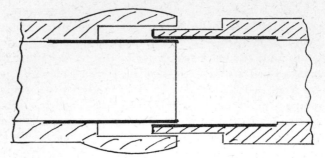

Fig. 24 Section of early type of tuning slide with
telescopic metal tubes—the tenon wood-covered but
not lapped. In later forms such tenons were graduated
to correspond to different *corps de réchange* and similar
graduations on the stem of the screw-stopper

several other notes. The fingerings are shown on p. 245. Quantz was
extremely proud of this instrument, and to the end of his life used no
other type, although he seems to have published no formal description
of it before 1752. To his chagrin, however, the instrument did not
'catch on' outside Germany and, in spite of Tromlitz's encomiums, it
disappeared entirely after some sixty or seventy years (see Plate 6J).

Before leaving Quantz as a source of information we must note two
more important facts that we glean from his writings. One is that about
1722 attempts were being made to extend the downward range of the
flute—presumably to match the contemporary oboe. Among his
supposed possessions there is recorded a flute by Biglioni of Rome[9]
which had on the foot an open-standing key which carried the lowest
note down to c'♯. According to Rockstro, who examined this instrument
while it formed part of the Carli Zoeller Collection,[10] its tone was poor,
and perhaps this may have influenced Quantz in his well-known dislike
of extended foot joints. He says in his *Versuch* of 1752 that the device
was not pursued because the added length was detrimental to tone and
intonation—a valid criticism, to be sure, if the rest of the tube were not
adjusted in accordance. Nevertheless, in spite of Quantz's no doubt
influential objections, we note that Majer (*Theatrum Musicum*, 1732)
gives a fingering chart for a flute with low C♮ and D♯ keys. It seems
probable that extension keys did not come into general use much
before the last quarter of the century. Presumably by this time the
lengthened foot would be regarded as part of the whole design of the
tube, and not just a supplement to an already standardised instrument.

In 1965 evidence came to light showing that English makers were prepared to supply such flutes some forty years earlier.[11]

The following are some of the instrument makers whose products illustrate the progress of the transverse flute in the first part of the 18th century:

I. Denner (Nürnberg), d. 1735
T. Stanesby, sen. (London), d. 1734
T. Stanesby, jun. (London), 1692–1754
C. Bizey (Paris), d. 1752
J. M. Anciuti (Milan), known to be working c. 1717–1740

and of course P. Bressan and J. Hotteterre already mentioned— though the collector who today finds an unrecorded example by any of them will secure a rare prize.

———

With the fourth quarter of the 18th century we find the beginning of what we might call a 'mechanical' instead of a purely acoustical approach to the intonation problems of the flute. The obvious notion that the chromatic semitones would be better sounded from their own individual holes, if these could be brought under control of the fingers, began to receive practical attention. Not that the idea was in itself anything new, and there is possibly some evidence that it had been seriously considered as long ago as the Hotteterre period. In the National Gallery painting referred to on p. 81 the player in the right foreground holds across his knee a most handsome ivory flute. Five of the six finger-holes are clearly to be seen, only the sixth is hidden by the fingers which are curled round the body of the instrument. The important thing is that beside the fourth hole there appears a second one offset from the line of the others, and in such a position that it could just be stopped by the tip of the left little finger. Now what could the purpose of such a hole be? It is placed just level with the A♮ hole, considerably higher than the keyed G♯ hole that was to come later, but if it were small and less undercut than the A♮ it might surely yield a usable G♯. If it were merely one of a pair of alternative holes, one of which was intended to be stopped up as in the older recorders, surely *both* would have been offset. If they were intended to be closed with a single finger surely they would have been placed much closer together as in the Baroque oboe. At this time the writer is not aware of any surviving three-piece flute that shows this feature, but the conjecture is supported by a specimen which came into his possession some four or five years ago. This is a four-piece ivory instrument, extremely worn round the finger-holes by years of use, and bearing the mark of Martin, London (see Plate 2F). It can be dated with some confidence at *c.* 1750.[12] At some period this instrument has been the subject of experiment: only 5 mm. below the A♮ hole a much smaller hole has been bored, just within reach of the left little finger. When opened this hole gives a respectable, if hardly full-bodied, G♯, certainly much better than the corresponding 'forked' note.

Turning again to the painting, a dark ellipse just appearing on the lower edge of the same flute, between the E and F♯ holes, suggests the presence of another hole on the inner side of the instrument. This, to be sure, is not very conveniently placed for the right thumb, but experiment has shown that, with practice, such a hole could be stopped. Does this perhaps represent an attempt to replace what was notoriously the poorest of all the 'forked' notes? The Martin flute gives us no help here for the unknown experimenter has tried nothing similar on the lower joint, but we may note as a matter of passing interest that he *did* try out both a C♮ and a B♭ hole for the left thumb. The writer's first introduction to the National Gallery picture was through the medium of a large photograph, but subsequent examination of the actual work, and the opinion of experts at the Gallery, confirm that these details do form part of the original painting.

So we come to the appearance of chromatic holes provided with closed keys, and we have to admit that we cannot name any one originator for any of these. The most that we can say is that they began to be mentioned in various writings *c.* 1775, though in that year they do not seem to have been known in Berlin which was then an important centre of flute playing. On the other hand, there is almost certain proof that they had penetrated there by 1780 for Ribock (1782)[13] speaks of having used them regularly for some time. He mentions Kusder[14] of London and Tromlitz of Leipzig as makers. In France the 'extra keys' seem to have waited longer for full recognition, for an *Encyclopédie Méthodique* issued in 1785 says 'it is pretended that an English musician has constructed a flute with seven keys in order to obtain all the semitones'. The only additional key known to the writer of this article was the enharmonic E♭ of Quantz. The most important English reference is found in the first issue of Wragg's highly esteemed *Flute Preceptor* which was published in 1792 and reached its thirteenth edition in 1795; but some evidence of English manufacture in 1774 is found in a biography of the Irish flautist Andrew Ashe, published in an anonymous *Dictionary of Musicians* in 1827 (see *Rockstro*, Articles 453 and 860). The rival London flautists Florio and Tacet have both been given credit for 'inventing' the new keys, on no better evidence, apparently, than that of several anonymous 'Compleat Tutors' and 'New Instructions' which appeared between 1770 and 1780. In three of these we read successively of a 'new invented German-Flute with additional keys— such as played by the two celebrated Masters, Tacet and Florio'; of 'Florio and Tacet's new invented German Flute with all the keys'; and of the 'German-Flute with all the additional keys, Invented by Mr Tacet'.[15] Of course we must in justice bear in mind that these works appeared at a time when the the word *invention* was customarily used with much more latitude than would be acceptable today, and by men who had either commercial or partisan interests to serve. On the authority of the maker Cornelius Ward (1844) we learn that Florio was much concerned with the re-introduction of the extended foot, and that he prized the low C and C♯ keys (which he had 're-invented') so much that while occupying the first flute desk in the Opera in London he attempted to keep them concealed from his colleagues.[16] This really seems to have been pointless, since the English makers Caleb Gedney and Richard Potter were producing them at the period, as is proved by surviving examples dated 1768, 1776, 1777, and 1778.[17]

The actual keys about which so much *brouhaha* was built up were, on the upper joint, a B♭ lying longways convenient to the left thumb, and a similar G♯ for the left little finger, which had hitherto been unemployed. On the lower joint an F♮ was set crosswise between the two lowest holes. This was less convenient since it could only be opened by the right third finger which had to leave the E♮ hole to do so. These three, together with the already established D♯, made up the equipment of the four-keyed flute, or, if the extended foot were favoured, the six-keyed type which we may regard as the professional player's standard instrument during the greater part of Beethoven's working life. Even so, instruction books by well-known players suggest that for some time the body keys were used mainly to provide shakes and graces rather than sustained notes. Both types of instrument are to be seen in plenty in many musical collections today. As to which, if any, among these keys had priority we have as yet no evidence, unless we try to draw some inference from the few three- or five-keyed flutes that are recorded. Among the known one-keyed flutes to which a second key has clearly been added at a later date we note that the G♯ seems to

H

have been the one of choice (see Plate 5C). Dayton Miller informs us
(1935) that in all collections then known to him there were only three
flutes with original D♯ and G♯ keys alone, and he quotes an engraved
plate in J. V. Rynvaan's *Muzykal kunst-woorden-boek*, published in
Amsterdam in 1795, as the only known illustration of such.

From the foregoing extracts the reader will no doubt have gathered
that documentation of the flute during the 18th century is confused
and sometimes contradictory.[18] However, before the end of the period
things become clearer, and the last few additions to the instrument are
accounted for reasonably well. At this time there still remained one note
in the fundamental scale that had to be produced by 'forking'—the
upper C♮ played with all holes, except the highest, closed. This was, in
fact, not at all a bad note because the full length of the tube below the
C♯ hole was sufficient to flatten that note by a good semitone. Nevertheless, the need was felt for something better and so a hole was made in
the desirable position between those for B♮ and C♯. Rockstro says that
this was at first governed by an *open-standing* key which had to be kept
closed most of the time by the left thumb—which, on the face of it,
seems difficult to imagine.[19] In 1782 Ribock claimed to have devised a
closed C♮ key, allotting it as a second duty to the left thumb, though
Rockstro doubts the originality of the idea. It was obviously a more
practical proposition, though still not ideal, and in a few years the hole
was transferred from the top to the near side of the joint where it could
conveniently be covered by a long key carried down to the right
forefinger. (See also p. 226.)

One by one the major inconveniences of the multi-keyed flute were
now being overcome, but there still remained one great difficulty with
the cross F♮. As this had to be opened by the same finger which
governed the E♮ hole, slurs between d' or d'♯ and f' could hardly be
played without sounding an intermediate e'. Ribock attacked the problem by giving the touch of the F♮ key to the right thumb, but this
interfered with the natural support of the instrument which was
important to the firm closing of the finger-holes. In 1786 Tromlitz
devised at least a partial solution by making a second F♮ hole on the far
side of the joint and covering it with a long key for the left little finger.
This, of course, doubled the duties of that digit, and even with the
duplicate hole there were still some combinations of notes that were
difficult to play cleanly. However, matters were much improved, and
the 'long F' in one form or another survives today. Curiously enough,
it seems to have attracted even more opposition than the earlier new

keys.[20] In spite of his invention Tromlitz seems to have preferred the Quantz type of flute for his own use, and although Furstenau (1832 *post*)[21] states that he played on an eight-keyed instrument in 1786, in 1791 he wrote of the extra keys: 'They are of great use for those who have been able to master their difficulties—but the most useful flutes have only the e♭ and d♯ keys, with the register and the screw-cork.'[22]

As the 18th century approached its close, then, the state of the flute was still far from settled. Professional players of repute were using anything from one to eight keys, and this situation was to continue for a good many years. The extent to which this instability may have affected the development of orchestral music is touched on in Chapter 9. Although the cone-bored flute almost certainly originated in France[23] the most important work towards improving it had been done in Germany. The position of the instrument in the former country *c*. 1795 can be gathered from a *Méthode* by Devienne, an excellent instruction book which, revised and brought up to date several times, was still esteemed for general teaching a hundred years later. From Devienne's first edition we learn that though the F♮, G♯, and B♭ keys were then becoming known in France, they were still not in general use. He himself appears to have used them principally for shakes, etc., but he recommends them to his pupils, as well as the low C and C♯ keys. The state of matters in Italy only a few years earlier appears to have been much the same, according to an instruction book by Lorenzoni of Vicenza.[24] Finally, the position in England, and the degree of refinement to which the best English makers had brought the art of flute-making, are indicated by the specification of a patent granted to Richard Potter of London in 1785. In the drawing annexed to the application the B♭, G♯, F♮, and D♯ keys are shown, as well as a head lined with metal and divided by a tuning slide, the outer tube of which is covered with wood (see Fig. 24). A screw-cork is shown, and a register on the foot joint. The projecting stem of the screw, the slide, and the register are marked with incised circles each of which is numbered, and it is explained that for optimum tuning the numbers exposed on each should agree. The low C and C♯ keys do not appear, as, presumably, the register was not thought compatible with the extended foot. That Potter did sometimes make this foot at the period is proved by the dated specimens referred to on p. 97. Potter's patent also covered the 'pewter plugs'—so-called—which he fitted to the keys (see p. 218). The idea was not new, according to Rockstro (Article 384), but Potter may not have been aware of this; and in any case patents in his day carried no protection beyond the country of origin, there being as yet no International Convention.[25]

Among the more distinguished instrument makers whose flutes, typical of the best later 18th-century work, may be seen in major public collections are:

T. Lot (Paris)
M. Lot (Paris)
Scherer (Paris ?), maker of Frederick the Great's favourite flute
Willems (Brussels)
Cahusac (London)
Eisenbrant (Göttingen)
A. Grenser (Dresden)
Schlegel (Basle)
R. Potter, 'Potter Senior' (London)

NOTES

[1] Probably the fullest bibliography of flute tutors extant is to be found in Dayton C. Miller's *Catalogue of Books and Literary Material relating to the Flute*, Cleveland, Ohio, 1935. Privately printed. Many of the Miller items are unique examples, and his commentary is invaluable. The original material is now in the Library of Congress, together with the instrumental part of the collection. In 1961 the Library issued an instrumental check-list compiled by Laura E. Gilliam and William Lichtenwanger.

[2] '[The German flute] still retains some degree of estimation among gentlemen whose ears are not nice enough to inform them that it is never in tune'. See Sir John Hawkins, *A General History of the Science and Practice of Music*, London, 1776. A new edition with the author's posthumous notes was published by J. Alfred Novello in London, 1853.

[3] See p. 174 below and note 19.

[4] Praetorius, Michael, *Syntagma Musicum*, Vol. II, English translation by Harold Blumenfeld, Bärenreiter, New York, etc., 1962, p. 35.

[5] Until quite recently a positive dating of *pre-1726* was accepted on the traditional assumption that a four-piece flute by F. Boie of Göttingen, presented to the collector Carli Zoeller by Albert Quantz, grand-nephew of the celebrated flautist, was actually an instrument used by him prior to his Paris visit in that year. See Rockstro, Day's *Catalogue*, Carse's *Musical Wind Instruments*, etc. In 1960, however, Pastor Gunther Hart of Zurich examined the church records of Göttingen and found that in fact J. F. Boie (the first instrument maker of that surname) was christened in Stolzenau in December 1762. Thus he can only have been eleven years old when Quantz died. The flute in question (now in the Adam Carse Collection) bears the name *Quantz* written in ink above the maker's brand of *F. Boie*. Thus the instrument becomes something of a mystery. How did Albert Quantz come to associate it with his illustrious forbear? And why was the name written on it? See note by Lyndesay G. Langwill in *Galpin Society Journal*, Vol. XIV, 1961, p. 72.

[6] It is common to find old fitted flute-cases with accommodation for no more than three.

[7] See Rockstro, *The Flute*, p. 121, Article 298, quoting A. J. Ellis, in *Journal of the Society of Arts*, London, March 1880. Also *Galpin Society Journal*, Vol. XIX, 1966, p. 136.

[8] Three such rings are included in the equipment of a Boehm 1832 model flute in the writer's collection, with slots for them in the case.

[9] Now No. 43 in the Boston Collection. This instrument also was presented to Zoeller by Albert Quantz and it is claimed (see Rockstro, Article 430) that it was bought in Rome by Quantz in 1724 or 1725. Its general appearance suggests a later date.

[10] *Ibid.* Article 430 *et seq.*

[11] Byrne, Maurice, 'Schuchart and the Extended Foot-joint' in *Galpin Society Journal*, Vol. XVIII, 1965, pp. 7 *et seq.*

[12] The only Martin of London appearing in Langwill's *Index* is an A. Martin, represented by a one-keyed flute in the Bull Collection, and entered as 'possibly Adam Martin, Mus. Instr. Mkr. Hermitage Bridge' in Kent's *London Directory* of 1796. The general appearance, style of key, and ornamentation of the present specimen are closely similar to those adopted by Charles Schuchart of London, and suggest a much earlier dating.

[13] Ribock, J. J. H., *Bemerkungen über die Flöte, und Versuch einer kurzen Anleitung zur bessern Einrichtung und Behandlung derselben*, 1782.

Dayton Miller, considering the appearance of an exhaustive table of shakes for the one-keyed flute in the third edition of Granom's *Tutor*, concluded that the additional keys were not known in the year of its publication (*c.* 1770). This may indeed have been so in England where Continental innovations have always been rather slow to appear—due more often to poor international communications than innate conservatism—but in France it seems that experimental keys were being made at least ten years earlier, following the lines suggested by the fashionable *musettes.*

[14] Langwill describes Kusder as a 'shadowy figure whose name occurs in many books of reference'. His name has so far been traced in only one *London Directory*, Holden's for 1799, but several examples of his work are known.

[15] The quotations in our text are taken respectively from: *The Compleat Tutor for the German-Flute Containing the easiest and most modern Methods for Learners to play*, etc., London, Printed for C. & S. Thompson, *c.* 1770; *The Compleat Tutor, For the German Flute etc.* (as above, but with a different frontispiece and some changes in the text), London, Jonathan Fentum, 1770; *New Instructions for the German Flute etc.*, London, Printed & Sold by Longman & Broderip, No. 26, Cheapside, *c.* 1780, all formerly in the Dayton C. Miller literary collection; now lodged in the Library of Congress, Washington, U.S.A.

[16] Ward, Cornelius, *The Flute Explained: being an Examination of the Principles of its Structure and Action* ... London, 1844 (published by the author).

[17] The later flutes quoted belong respectively to the Collections of the Historical Society of Chicago, the late Adam Carse, and the late Dayton C. Miller.

The Gedney example is particularly important as its date of 1769 makes it the earliest six-keyed flute so far recorded. It is one of the gems of the Max Champion Collection, and has two alternative upper joints and its own fitted case all in superb condition.

[18] Making allowance for the fact that some of the dates accepted by him have had to be modified in the light of more recent discoveries, Rockstro's compilation and comments still remain the fullest and most useful that are generally available. They should, however, be read in conjunction with the commentaries in Dayton Miller's *Bibliography of the Flute*.

[19] Rockstro, R. S., *The Flute*, London, Rudall, Carte and Co., 1890, Article 445.

[20] Both Tulou and Nicholson (until the last few years of his life) seem to have objected strongly to it. The limit of bigoted conservatism seems to have been reached by W. N. James, editor of *The Flautist's Magazine* and other periodicals between 1826 and 1832. In the course of his 'Six Essays on the fingering of the Flute', published as supplements to the *Flutonicon* (1841–46), he says that the c′ and c′♯ 'have no business on the flute at all; that these notes are excrescences, and engrafted most artificially on the tube of the natural flute. The addition of these two long keys was the invention of a German, as are also a great number of other keys, the value of which the English flute-player has had sufficient common sense to repudiate.'—and a good deal more in the same vein. See also *A word or two to Mr. W. N. James*, by Nicholson, London, Clementi, Collard and Collard, 1829.

[21] Furstenau, A. B., *Die Kunst des Flötenspiels in theoretischpraktischer Beziehung dargestellt*, Leipzig, Breitkopf and Härtel, 1834 (?).

[22] Tromlitz, J. G., *Ausfürlicher und gründlicher Unterricht die Flöte zu spielen*, Leipzig, A. F. Böhme, 1791.

[23] Theobald Boehm's attribution of the cone-bore to J. C. Denner of Nürnberg does not seem capable of support. *Die Flöte und das Flötenspiel*, Munich, 1871; translation by Dayton C. Miller, London, Rudall, Carte & Co., 1922, p. 10.

[24] Lorenzoni, Antonio, *Saggio per ben sonare il flauto traverso*, Vicenza, F. Modena, 1779.

[25] The International Patents Convention, by which a number of nations agreed to respect each other's patents, was not signed until 1883. Before 1870 the various independent German-speaking states granted their own patents or privileges, but would not necessarily recognise one another's unless specific trade agreements were in force.

CHAPTER 6

The First Part of the 19th Century

WHEN WE have passed the year 1800, the first thing that we notice in flute literature is the intense activity among improvers and experimenters that occurred in the first thirty years of the new century. At this period the flute was approaching the peak of its popularity as a solo instrument,[1] and its possibilities in the orchestra were becoming better understood and exploited.

As we noticed in the previous chapter, the most up-to-date flute—though possibly not the most favoured—in the last years of the 18th century had eight keys, and it was this instrument that became the subject of the 19th-century improvers. Of course many of the older makers were still in the field, and first among them with new ideas was the redoubtable Tromlitz. In spite of his own modest requirements, he continued to think of those who wanted all possible mechanical assistance, and in 1800 he devised an improvement in the 'long F'. In this arrangement a lever for the left little finger merely raised the head of the older cross-key, thus avoiding the need for a second F♮ hole, and by so much reducing the risk of leakage. Possible leakage due to ill fitting or unsteady keys, we may observe, was one of the most frequent objections urged against keys in general by the more conservative older players—and with poorly made instruments justice was certainly on their side. Being concerned by the double duty imposed on the left thumb by the B♭ and C♮ keys, Tromlitz proposed for the former an additional long lever on the same principle as his version of the 'long F'. Neither idea seems to have been well received at first, but very shortly many other makers had 'borrowed' them. Another point which attracted Tromlitz's attention was the unduly high position of the G♯ key and hole on many flutes, notably English ones. This, we may suppose, followed from the grafting of a new key on to an instrument which had already assumed a more or less standardised form. As later makers were to show, a more just position for the G♯ hole could be found either on the upper or the lower joint if the relative lengths of these were adjusted and the position of the tenon and socket carefully considered[2] (compare Plate 7E and F).

The most interesting of all Tromlitz's ideas, however, does not seem to have been realised in practice. This was nothing less than a scheme for a keyless flute (see also *Giorgi Flute*, p. 196), though he admits that his experiments showed that it presented some serious difficulties in fingering which prevented him bringing it forward at the time.[3] Tromlitz's scheme is of historic importance because it contains the germ of one of the most important concepts of flute-playing theory— that of the 'open key' system. This postulates that properly all keys should stand open when at rest, and it has been hotly debated both *pro* and *con*.

The year 1802 saw an interesting proposal by one William Close, of Dalton, Lancashire, eliminating the need for a special hole for each note of the chromatic scale. Employing a principle used successfully with certain flageolets and whistle flutes, he suggested providing one or more pin-holes located near the mouth-hole which when opened should raise the pitch equally throughout the compass of the fundamental scale, thus virtually transposing the whole flute instantaneously as required.[4]

In 1803 there appeared another and more plausible attempt to re-model the flute, which has been referred to more or less extensively by almost all writers on the instrument. Dr. H. W. Pottgeisser, a medical man, published in the *Allgemeine Musikalische Zeitung* an anonymous article on the flute since the time of Quantz, and presented his plan for a radical revision. As things were at the time, there was no doubt something to be said for Pottgeisser's plan, but the article itself is far too long for critical discussion here. Fig. 25, which is a sectional drawing reprinted from the original—with Rockstro's translation of the captions —gives a clear idea of the scheme. It will be noticed that Pottgeisser proposed a rather more pronounced taper to the bore than was custo- mary at the time and this resulted in a slightly shorter tube, and allowed the holes to be placed slightly closer together. Each finger and thumb was to have its own hole (the right thumb actually operating the one key necessary) and these were to be equalised in size, a consider- able advance on the standard arrangement. A second key, presumably open-standing, was to be permitted if the left little finger should prove too short to reach the G♯ hole without this assistance. In addition one- piece construction was envisaged for the whole body and foot. By his own account (1844) Cornelius Ward once possessed such a flute, but Rockstro, having failed over some years to get a sight of it, inclined to the view that Ward had constructed it himself after the original drawing. Ward is known to have spoken highly of this instrument, but one rather

wonders if his reluctance in later years to show it was due to its similarity
in some respects to various flute designs which he patented in 1842 as a
commercial reply to Boehm's revolutionary design of ten years earlier.

Tebaldo Monzani, a leading flautist and one of the most prolific of
London makers,[5] comes prominently into the picture about this time.
Established in 1790, he produced many flutes of current types which
are notable for their fine workmanship, if not remarkable for tone.
Characteristically he omitted the tuning slide in the head, made all
tenons point downwards, and constructed the lower and foot joints

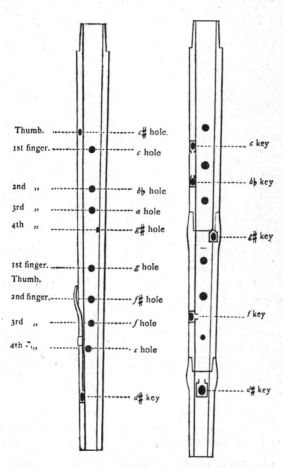

Fig. 25   Comparative sections of Pottgeisser's proposed flute and four-keyed flute of the period

in one piece. Monzani's recorded addresses, and changes in the style of the firm, make his instruments easy to date fairly accurately.[6] While discussing efforts to improve the defective semitones in the early 19th century Rockstro draws particular attention (Article 500) to a Monzani instrument dated 1807 which carries, in addition to the usual eight, what he calls 'two wretched little keys intended to improve the notes *a* and *g*.' This type of flute cannot have been common, and a specimen in the writer's collection suggests that these two keys may have been additions rather than features of a standard model (see Plate 7B). In the present state of this example it is difficult to assess the effectiveness of the tiny supplementary holes, but Rockstro seems to have been in no doubt—he condemned them. Incidentally, the finger-holes on this instrument are the smallest that are to be found in any English instrument of the time, though some French examples go even further. An excellent feature which is also uncommon in English instruments is the use of telescopic metal tubes instead of wooden tenons to unite the joints.[7]

The year 1808 showed something of a record for English flute patents, some of them of more than passing interest. On 9 August a patent was granted to Charles Townley for 'A Key—causing the Bore —to lengthen or contract at Pleasure.' This was effected by two levers operated by the left thumb which acted on the tuning slide, and which could be used during performance. The idea was more than once revived in Germany (see Rockstro) but the absence of examples in present-day collections suggests that the device was seldom, if ever, made. In November a second patent was secured by Townley, this time a comprehensive one covering a number of ideas. The only important one was an extra key which covered a small hole designed to sharpen the d' on flutes with the extended foot. At that time the hole required for that note was often bored lower than its just position because when so displaced it improved the f'''# and several other of the higher notes for those players who adhered obstinately to the traditional fingerings of the one-keyed flute. That the d' was hard to bring up to pitch appears to have been accepted as the less of two evils. Townley's grant also covered a sort of 'clip-on' mouthpiece designed to assist in directing the air stream against the edge of the mouth-hole. From the description furnished it seems that the idea was not completely new, and another rather better design of the same thing was to be patented by W. Wheatstone in 1820. It seems obvious that any such device is bound to interfere to some extent with the player's free control of *embouchure* which is one of the great artistic qualities of the transverse flute, and we need not consider the matter again.

On the same day in November 1808 another comprehensive patent was granted to the Rev. Frederick Nolan, part of which is of great historical importance. Part three of the specification proposed the construction of open-standing keys (either as a second order lever, or as a linked pair of the first order), the touch-pieces of which were in the form of rings surrounding one or other of the simple finger-holes. The original drawings, though poor in perspective and not complete as to detail, are reproduced in Fig. 26.

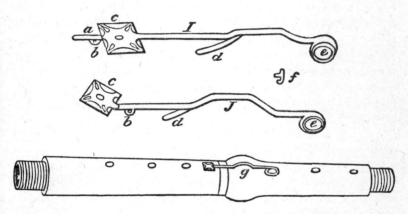

Fig. 26   Ring-keys as proposed by Nolan (1808)

This constitutes, as far as we are aware, the first contrivance for closing both an open key and a normal hole with the same finger. By sliding the finger off the ring, but keeping it on the shank of the key, the latter could be kept closed while the hole sounded its proper note. The basic principle is fundamental to the organisation of most of the highly mechanised flutes of today. Nolan envisaged the use of a tiny catch which could render the device inoperative at will, but this seems merely to complicate matters.

During the next decade or so, the race to secure patent protection continued. Many ideas were proposed, some not original, others of little practical value, but some also of considerable importance. In 1811 C. M. von Weber wrote to the *Allgemeine Musikalische Zeitung* describing a flute allegedly devised by J. N. Capeller, a member of the Court orchestra in Munich. The body of this instrument was made in one piece, and the G$\sharp$ key had a second touch for the right hand. The great feature was, however, the mouth-hole which was movable longwise in the head. We shall have more to say of this device in the next chapter— here it will be enough to quote that 'By this arrangement [including the screw cork] the pitch of the whole instrument can be rapidly altered, without any detriment, on the whole, to the general intonation.' Capeller also added a supernumerary shake-key for d″ which in different forms is incorporated in most good flutes today. The next year Monzani secured an umbrella patent covering several details, among them the cork lapping and metal lining to sockets which had in fact been used by French makers for some time. He also specified his combined lower and foot joint, although that had been before the public at least since 1807; and finally a 'nob' [sic] on each side of the mouth-hole (see Reform-mundstüke, p. 9). In 1814 James Wood, one of a family whose name appears in different contexts on many woodwinds from 1807 to the mid-century, obtained protection for the use of telescopic metal tubes at each joint of the flute although, as we have seen, Monzani was using these as early as 1807.

At this period also foreign patents were being granted with equal facility though few of them seem to have embodied anything revolutionary. The cut-glass flutes of the Parisian Laurent which, with their 'jewelled' head-caps and silver keys, make show-pieces in many a collector's cabinet were patented in 1806, though they were in fact no more advanced than their less flamboyant contemporaries. The fitness of glass for the tube has often been criticised, and certainly a specimen in the writer's collection is tonally meagre. The intractability of the material, however, gave rise to one interesting minor point of construction. Although the joints could be ground down to form tenons fairly easily, the mating socket was both difficult to form and mechanically weak. Silver sleeves were therefore cemented on to form the female part of the joint. This scheme of Laurent's may have suggested a similar, though mechanically unsound, device to Monzani. A highly fanciful instrument in the writer's possession has the head deeply fluted in the manner of an Ionic column except where a silver lip-plate is inlaid. The sockets take the form of silver sleeves, also fluted, but these are not cemented to the joints. Instead they are riveted to rings of soft alloy rather like thick washers, and these in turn are threaded, and screw on to a spigot turned from the wood of the joint (see Fig. 27). The instrument has evidently been well though not excessively used, and these elaborate sockets have clearly not stood up.

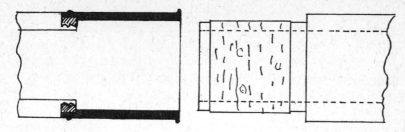

Fig. 27   Section of Monzani's silver sockets

A flautist of distinction of whom we hear from time to time during the first quarter of the 19th century is P. Petersen of Hamburg. Fétis attributes to him the invention of the G♯, B♭, and C♮ keys, though without any traceable support. In fact he seems rather to have concentrated on doing without keys (Rockstro, Article 683). His one authenticated addition to the instrument appears to have been a lever device acting on the tuning slide, possibly something like Townley's.[8] In 1824 Dr. Pottgeisser came to the fore again after a silence of twenty-one years. In the *Allgemeine Musikalische Zeitung* during 1824 he expressed some disappointment that his earlier anonymous article had attracted little notice, and explained that circumstances had thereafter kept him from musical activities for nearly twenty years. Renewed leisure had, however, allowed him to resume his studies of the flute, and he proceeded to give an account of the multi-keyed instrument as he then found it. He admitted its elegance and efficiency, but thought it little improved in intonation or purity of tone, and he felt more than ever convinced that the flute required radical re-thinking. In consequence he began a series of experiments which led again to the design of a new instrument. Once more Pottgeisser adhered to the principle of giving open holes to the four fingers of each hand, but this time he added several keys, including Capeller's d″ shake. The most important feature of the design is, however, the equalisation of all holes except the c′♯ and d′ with a diameter of 6·4 mm. regardless of the taper of the bore, and his insistence on correctness of placing rather than convenience to the fingers as the criterion of position. The c′♯ and d′ holes had the larger diameter of 7·9 mm. This, of course, foreshadows the great work that Theobald Boehm was to begin less than ten years later. Pottgeisser's treatise is accompanied by a detailed drawing[9] from which Fig. 28 is reproduced.

The key shown is the second historically important feature of Pott-geisser's 1824 flute. A bar pivoted as a lever of the second order lies along the body of the tube. At the right hand end it carries a carefully shaped crescent verging closely on the B♮ hole, and so adjusted that it can be depressed by the finger that closes that hole without causing

Fig. 28   Pottgeisser's ring-key and crescent touch-
piece

leakage. Where the bar crosses the c″♯ hole it carries a ring fitted with a perforated pad, and this serves to reduce the area of that hole when the key is down. This has the advantage of flattening the 'forked' c″♭ and sharpening the c″♯ with all fingers raised. The principle of the ring-pad to adjust the diameter of a hole is today employed in many flutes as well as in other woodwinds. Pottgeisser deposited the actual instrument with the publishers Breitkopf and Härtel in Leipzig, and there it was examined by Carl Grenser, the principal flautist of the town, and nephew of the Dresden instrument maker, J. H. Grenser. Grenser sub-mitted a lengthy criticism to the *Allgemeine Musikalische Zeitung* in the same year. Doubtless some of his strictures were well founded, but the patronising tone of his closing remarks must have been galling to the inventor. Though Pottgeisser's flute was itself stillborn, posterity values at least two of the principles he formulated.

———————

If at this stage we look critically at a typical series of cone-flutes, from the Hotteterre type to, say, 1815, we notice a changing feature which we have not so far mentioned—the finger-holes in general have become progressively smaller and at the same time more variable in size among themselves. Compare, for instance, three instruments that have already been mentioned; the Glasgow *Rippert* (*c.* 1690); the V. and A. *Bressan* (*c.* 1710); and the *Monzani* of 1807. The following table shows the diameters of the six finger-holes as they emerge on the surface:

	Rippert	Bressan	Monzani
Hole 1	6·8 mm.	6·7 mm.	6·6 mm.
,, 2	6·9 ,,	7·5 ,,	6·6 ,,
,, 3	6·7 ,,	6·8 ,,	6·3 ,,
,, 4	6·7 ,,	6·7 ,,	6·4 ,,
,, 5	6·7 ,,	7·0 ,,	6·6 ,,
,, 6	6·7 ,,	6·0 ,,	5·4 ,,

Of course in absolute terms these variations in diameter are only fractional, but they are enough to be critical in the matter of internal tuning. In any case all three examples show a great reduction in the average size of the holes compared with those of the 17th-century cylindrical flute. In 1637, Mersenne (Vol. II) quotes these as ranging from 7 to 11·3 mm. in diameter. We conclude, then, that a general reduction in the size of finger-holes was a part of the Hotteterre re-design of the flute—possibly suggested by a similar and successful feature of the true oboes as distinct from the shawms—and secondly that the relative irregularity of the holes developed in the course of continued efforts to improve intonation. We notice from the above table that between the times of Rippert and Bressan, in his latter phase, this feature has already become obvious, and Halfpenny says that the specimen quoted is particularly good on the 'forked' Fs.[10] Our comparative table does not, of course, indicate the extent to which under-cutting—practised by all the makers mentioned—affected the matter, but it does illustrate an unmistakable trend.

During the early years of the 19th century a number of English players, unlike the majority of their Continental brethren, began to be dissatisfied with the small tone of their instruments which they attributed to the small size of the mouth- and finger-holes in relation to the bore. The elder Charles Nicholson was probably the first to advocate larger holes, and certainly in his hands they seem to have yielded a fuller tone. It was, however, his son, Nicholson the younger, who carried matters to an extreme. The most celebrated English flautist of his day, he had his instruments built with the largest holes that have ever been applied to the ordinary eight-keyed flute. To be sure, these were as irregular as ever, but his great lung power and iron lip enabled him to overcome the tonal inequalities and produce a volume of sound that was the despair of his rivals. Both Nicholsons had, it seems, ideals of flute tone that were somewhat unorthodox in their day, and the younger was to write in his *Tutor* that 'the tone ought to be as reedy as possible;

as much like the hautboy as you can get it, but embodying the round mellowness of the clarionet'. Contemporary writers record that Nicholson's tone was somewhat hard though infused with grandeur, but we can hardly wonder that it was not admired everywhere. Nicholson's reputation both for volume and dazzling technique started a positive craze in England for large-holed flutes and these were made and sold in quantity. Plate 61, shows one of an extremely popular model made by T. Prowse the elder, and marketed by Clementi and Co. of London. For the privilege of stamping these instruments 'C. Nicholson's Improved' the makers paid handsome royalties which added substantially to the virtuoso's income, but it is to be noted that for his own use he preferred flutes by Potter or Astor. The example illustrated has not the largest size of holes, but belongs to what was termed the 'medium hole' category. Rockstro very justly points out that the Clementi flutes were not the equal of similar instruments by Rudall and Rose who had formed a partnership c. 1821.[11] The workmanship of Rudall and Rose has about it an almost indefinable air of artistry, even when they made instruments to other designs than their own—and they adopted no dog-in-the-manger attitude to this. For example, the curious 'waisting down' of the head in the region of the mouth-hole which was a feature of the 'Nicholson Improved' model they reproduced if required, though, as far as I am aware, they never went so far as to copy the alleged ornamental turning which disfigured many of the kind. Mention of Rudall and Rose brings to mind another manufacturing process with which they were particularly successful—the 'chambering' or making of minute local expansions in the bore the acoustical significance of which we have already discussed on p. 35.

Within the period determined for this chapter there remains one further innovation of importance to record. While England was becoming increasingly concerned with enhanced volume of tone, some Continental players were beginning to think of extending the *compass* of their flute, and c. 1815 Trexler of Vienna, for one, had added no less than seven open-standing keys to a super-extended foot thus carrying the lowest note down to g♮.[12] The touches of these were distributed in various ways between the two little fingers and the left thumb, and were made to overlap so that closing a lower one automatically closed those immediately above. Sometimes the tube was turned back on itself near the b♮ hole to reduce the overall length of the instrument. Such flutes can hardly have been common at any time, and specimens are prized by collectors today. Possibly the idea was specifically a

Viennese one, for S. Koch, also of that city, was noted for his particularly fine examples. Plate 7 shows a very ornate specimen by the latter maker, *c.* 1820, built on the straight model down to a♮. It will be noticed that all the normal keys of the period, including the d″ shake and duplicate touch to the B♭, are provided. Surviving specimens suggest that at no time can these instruments have been very efficient. The beauty of their workmanship is beyond question, but with only long simple levers to span such long distances 'whip' and backlash must have made airtight closing a matter of uncertainty.

Leading flute suppliers who were active in London from the end of the 18th century till about 1830 include:

Astor	Metzler
Clementi	Milhouse
Drouet	Monzani
Gerock and Wolf	Prowse
Goulding	Potter (William Henry)
D'Almaine	Wood (James)
Rudall and Rose	

and their various partnerships, who made for whom, etc., form a fascinating study which has not as yet been fully worked out. On the Continent we may add Buffet, Godefroy, Laurent, and Nonon in Paris; Grenser of Dresden; Griesling and Schlott of Berlin; Trexler, Koch, and Liebel in Vienna, to mention but a few. In Albany, New York, Meacham and Pond were supplying typical flutes and clarinets but there is some reason to think that these were mainly imported instruments.

NOTES

[1] Shortly after 1776, Mr Coningham, an equestrian, advertised in London that as part of his entertainment he would ride two horses simultaneously while *playing the flute*.

[2] The same problem affects many 'simple system' clarinets and some makers have solved it by boring the hole in its required position through both socket and tenon. This obviously rules out the use of anything other than cork lapping for the tenon, and it requires some device to prevent relative rotation. It could not, of course, be applied if the joint had to be pulled out at all for tuning purposes.

[3] Tromlitz, J. G., *Ueber die Flöten mit mehren Klappen*, Leipzig, A. F. Böhme, 1800, Chapter VII. An English translation of the passages concerned, with an interpretation of Tromlitz's rather unusual terminology and a commentary, will be found in Rockstro, Articles 482–6.

[4] Close, William, 'Experiments and Observations on the Properties of Wind Instruments—' ex *Nicholson's Journal of Natural Philosophy, Chemistry, and the Arts*, Series I, Vol. V, London, William Nicholson, 1802.

I

Halfpenny, E., 'The Sound-hole in a Flute', letter to the Editor, *Galpin Society Journal*, Vol. VII, 1954, p. 53.

[5] Monzani in his youth played both flute and oboe, a not uncommon combination in the later 18th century. In England he used the one-keyed flute professionally for some time after both Tacet and Florio had adopted the extra keys. The variety of instruments that bear his name points, either to a very open mind, or to great commercial acumen.

[6] On Monzani flutes, unlike many of their contemporaries, silver keys and mounts are almost invariably hall-marked. This provides a second useful means of dating. No doubt keys for standard models were made in batches, but where special keywork was involved we may reasonably expect the hall-mark to indicate the actual year of construction.

[7] Rockstro (Article 324) condemns this practice on the grounds that such telescopic tubes soon tend to be spoiled by 'the inevitable friction'. This is manifest nonsense. Modern metal flutes are inevitably built this way and, with no more care than is demanded by lapped joints, behave perfectly. Unfortunately many of Rockstro's excellent descriptions and commentaries are often marred by violently expressed personal prejudices.

[8] 'Ueber P. N. Petersen's Verbesserungen an der Flöte', *Allgemeine Musikalische Zeitung*, Leipzig, May 1822. An account in English appeared in *The Harmonicon* in 1823.

[9] *Ibid.* 1824.

[10] *Galpin Society Journal*, Vol. XIII, London, 1960, p. 42.

[11] Langwill in his *Index of Musical Wind Instrument Makers*, p. 101, notes that Rockstro quotes a wrong series of addresses for this firm.

[12] Rockstro, R. J., *The Flute*, p. 303, Article 559.

CHAPTER 7

The Work of Theobald Boehm

IN ANY account of the flute the work of Theobald Boehm commands a chapter to itself. It was he who, through a combination of musicianship, vision, and mechanical ability of a high order, fathered the instrument which is used by the great majority of players today, and though modifications and some improvements may have been made since his time, none of these has fundamentally altered the instrument as he left it. One is tempted to say that the position of Boehm is unique in musical instrument history. Cases are known where *dynasties* of *artiste-ouvriers* have entirely remodelled an instrument—as the oboe in the hands of the Triébert family, or the bassoon with the Heckels— but no other one man is known to have started his playing life with an instrument unmechanised save for one primitive key, and to have left it as one of the most perfect and efficient of all. It is therefore sad to record that this chapter in musical history has been marred by one of the bitterest and most unseemly controversies known. During his lifetime Boehm was (as we now know, wrongly) accused of helping himself to another man's ideas, and his work was denigrated by interested parties in the musical instrument trade. After his death in 1881 at the venerable age of eighty-seven the charge of misappropriation was revived by R. S. Rockstro with a violent attack in his great *Treatise on the Flute*,[1] and this in turn called forth a book-sized defence and enquiry into the facts of the case by Christopher Welch. In the light of the present status of the Boehm flute it would be best if these wretched matters could be forgotten, but because of the great value to students of much of Rockstro's book we are constantly and unavoidably reminded of them. I have, therefore, for the sake of completeness thought it necessary to give a short account of the controversy, but I believe that the most fitting place for it is in an Appendix (see p. 238).

Theobald Boehm was born in Munich on 9 April 1794, son of a well-known jeweller and goldsmith. In his father's profession he displayed considerable precocity so that, according to his biographer von Schafhäutl, he was by the age of fourteen entrusted with most important repair work. Certainly the technical skill acquired in these early years proved invaluable later on and rendered him, unlike many inventors, independent of others for the practical realisation of his ideas. When still a child Boehm showed a great aptitude for music and, it is said, taught himself to play a flageolet which, however, he soon gave up in favour of a flute. A one-keyed specimen made by Proser,[2] now No. 152 in the Dayton Miller Collection, and well documented as once belonging to Boehm, is probably the actual instrument. By the age of seventeen the young jeweller was finding the deficiencies of such a simple instrument irksome, and in 1810 he made himself a copy of a four-keyed flute by the celebrated C. A. Grenser of Dresden which he had borrowed from a friend. It is recorded that his self-taught performance on this instrument gave no great pleasure to neighbours and friends, but it did attract the attention of J. N. Capeller, then flautist in the Court orchestra, who in defence of his own ears, offered the boy some formal instruction. For two years thereafter Boehm was Capeller's most zealous pupil and with interesting results, for both the young mechanic and his professor were well aware of the defects of the contemporary flute. They sought particularly to smooth out the discrepancies between lower and higher registers, and Boehm made new instruments both for himself and his teacher. There are conflicting reports at this time concerning a flute fitted with a sliding gold plate which allowed the position of the mouth-hole to be varied. Boehm in later life included this idea in an account of original improvements he devised during the years 1812–17, but the article by C. M. von Weber to which we have already referred (p. 107) mentions it as a feature of the new flute introduced by Capeller in 1811. Whichever was in fact the originator of the idea, there is little doubt that its practical construction was due to the skill of the young Boehm.[3]

By 1812 Boehm had made such progress as a flautist that Capeller admitted that he had no more to teach him, and in that year he was appointed to the orchestra of the newly opened Isartor Theatre in Munich. For the next five years gold-smithing and flute-making by day and flute playing in the evenings occupied Boehm's time, but in 1818 an appointment in the Royal Court service led him to turn wholly to music. Thereafter, for some years, his requirements in flute-making were fulfilled by others, though not always to his complete satisfaction, and in 1828 he established a flute factory of his own. The instruments produced there were of the highest quality, fitted with tuning slides, hardened gold springs, and with the keys mounted on screwed-in pillars, a very advanced feature for the time (see p. 223). Boehm, in his *mémoirs*,[4] tells us that he himself designed an apparatus for accurately setting these pillars on the radius of the bore. One of these flutes of *c.* 1829, now in the Dayton Miller Collection, was described by that authority as 'perfect' in workmanship and finish, with a sweet and mellow tone and astonishingly good tuning for a flute on the old system. The mark carried was 'Boehm and Grève à Munich', Grève being Boehm's chief workman and partner at least between 1830 and 1843. Specimens are much prized by collectors today. Fig. 29, which is taken from the above pamphlet, depicts one of these instruments, and from it we learn one very important point, *viz.* that Boehm was even then using the longitudinal 'rod-axle' in a limited way although he apparently did not employ it on a London-made flute of 1831.

Fig. 29   Flute—'old system'—from Boehm's factory,
c. 1829

In that year Boehm appeared both in Paris and London as a travelling virtuoso and had considerable success. In the latter capital, he had, however, to encounter the rivalry of the great Nicholson whose facility, and above all power, on a large-holed flute had set a standard that few could emulate. Many years later, in a letter to Mr W. S. Broadwood,[5] Boehm recalled: 'I did as well as any continental flautist could have done, in London, in 1831, but I could not match Nicholson in power of tone, wherefore, I set to work to remodel my flute. Had I not heard him, probably the Boehm flute would never have been made.' Here we have a clear admission of one reason for Boehm's efforts to redesign the flute of his time. He could hardly have missed the point that Nicholson's large holes, albeit very unequal in size, contributed materially to his enormous tone, but whether Boehm was in any way influenced in his intentions by what had already been done in this connection by the amateur player Captain Gordon[6] whom he met at this time seems very doubtful. In any case it is clear that even before he left London Boehm had some plans in mind, for he caused to be made or—according to a letter he wrote in 1843—himself made an instrument in the workshops of Gerock and Wolf. These makers issued a descriptive pamphlet and scale for this flute,[7] with an engraving (Fig. 30) which they described as 'Boehm's Newly-invented Patent

Flute' with the additional claim 'manufactured and sold by the Patentees only, Gerock and Wolf, 79 Cornhill.' In spite of the typically extravagant claims set out in the pamphlet, this flute evidently did not succeed—probably Boehm never saw it in commercial production, if indeed it ever got so far—and early in 1832 he produced the first real 'Boehm System' instrument in his Munich factory.

Fig. 30   Boehm's 'London' flute, *c.* 1831 (*from Gerock and Wolf's pamphlet*)

In the London model Boehm seems to have made little basic change in the standard flute of the time, except to place the holes for E, F♯, and G, and an *open* hole for F♮, rather lower down and in a better acoustical relationship both as to position and size. This was not a new idea, as Dr. Pottgeisser had proposed something similar as early as 1803 (p. 104), but Boehm's method of controlling the holes was an innovation, and was the foundation of his version of the 'open-keyed' system which he was to develop fully in his later instruments. A pair of first order levers linked together were pivoted one each side of the F hole. That below carried a ring surrounding the E hole, and that above had a ring surrounding the F♯ hole, and a padded cup at its extremity covered the G hole. Thus four holes were controlled by three fingers only. The notoriously bad 'forked' F on the old flute was eliminated, and the F♯, though now technically a 'forked' note, had the F hole open at the same time, and was therefore comparatively little veiled. Fig. 31, extracted from Gerock and Wolf's pamphlet, shows the fingerings used. On the upper part of this flute the A hole was placed lower (and more correctly) than usual and was brought under the control of the left third finger by an open-standing second order lever with a touch-plate. Various such mechanisms for closing inaccessible holes had of course long been known.

When we compare the available documents concerning Pottgeisser and Boehm we cannot fail to notice the similar attitude of the two men, one an amateur flautist, the other a professional. Neither was prepared to accept that the defects of the standard flute were just something put there by Nature to be endured or overcome according to inclination or ability, and one rather wonders what might have happened had Pottgeisser been a younger man when he resumed his

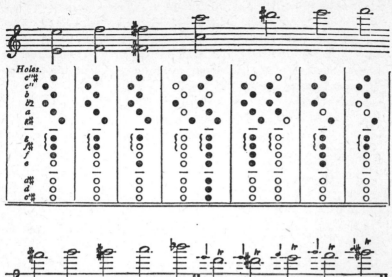

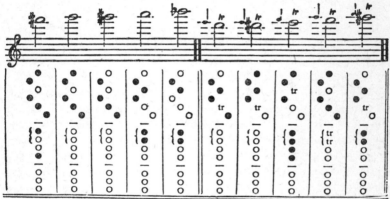

Fig. 31   'Scale of Notes affected by Gerock and Wolf's
Newly Invented Flutes' (i.e. Boehm's) from pamphlet
published *c.* 1831

studies in 1822, and with mechanical ability such as Boehm's to draw
upon. As it was, he left his second flute with the placing of the holes
much improved, but with no apparent rationalisation of the fingering.
Boehm's approach was no more radical than Pottgeisser's, but until
he had satisfied himself by practical experiments as to the optimum size
of bore, and the size and placing of the holes for musical requirements,
he left out of consideration the question of controlling them. His
mechanical mind suggested that once the proportions had been fixed

means of control with the available number of fingers could be devised. As Adam Carse has wisely pointed out,[8] the Boehm *mechanism* is what he designed for this purpose, while the Boehm *system* was his allocation of the holes to the different fingers and his method of securing adequate 'venting' for each note. In common usage there is sometimes a little confusion between them.

Boehm's flute of 1832 is perhaps best understood by taking the right- and left-hand sections separately at first. Of course the body had to be made in a single piece for mechanical reasons, but Fig. 32 will make the matter clear.

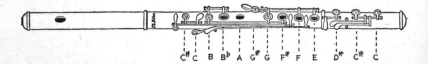

Fig. 32   Boehm's 1832 flute. Reproduced from his pamphlet of 1847

Starting with the right little finger in its accustomed position over the foot keys, the E, F, and F♯ holes lay comfortably under the third, second, and index fingers, but the G hole was unprovided. A padded cup was therefore placed over this hole and attached to an axle which also carried two rings surrounding the F and E holes. Thus the G hole could be kept closed when either the second or third finger was down. Another ring surrounding the F♯ hole was attached to a long axle extending into the left-hand territory as far as the B hole, and this had a projecting arm over the G cup. By this means the G hole was also closed when the right forefinger was lowered. In this way three fingers were enabled to govern four holes.

On the upper half of the flute the left little finger lay over an open-standing key for the G♯, and this allowed the first and second fingers to close the A and B♭ holes with comfort. The B was provided with a padded cup and this was attached to another short axle with a ring surrounding the B♭ hole. Thus, again, three fingers controlled four holes, but this time something further was needed. The long axle carrying the F♯ ring was provided with a second lateral arm over the B cup so that lowering the right forefinger would keep that hole closed. Otherwise opening the B♭ hole would automatically have sounded the B♮. The C hole was placed on the near side of the flute and was governed by an open key for the left thumb. C♯ required a hole too far up the tube to be comfortably covered by the left forefinger, so that too was furnished with an open key on a short axle with a convenient touch-piece.

This completed the basic equipment of the flute, and it will be seen that, except for the D♯, all keys were open-standing—the nearest approach to a theoretically 'open-keyed' system that had been achieved. At this time, however, many players were finding Capeller's special d″ shake key indispensable, so the necessary small hole was provided above the C♯ and covered by a closed key with a long axle carried down to the right second finger. To facilitate shakes involving the left thumb another long axle was connected with the C key so that this could also be operated by the right third finger.

For some years after 1832 Boehm played and exhibited his new flute, visiting both Paris and London. He submitted it to the Paris Academy of Sciences where it might have received valuable commendation, but its proper consideration was effectively interfered with by the Paris player Victor Coche, whose professional jealousy was disguised behind a show of friendly help. We shall have more to say of this astute man later.

In spite of its manifest advantages the 1832 flute was slow of accept-ance, especially in Germany, where its admittedly more 'open' tone was compared unfavourably with that of the older instrument, and probably proved more of an obstacle than the changes of fingering involved. Between the years 1833 and 1846 Boehm's other concerns (improvements in the steel industry in Bavaria, etc.) took up so much of his time that he had to give up flute-making in any personal sense, and his factory was closed in 1839. About 1840, however, there were signs that the instrument was gaining some ground outside Germany, and respected players in both England and France were taking it up.[9] In 1843, therefore, Boehm made formal arrangements for the flute on his model to be manufactured in Paris by Clair Godefroy *ainé*, and in London by Rudall and Rose. Some years before this, however, both Cornelius Ward and Auguste Buffet (advised and assisted by Victor Coche) had helped themselves to the design, and the latter, it must be admitted, had improved some details of the mechanism.[10] For example, if we turn back to Fig. 32 we see that the top key, the d″, set across the tube, although mounted on an axle, appears to have a touch-piece where no finger could possibly reach it. This projection is in fact not a touch-piece at all, but an extension of the key shank which was necessary to carry the *leaf-spring* that kept the key closed. Boehm, in his earlier designs, depended entirely on flat springs, and the *needle-spring*, which he adopted later, must be credited to the Buffet workshop. The best class of Buffet instruments have always been remarkable for fine craftsmanship.

One of the charges levelled at the 1832 flute by Rockstro was that 'the arms closing the G and B holes were a perpetual source of annoyance, and though they were provided with regulating screws their action was extremely uncertain'. This can have been nothing but prejudice, as good specimens prove. Boehm was far too good an engineer to have left any doubt in such a matter, and Rockstro admits that the specimen he examined was in a poor state, with loosened pillars, etc.[11] Nevertheless, when we consider the position naturally assumed by the fingers in holding a flute comfortably, we recognise that there were certain justifiable objections to placing axles on both sides of the tube, and shortly both the authorised and the unauthorised makers had transferred them all to the *inner* side (compare Plate 8A and B). This, of course, called for some other device than a separate rod with projecting arms to convey the motion of the F♯ ring to the G and B cups if things were not to get inconveniently crowded, and Buffet seems to have been the first to come up with a most elegant solution. He attached the E and F rings and the G cup to one axle, but the F♯ ring was mounted on a loose sleeve through which the axle passed. A lug soldered to this tube lay beneath a similar lug pinned to the axle above the sleeve. On the upper part of the tube the C♯ cup and its touch-piece, and the B♭ ring and B cup combination, were both attached to loose sleeves threaded on a fixed rod. The latter sleeve carried yet a third lug which lay on top of the other two, forming with them what was called the 'clutch'. Thus the old function remained the same. The E, F, and F♯ rings could each close the G hole, and the latter ring also closed the B hole. The C♯ cup and touch-piece were unaffected and merely shared the fixed rod as a pivot. Clearly leaf-springs were inappropriate to such an arrangement, and needles were used where required. The workmanship called for was almost of 'watchmaker' quality, and even today the difference between a fine flute and a second-rate one often lies in this feature alone.

An aspect of the new Boehm flute to which serious objection was made, especially by French players, was the open-standing G♯ key, although this was obviously essential to the full realisation of the 'open-keyed' plan. Originally a simple lever lying *along* the tube (Fig. 32

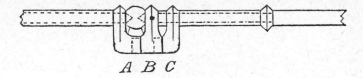

A B C

Fig. 33   The 'clutch' devised by Buffet
    A. Lug attached to sleeve carrying B♭ ring,
       etc.
    B. Lug pinned to axle carrying G cup and E
       and F rings
    C. Lug attached to loose sleeve carrying F♯
       ring

above), both Godefroy and Buffet, in their improved instruments, adopted the 'sleeve and pivot rod' form and so made it more elegant and less liable to accidental damage. Nevertheless the objection persisted, and the Paris professor Vincent Dorus, who had adopted the new instrument with enthusiasm, devised a form of closed key shown in Fig. 34. The action was such that when the A hole was open so was the G♯ as theory demanded, but on lowering the right third finger the G♯ hole was automatically closed until opened again by the little finger to make the note by the traditional fingering. Unfortunately this ingenious arrangement depended on two opposed springs, one stronger than the other, which always entails some element of risk in performance. Moreover, the necessary power of the stronger spring made the touch rather heavy and difficult in the G♯–A shake.[12] This same question of 'open' versus 'closed' G♯ continued, as we shall see, when Boehm introduced his later flute, and it has not been entirely resolved even today.

A further addition which became necessary about this time was a key for the d″♯ shake, so a small hole was provided above that for the d″. Control of this was given to the right third finger which had therefore to relinquish its connection with the C♮ thumb-hole. Assistance with shakes on this note was, however, still required so the right forefinger was again called into service. Many flutes of Godefroy and Buffet make show this arrangement, and all three linkages were most elegantly arranged to make use of the axle and loose sleeves with appropriated clutches, and needle-springs. Specimens that have been well cared for show that this beautiful mechanism could be in every way satisfactory. At the same time the rod and sleeve device was applied

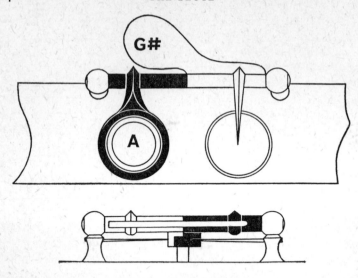

Fig. 34   Dorus' G♯ key

to the keys on the foot joint making their action more positive by
eliminating a possible source of backlash at the point where Boehm's
longitudinal c′ and c′♯ levers passed under the tails of the keys proper
(compare Plate 8A and c). It is said that during these years the French
workers made other improvements of an acoustical nature, but these
have not been identified, unless the substitution of two small holes side
by side for the larger single C♮ thumb-hole be one. The advantages
of the duplication are difficult to imagine, but paired holes opened and
closed as one are not uncommon on so-called 'cone-Boehm' flutes.

Boehm's crowning musical achievement came in 1847, and in
starting to examine it we cannot do better than quote some of his own
words written twenty-four years later. 'I was never able to understand
why, of all wind instruments with tone-holes and conical bore, the
flute alone should be blown at its wider end: it seems much more natural
that, with a rising pitch and shorter length of air column, the diameter
should become smaller. I experimented with tubes of various bores but
I soon found that, with only empirical experiments, a satisfactory result
would be difficult of attainment.' (One can only suppose that Boehm
regarded the recorder as an obsolete instrument, and therefore outside

his context. Incidentally he attributed the invention of the cone-bored transverse flute to J. C. Denner of Nürnberg (p. 102, note 23).)

'I finally called science to my aid and gave two years [13] to the study of the principles of acoustics under the excellent guidance of Herr Professor Dr von Schafhäutl.[14] After making many experiments, as precise as possible, I finished a flute in the latter part of 1847, founded on scientific principles, for which I received the highest prizes at the World's Expositions, in London in 1851, and in Paris in 1855.'

It seems, then, that although Boehm had improved the conventional flute of his time beyond recognition, he still felt some doubts about its basic *rationale*. This may to some extent account for his re-entry on a field which he had left for some years, for we have no evidence that he was at all worried by the various modifications that had been applied to the original 1832 model, though he must have observed them with interest.[15]

The extent to which Boehm's work of 1846–47 could today be called scientific may perhaps be questioned. The physics which he learned from von Schafhäutl could only have been the classical acoustics as understood at that time, and the basic length of the flute tube, and its relative diameter for a given pitch, as well as the size of holes which best satisfied his stringent requirements as a musician, still had to be determined by experiment. But, as Dayton Miller has pointed out, once these data had been obtained, Boehm's application of them was truly the work of a scientific mind.[16] The relative positions of the holes were obtained by calculation based on a simple law of acoustics, and in the course of his ensuing work Boehm devised a geometrical diagram which he called his *Schema*, from which the necessary dimensions could be read off directly for a flute of the right length to conform to any of the different pitch standards then in use. The *Schema* was submitted to the authorities of the Paris Exposition of 1868, but the jury expressed themselves as unqualified to assess it. Had it secured the seal of their approval it would no doubt have proved useful in the musical instrument industry, but, as it was, a limited publication by the Bavarian Polytechnic Society in their *Kunst und Gewerbeblatt* for October 1886 was all that it received. Boehm has been accused of himself departing from the *Schema*, but Miller, in 1921, found among some fifty unaltered specimens from the Boehm workshop no single example which did so. In making such a comparison we must, of course, look carefully for evidence of alteration which may have occurred during repair work, or even deliberately in the course of adjustment to a different pitch

standard. It is not unknown also for a flute to be 'retuned' internally
when passing from one ownership to another—there are few players
who have not some idiosyncrasy of blowing, favourite fingerings, etc.,
which may have led to minor adjustment of the original size of one or
more holes.

The new flute which Boehm introduced in 1847 as the result of his
experiments and calculations had a length (air column) of 623 mm. for
a pitch of A = 435 c.p.s., allowing for end correction (p. 30 above),
and a diameter in the cylindrical portion of 19 mm. The designer, in
fact, preferred a diameter of 20 mm. which satisfied him as to volume
and richness of tone in the first two octaves. The third octave, however,
he found rather difficult to sound softly, so he compromised on a
slightly narrower tube which eased the matter. In the uppermost quarter
of its length the tube tapered in a very gentle curve to 17 mm. at the
stopper. This contraction, Boehm decided, was necessary and had an
important effect on tone production and the relative intonation of the
octaves. The actual form of this contraction is difficult to express—
Boehm himself said it 'closely approached the curve of the parabola'
but in fact it appears to have been determined quite empirically. Miller
took up this point, and after measuring and plotting the shape of nearly
a hundred flute heads of many makes, concluded in 1922 that there
was no consistency among makers as to its proportions.[17] The only
thing in common was that all employed a taper of some 2 mm. in this
part of the tube. The 'Cylinder Flute with Parabolic Head', nevertheless, became the recognised appellation of the new instrument, and in
1847 Boehm obtained patents for the tube in this form. That year he
reopened his flute factory and from then on proceeded to make the
instrument with both wood and metal bodies, sometimes fitting wooden
heads to metal lower parts.

Boehm argued very justly that the note-holes should be as large as
possible, certainly not less than three-quarters of the bore diameter,[18]
which worked out at 14·5 mm. on his scale. But with wooden tubes
this introduced almost insuperable difficulties in manufacture, and
again a compromise was adopted—for metal flutes 13·5 mm. and for
wooden ones 13·0 mm.[19] At first it seemed to Boehm that it would be
desirable to graduate the holes from the lowest to the highest, and a
few flutes were made on this principle, but again manufacturing
difficulties were greatly increased, and the practical advantages proving
small, the idea was given up. The theory was, however, taken into
account when the standard size for the holes was fixed. Today some

high-class flute makers do employ graduated holes, not consistently in series, to be sure, but in groups of two or three sizes. The holes on the foot joint are very commonly slightly larger than the others.

The system of fingering Boehm had already worked out for his 1832 instrument, but the new large holes which could not well be stopped directly by the fingers presented a problem. Padded covers had to be provided for each hole, and as each one had to open independently (corresponding to the lifting of a finger on the former ring-keyed instrument) yet be coupled to others, new mechanism was required. The tubes and axles of the French makers provided the solution, and these Boehm now adopted. Each cover was attached to its own sleeve and sprung 'open' by a light needle spring. Where movement had to be transferred from one key to an adjacent one this was accomplished by means of overlapping lugs provided with set screws to adjust the relative rise and fall. Control of the B hole from the F$\sharp$ plate was brought about in a similar manner, using a clutch like that of Buffet, but with only two elements.

Before the cylinder flute had settled down to the definitive form just described, however, some intermediate types seem to have been made. Flutes made in Boehm's own workshop between 1847 and 1867 were marked 'Th. Boehm in München' and carried serial numbers. In 1854 Carl Mendler entered Boehm's employment. He was a watchmaker by training, and no doubt his skill did much to maintain the high mechanical standard of the instruments produced. In 1862 he became foreman, and five years later a partner in the concern. Thereafter the makers' mark became 'Th. Boehm & Mendler' but the serial numbers were discontinued. After Boehm's death the business was carried on successively by Mendler, and his son Carl junior, from about 1895, but the old makers' mark was retained.[20]

A considerable number of early 'Th. Boehm' cylinder flutes are now in the Dayton C. Miller Collection, and using the serial numbers as a guide some very interesting conclusions can be drawn from them. No. 1 (D.C.M. 625) appears to have been a straightforward application of the 1832 mechanism to the newly devised tube, with finger-holes of 11·54 to 11·56 mm., as was also No. 2; but No. 5, made in 1848, now in the Deutsches Museum, Munich, has the holes covered. No. 7, also of 1848, in the same collection, shows a reversion to the open rings but with some differences in the mechanism. All these are metal flutes with the barrel-shaped *embouchure* (p. 9) but by about 1850 Boehm had evidently begun to make the built-up type with lip-plate

and 'chimney'.[21] With the grant of English and French patents for
the cylinder flute of 1847 Boehm again assigned manufacturing rights
to his former representatives, Rudall and Rose, and Godefroy *ainé*.
Adam Carse says that Louis Lot of Paris also secured French rights,
but this seems to have been rather later, possibly a second assignment.
Lot is believed to have been Godefroy's son-in-law, and there is correspondence between him and Boehm preserved (p. 157, note 7). A large
number of beautifully made cylinder flutes bear the Lot mark. Evidence
of the close association of Boehm with the London firm is afforded by
the specimen shown in Plate 8D. This is an exact copy of the above
mentioned Nos. 1 and 2 except that the head section is made a little
longer and the socket placed proportionately lower down. It is a beautiful instrument, gold plated, and evidently much worn in use. The
embouchure has been renewed.

In 1851 Boehm paid another visit to England. This was the year of
the Great Exhibition at which the new cylinder flute gained first prize,
and at that time he was playing on an instrument with graduated holes
progressing evenly from 12 to 15 mm. in diameter. One wonders if this
visit, were more known about it, might not shed light on a very curious
specimen which the writer found in a London pawnbroker's some
years ago, and which does not seem to be duplicated in any other collection. It is beautifully made of silver, with the lip-plate in gold, and
several gold springs of the type used in the 1832 model (see Plate 8F).
The tube, which is very light, has the typical Boehm profile and proportions, notably the very short space between the *embouchure* and the
end-cap. The mechanism is very delicate though quite positive in
action, and the covers are riveted to the key shanks in the manner of
the earliest numbered examples. Longitudinal axles are all kept to the
inner side of the body, a feature that does not seem to have been fully
established before about 1860. The most unusual point, however, is
the placing of four of the holes; the G, B♮, and C are all set on the
inside and are covered by simple lever keys pivoted *across* the tube, and
the G♯ is offset on the other side and covered by a second order lever
as on the very first design of the 1832 model (see Fig. 32). Both the G
and B♮ keys are closed by long tails soldered to the sleeves of the
associated keys, and the rise and fall is adjusted by set-screws. The
C key is closed as usual by the left thumb, but it has an extended touch-
piece so that the B♮ below can be closed simultaneously to sound A♯
from the usual hole. This arrangement was occasionally made by
Boehm *c.* 1860—it is to be seen on the Gustave Oeschule/Honeyman

flute, No. 177 in the Dayton C. Miller Collection and which that authority regarded as an experiment.

Mention of the primitive G♯ key on the last instrument reminds us again of 'open' versus 'closed', which was as controversial a matter in 1847 as it had been in 1832. Boehm remained convinced of the superiority of the open key, and produced a very elegant and effective version for the new flute. His French licencees, however, to meet the views of their countrymen, soon added the Dorus G♯ key. This, though good on metal flutes, was less satisfactory on wooden ones since the necessary axle on the outer side of a stouter tube sometimes got in the way of the left third finger. The objection to opposed springs of course remained. Although Boehm favoured the open G♯ entirely, he was open-minded enough to make a few closed keys for special clients. One such is found on the Macauley flute (D.C.M. 161). In appearance it is similar to his standard open key, but the cover is sprung *closed* and the attached lever is divided in the middle and provided with an additional fulcrum, thus reversing its effect (see Fig. 35). This was probably the best type of closed G♯ ever designed but it does not seem to have been copied by any other maker. No doubt Boehm did little to publicise it. It is to be noted that with this type of G♯ Boehm placed the A hole 1·2 mm. *above* its *Schema* position to compensate for the inevitable flattening of that note due to the presence of a closed hole immediately below. Both he and later makers applied a similar compensation to the F♯, and for a similar reason.

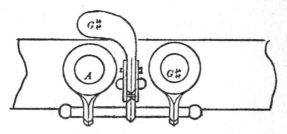

Fig. 35   Boehm's closed G♯ action

The keys allocated to the left thumb form another feature in which the original cylinder flute differed from its present-day descendant. At first Boehm envisaged no more than a single open key to cover the C hole, so that simply lowering the thumb would sound the B♮. In 1849, however, a celebrated Italian flautist, Giulio Briccialdi,

K

devised the arrangement shown in Fig. 36. By this mechanism the C hole was closed by the left thumb on touch-piece *x*. A slight sideways shift on to touch-piece *y* kept the C hole shut but also closed the B♮ hole at the same time, thus sounding B♭ and giving an alternative to

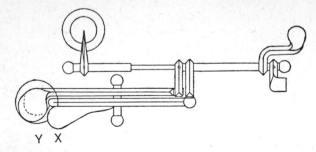

Y X

Fig. 36   Briccialdi B♭ action

the usual fingering with the right forefinger on its own key. This same forefinger could operate a shake-key when the thumb was released. The arrangement is in universal use today. Boehm regarded the movement *upward* along the tube as irrational in passing from a higher to a lower note and shortly came out with the key-work shown in Fig. 37. The thumb now moved in downward direction from B to B♭. It will be noticed that a second touch for the right-hand shake was also added.

In considering the key-work of the classical cylinder flute as outlined above it is rather easy, while admiring Boehm's mechanical ingenuity, to forget that everything he designed had no purpose but to implement the acoustic principles that he had worked out. His final contribution

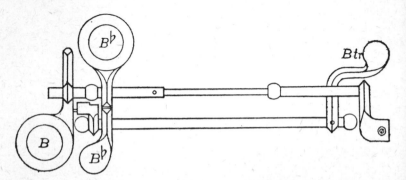

Fig. 37   Boehm's B♭ thumb levers

reminds us again of this fact. Some time, *c.* 1854, Boehm produced an *Alt-Flöte* in G, now commonly called a bass flute—and we may note in passing that he would never extend the compass of the ordinary concert flute below b♮, as many examples prove. The G flute, and his intentions in designing it, are considered in a later chapter, among other large flutes, but here we require to notice one feature of it. Finding that, however well designed the instrument was, some of the higher harmonics lacked freedom of speech and purity of tone, Boehm returned to basic acoustics and, at a position calculated to assist the formation of an antinode in the air column, he introduced a tiny vent-hole and key on the lines of the 'speaker' keys used in reed instruments. Satisfied of its value on the G flute, Boehm applied it also to the concert instrument, and it is sometimes to be found between the c♯ and d″ holes on both wooden and metal examples from his own workshop. The idea has not survived and present-day players seem to get on perfectly well without it.

The last observation we have to make in this short survey of Boehm's work is also concerned with basic acoustics. His preliminary studies convinced him that the ideal shape for the mouth-hole would be a rectangle with rounded corners, undercut to an angle of some 7 degrees. Here he seems to be on debatable ground and his arguments are not very convincing. Certainly he did not adhere rigidly in practice to this theory[22] and he seems to have bowed to the inescapable fact that the *embouchure* which suits one player is often useless to another, even on the same flute. Boehm's acceptance of the fact, even if unexpressed, is another testimony to the fair-mindedness of a very remarkable man.

NOTES

[1] Yet, be it noted that, as a pupil of Richard Carte, Rockstro was not above adopting Boehm's model of 1832, the first really satisfactory version—see Rockstro, *The Flute*, p. 633, Article 925—nor did he later contemn the cylinder model of 1847, but indeed added his own improvements to it with some success. By 1864 he was sponsoring a 'Rockstro Model' and in 1884 he published a descriptive pamphlet and a supplementary fingering chart for this instrument while still obstinately crediting the original basic scheme to Gordon rather than to Boehm (see Appendix I).

[2] According to Lyndesay Langwill's *Index of Musical Wind Instrument Makers*, 2nd edn., Edinburgh, 1962, Proser is known only as a London maker, 1777–95. It seems curious that an example of his work should turn up in Munich during that period—or was he perhaps a German who set up in England after commencing in Bavaria? An almost identical instrument, now in the writer's collection, was bought in a London street market in 1936.

[3] *Allgemeine Musikalische Zeitung*, May 1811. An attack on the instrument

by Heinrich Grenser appeared later in the year in the same periodical (p. 778), and a rejoinder by Capeller in the first issue of the *Münchener Gesellschaftblatt* in 1812. See also a translation of von Weber's account in Rockstro, p. 179, Article 521. The opportunity for a sneer at Boehm is not missed.

[4] Boehm, Theobald, *Ueber den Flötenbau und die neuesten Verbesserungen desselben*, B. Schott's Söhnen, 1847.

[5] Th. Boehm to W. S. Broadwood, London, August 1871. See Boehm–Miller's *The Flute and Flute-Playing*, London, Rudall, Carte and Co., 1922, p. 8.

[6] William Gordon, generally stated to have been a Swiss by birth, Captain in a regiment of Charles X's Swiss Guards. A keen amateur of the flute, he was a pupil of both Drouet and Tulou (see also Appendix I).

[7] Gerock and Wolf, *Scale and Description of Boehm's Newly-Invented Patent Flute, etc.*, London, n.d., *c.* 1831.

[8] Carse, Adam, *Musical Wind Instruments*, London, Macmillan and Co., 1939, p. 95.

[9] In England Richard Carte (*c.* 1843) and Clinton took up the new flute with enthusiasm, and to their names Fitzgibbon (*Story of the Flute*, London, William Reeves, 1913) adds those of Folz and Card, who later brought out a model of his own which did him no credit. In Paris Dorus, a highly esteemed professor in the *Conservatoire*, adopted the Boehm instrument, though probably after the well-known soloists Camus and Coche had done so. His modification has already been alluded to on p. 123. Although Coche must be given credit for an extremely fine instruction *Méthode*, his gerrymanderings concerning the acceptance of the new model, and the claims he made on his own behalf, leave an unpleasant impression. His letters figured prominently in the 'Boehm–Gordon Controversy' (see Appendix I).

In spite of obstructive conservatism in Germany Boehm was not entirely without supporters there, and John Finn, in *Musical Opinion*, No. 273, April 1894, names Stettmaier, Furstenau, and Heindl as advocates of the 1832 flute. Heindl's own instrument of the later cylinder model is now No. 99 in the Dayton Miller Collection.

[10] There was, of course, no reason why Buffet should not do this. Boehm had made no efforts to secure protection, presumably because he did not regard his refinement of mechanisms that had long been known in a crude form as patentable. He was never slow to apply for protection for anything he regarded as a true invention.

[11] Rockstro, *The Flute*, London, Rudall, Carte and Co., 1890, p. 331, Article 594.

[12] Dayton Miller, in a comment included in his translation of *Die Flöte und das Flötenspiel*, p. 71, compares his personal experiences of all three types of flute and gives a balanced judgment. On the whole he supports Boehm's arguments in favour of the open G♯.

[13] 1846 and 1847.

[14] Von Schafhäutl of the University of Munich was undoubtedly an able acoustician. An account of his life and work by Ludwig Boehm appeared in the *Bayer Industrie und Gewerblatt*, No. 17, 1890, and a translation will be found in Welch's *History of the Boehm Flute*, London, Rudall, Carte and Co., 1892.

[15] This would appear to be in the character of the man. In spite of Rockstro's accusations of grandiloquence, etc., Boehm seems to have impressed all who knew him as a warm and generous personality, perhaps tinged with Teutonic formality, but attractive and amiable. See C. von Schafhäutl, 'Ein merkwürdiges Künstlerleben' in *Allgemeine Musikalische Zeitung*, 1882. An English translation

will be found in Welch's *History of the Boehm Flute*. See also John Finn's appreciation, note 9 above, and 'Theobald Boehm—an Appreciation', by James S. Wilkins, jnr., included in Miller's *The Flute and Flute-Playing*, p. 167. In the latest book on the Boehm flute by Carl Ventzke, Frankfurt-am-Main, Verlag das Musikinstrument, 1966, much new Boehm lore has been accumulated, and fresh light, all to his credit, shed on his character.

[16] Dayton C. Miller, *op. cit.* pp. xxiv and 39. Writing in 1922 Miller said 'no complete set of laws has yet been formulated which enable one to calculate all the dimensions of a flute'—at the present time it seems that the work being done by Arthur Benade in Miller's old Institution, the Case Institute of Technology, Cleveland, Ohio, may soon lead to something of the sort, though they will no doubt prove very complex.

[17] *Ibid.* p. 17.

[18] *Ibid.* p. 27.

[19] *Ibid.* p. 27.

[20] According to Karl Ventzke, E. L. Leibl of Munich took over the goodwill of the Mendlers' business in 1895 and continued to use the trade mark *Böhm u. Mendler* at least as late as 1920.

[21] Both thinned wood heads with a raised and moulded *embouchure*, and moulded ebonite *embouchures*, are to be found among genuine Boehm instruments, though it seems somewhat rarely.

[22] D. C. Miller, *op. cit.*, illustrates on p. 23 a sectioned wax impression of a typical 'Boehm and Mendler' mouth-hole. The extreme in this matter seems to have been achieved by James Mathews of Birmingham, an enthusiastic amateur, and founder in 1856 of the Birmingham Flute Trio and Quartett [*sic*] Society. Mathews's flute had an ivory barrel-shaped *embouchure* with a perfectly square mouth-hole.

CHAPTER 8

The Flute after Boehm

ALTHOUGH THE cylinder flute of 1847 remains basically the dominant instrument of today, much has been done since Boehm's two interventions in flute history.

This work may conveniently be considered in three sections: (1) Completely new designs introduced either between 1832 and 1847, or after that year; (2) Additions and modifications based on the classic cylinder flute; and (3) Further work on the traditional cone-flute for those players who, for one reason or another, still prefer the 'old' fingering and bore.[1]

Once again we must stress that such divisions are, however, artificial, and imply no rigid lines of demarcation. Further, many instruments which are extremely interesting in themselves were produced as single examples to meet the requirements of individual players, and, although they did good service, had little general influence. We begin, then, with the period 1832–47.

The first new design which had any claim to real novelty was presented to the public in 1842 by Cornelius Ward, whom we remember as one of the unauthorised makers of Boehm's 1832 instrument. In January 1842 Ward secured British patents for no less than seven flutes, each with some difference in fingering. Two of them showed affinities with the designs respectively of Tromlitz and of Pottgeisser, with whose work we might expect a knowledgeable flute-maker to be conversant. The model he finally produced is shown in Fig. 38. It was a cone-bored

Fig. 38   Cornelius Ward's flute, final form. From his
pamphlet of 1844

flute on the 'open-keyed' system, with holes allocated directly to all four fingers of the right hand, and to the first, second, and third of the left. The left little finger controlled both the G♯ and A holes by a device similar to the Dorus G♯. A d″ shake-key was given to the right fore-finger. The most interesting feature is probably the C♯ arrangement for the left forefinger, which Ward made double, with holes of different sizes closing together, one with a padded cup and the other directly by the finger applied to a ring. Even Rockstro could find no virtue in this idea, though later on he adapted it in a much more reasonable form to his own version of the cylinder flute. According to Ward's *The Flute Explained*, which, in spite of its intemperate language, has been valuable to music historians, his idea was 'the construction of a flute on the open-keyed system which should afford greater mechanical facilities than had been attained by Gordon, Boehm, or Coche'. Certainly he borrowed extensively from all three, not to mention Dorus, the most conspicuous 'crib' being the bell-cranks and tracker wires by which he brought the c and c♯ keys up to the *left thumb*. The d♯ hole was closed by a ring surrounding the next hole above, the E♮, and released by another touch-piece for the left thumb, again on the Dorus principle. Rockstro tells us that both he and the well-known amateur, Alfred Chittenden, suggested further additions, and Ward flutes are known with various extra touches, etc. Plate 9A shows the standard form of the instrument. Whatever view we may take of Ward's ideas or his business probity (and Rockstro, rather surprisingly it may seem, quotes him as a disinterested witness) there can be no doubt about the beauty of his workmanship. Instruments made to other designs than his own, but bearing his *fecit*, are equally fine. Ward's 'Patent Flutes' were furnished with graduated metal tuning slides, and to move the stoppers he provided, not a screw, but a sort of eccentric with a tiny connecting rod. An indicator mounted on the eccentric spindle outside the head showed the setting of the cork, and had to be matched with corresponding numbers on the slide. Ten years before this Rudall and Rose had patented a much more ingenious mechanised head which obviated any matching up of graduations. Two screws, one of fine, the other of coarse, pitch, were attached respectively to the stopper and to a metal tube lining the head right down to what would have been the tuning slide in normal circumstances. Turning the end-cap operated the screws and thus extended the slide, and at the same time adjusted the cork proportionately. Unfortunately this added much weight to the head and the device found comparatively little use (see Plate 7D).

On its appearance the Ward flute created considerable excitement in England, and many amateur players adopted it. Unfortunately for the

maker no professionals of any standing at the time took it up, and
Rockstro goes so far as to suggest that its arrival rather stimulated a
renewed interest in the 1832 instrument. The implication is surely
clear. About this time, too, Folz, Camus, and Dorus had all visited
London, playing on the Boehm instrument, and in 1843 Rudall and
Rose entered into their manufacturing agreement with the originator.
Richard Carte and next Clinton adopted the Boehm flute, and even
Rockstro, then a pupil of Carte, turned away from Ward's instrument,
for which disloyalty he was never really forgiven.

It is possibly a little difficult for the present-day flautist to imagine
the professional heart-searchings which followed on the appearance of
a radically redesigned instrument, especially one involving a change of
fingering. It is the writer's experience that among instrumentalists
there are always a fortunate few to whom fingering is the least of their
worries; but many more who find it a constant challenge. The benefit
of an F♮ which was automatically well in tune must have been evident
to all but the most crusted conservatives, and so about this time a
number of individual efforts were made to adapt Boehm's right-hand
arrangement to the traditional flute. Most of these betrayed a complete
misunderstanding of the acoustic principles of the 'open-keyed' system,
but some were moderately successful. Typical of these efforts is the
instrument shown in Plate 9D built by Whitaker, formerly employed
by Rudall and Rose, and showing the quality always associated with
that firm. It is essentially a normal cone-flute of the time except that
it has an open-standing F♯ closed by rings for the right first and second
fingers only. There is a closed G♯, a d″ shake, and a B♮ shake for the
right forefinger. This arrangement was worked out by a well-known
London flautist, William Card, who is recorded as active between
1825 and 1861. A similar flute of Card's own make appears as No. 236
in the Dayton Miller Collection, but in this case all three rings for the
right hand are present. The instrument has been altered at some time
and probably once had a Dorus G♯. In the writer's example there is a
simple closed G♯ with a second touch for the right forefinger. Card
was born in 1788, so would have been one of the older professionals of
the period.[2] His later work falls mainly into our third category.

The portrait we now have of Abel Siccama, who was certainly one
of the most interesting innovators of the 1840s, is a little clouded.
Rockstro treated him with lavish scorn, but Welch, in his rejoinder,
seems to have gone rather too far the other way. According to the latter,
who knew him personally, Siccama in the earlier part of his life was a

fine classical scholar and a modern languages tutor of some distinction. As a great amateur enthusiast for the flute he observed the transformation that his favourite instrument had undergone in the early decades of his century and formed the opinion that, by the proliferation of key-work, it had probably lost more than it had gained. Like others before him he became enamoured with the concept of a completely keyless flute. He therefore set to work to design such an instrument and got as far as a scheme involving only one key (see Fig. 39). Unfortunately this design involved giving the G♮ hole directly to the right thumb, which has always been an uncomfortable expedient. From the year 1842 onwards Siccama devised a number of flutes of different designs which show that by degrees he had to abandon, more or less, the keyless principle as his experience grew.[3] Rockstro records that, through the agency of Alfred Chittenden, his model as at 1842 was brought to the notice of Rudall and Rose who decided not to take up its manufacture.

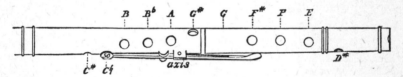

Fig. 39   Siccama's one-keyed flute design

Not unduly discouraged, Siccama continued his researches and in 1845 patented four designs, in one of which he incorporated the right-hand rings and open key of Boehm, with an extra touch-piece (see Fig. 40). In this plan, however, the ring device was moved one note

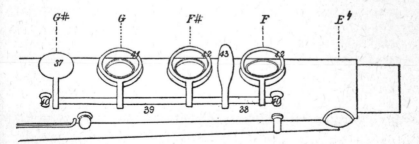

Fig. 40   Siccama's adaptation of Boehm's rings, c.
1845

further up leaving the E♮ hole to be covered by a *closed* key for the left thumb. Although Rudall and Rose had not found Siccama's first flute worth pursuing, the inventor managed to secure some financial backing, and in due course entered the field as a manufacturer on his own. In 1846 he issued a prospectus for a model which he styled the 'Chromatic Flute' and described also his 'Diatonic Flute'.

The next year he issued a larger pamphlet on this instrument, in which, it must be admitted, he made extravagant claims. Nevertheless the diatonic flute, which, we are told, was similar to his first design, achieved considerable success and was adopted by two most distinguished players, Joseph Richardson and R. S. Pratten, both of whom gave up the eight-keyed flute in its favour. It was in essence a simple cone-flute with rather large holes, well though not scientifically placed (in the Boehm sense), and fitted with the essential minimum of keys. The 'long F' was the only duplicate (see Fig. 41).

Fig. 41   Siccama's 'Diatonic' flute, *c.* 1847

Siccama's placing of the A and E holes put them beyond the reach of the two third fingers, so he applied two open keys with touch-plates in the middle of the shank. It is this feature which characterises unmistakably the instrument which is now generally known as 'The Siccama Flute'.[4] A quite incidental advantage of the A and E keys lay in the fact that the touch-plates could easily be adjusted to the hands of the player without affecting the mechanism in any way, and quite a number of Siccama flutes are known which have been so 'tailored' to measure. The Great Exhibition of 1851 saw quite a display of Siccama flutes in rivalry to Boehm's new cylinder model which, however, gained the first prize. Besides the inventor, several other firms manufactured the diatonic flute—presumably by arrangement—notably Mahillon and Co. of Brussels and London, who added a vent-key with two rings in control on the upper half to improve the c″ and c″♯. As late as 1902 Boosey and Co. were advertising what they called their 'improved Siccama Flute', the principles being the same as in the original, but with all holes except the highest two covered by open keys mounted on axles, and the c″–c″♯ vent added. This design was probably due to R. S. Pratten, of whom we shall have more to say.

The extent to which the idea of a *keyless* flute recurred amidst all the turmoil of rival *key-systems* in the mid-19th century is emphasised by the work of yet another interesting man, and in considering it we move from the 'amateur-turned-professional' to the true amateur. In the records of collections, exhibitions, etc., from 1890 onward the name of Dr Burghley of Camden Town, London, occurs with some regularity. Little is known of the doctor beyond what Rockstro says on p. 376—'a well-known amateur, an intimate friend of mine, Dr Burghley of Camden Town',[5] but a considerable number of his experimental instruments exist. There are eight in the Dayton Miller Collection, one at Boston, and three in the writer's collection, but they have seldom been illustrated. In describing the Boston example (which is similar to that shown in Plate 11D except for the angled head and separate tuning barrel) Bessaraboff says 'made for Dr Burghley', but the style of none of them suggests professional work. The tubes are made of mahogany embellished with black stained wood and ivory, and some have sub-sections of highly figured ornamental woods—all materials beloved of the mid-Victorian 'ornamental turner'. The keys, when fitted, are also of stained wood and rely for their 'set' on the natural springiness of the material. It would be nice to think that the good doctor made them himself, but we have no evidence so far to go on. In the simplest of the Burghley flutes the holes are arranged in a straight chromatic sequence for the fingers and thumbs of both hands, the highest (left thumb) being in the form of two oval slots set side by side at a convenient angle. The very short foot has one open key carrying the compass down to d'. A simple screw-cork is provided. In Bessaraboff's opinion the anonymous (Pottgeisser) drawing of 1803 (see Fig. 25 above) may have been the direct inspiration of these flutes, especially in view of the proportions of the bore. The head of example c (Plate 11) is made up of no less than seven separate sections which move upon each other so that the angle of the *embouchure* can be adjusted almost infinitely—truly a turner's *tour de force*. No. 1093 in the Dayton Miller Collection shows this feature but differs in other details. In the writer's specimen the work of the two thumbs is somewhat eased by the provision of two open keys. We have no information as to why Dr Burghley adopted a bent head in the majority of his instruments, possibly it favoured a more comfortable playing position— or did he have some medical objection to 'the shrieking wry-necked fife'? Bessaraboff draws attention in his description to the screwed plug which appears on the inner side of the body on a level with the fourth hole, but does not attempt to explain it. The writer suggests that this may have been an attachment for a sort of support similar to that used by some players on the German type bassoon. With the thumb doing double duty no doubt something of the kind would be a considerable help. The specimen E on Plate 11 will be discussed later.

Eleven out of the twelve instruments mentioned cover the flute in all sizes from piccolo in C, through concert flute, flute in G and flute in F, to bass flute in C, and while all have individual features, some share common characteristics. It would seem, then, that together they make up a series covering all Burghley's experiments with the direct open hole system. The twelfth, No. 1238 in the Dayton Miller Collection, has four covered finger-holes and seven keys, but is still based on the open hole theory.

In following the span of Siccama's activities we have bypassed the year 1847 in which the Boehm cylinder flute was introduced. It was immediately put into production by Rudall and Rose, but in spite of this, rival designs continued to appear. The most significant of these was due to John Clinton.

It will be remembered that Clinton, then a professor in the Royal Academy of Music, had been one of the first London players to adopt the ring-keyed Boehm when Rudall and Rose began to make it in 1843. That year he produced the first English instruction book for it, *An Essay on the Boehm Flute*, confining himself to the model with the Dorus G♯, and addressing his remarks expressly to those who were already familiar with the old instrument. This was a poor work, prepared in some haste, which he bettered greatly in his second effort (1846). It seems that Clinton was somewhat addicted to polemics, and it has been suggested that his extravagant advocacy may have done the new instrument more harm than good in some quarters. Be that as it may, by 1852 he had completely changed his views and had become as violent an opponent of the open-keyed system as he had formerly been a supporter. It is a little difficult to account for Clinton's *volte face* unless it was purely a commercial matter—in which he had, of course, a shining example in the antics of Victor Coche of Paris (see Appendix I). The writer is loth to take this view on the grounds that there is some evidence that about 1848 Clinton was beginning to find the 'Cone–Boehm' not entirely living up to the praise that he had at one time lavished on it. In that year he secured patents for some minor modifications, notably a device that permitted fingering the c″ according to the 'old' method. At the same time he substituted a single longitudinal bar for the three right hand rings, which would seem to be a retrograde step.

By 1855 Clinton had 'gone the whole hog' and published a pamphlet introducing a new design—the 'Equisonant Flute'. Welch tells us that well before that date he had been toying with an 'old fingered' model which was made for him by W. H. Potter.[6] The 'Equisonant' design appeared in a number of different modifications between 1855 and about 1863, which makes a definitive description somewhat difficult. Specimens showing minor variations are to be found in many collections. The examples shown in Plate 9B and C may, however, be taken as typical. Basically the instrument was a cone-flute with rather large holes redistributed and provided with elegant rod mechanism which preserved the traditional fingering almost entirely. This was achieved by the use of rings which closed an F♮ hole placed on the outer side of the instrument. Sometimes these also closed the G♮ above, but at others this hole was merely controlled by a plate for the right forefinger necessitated by its extremely high position. The G♯ was, according to tradition, a closed key, though on one model at least there was a duplicate hole which provided an alternative fingering (patent of 1863; see Plate 9B). The c″–c″♯ vent and rings appeared on the upper part, and sometimes Ward's duplicated C♯ hole.

In his next publication (*A Few Practical Hints to Flute Players, etc.*, London, Clinton and Co., 1855) Clinton did justice to Boehm in so far as he wrote, 'his system, too, is by far the best for *open keys* that has ever appeared', but he condemned the principle itself in strong terms. 'The conclusion I have drawn from the end of my labours is, that no other system than the shut-keyed can ultimately succeed, while any attempt to improve the open-keyed must end in disappointment and failure.' It is to be noted that the Boehm instrument of Clinton's strictures was the 1832 model. He must have been aware of the cylinder flute, but no doubt his revised views of the open-keyed system had crystallised pretty much before that appeared. On the expiry of the English patent for the cylinder flute, Clinton did, in fact, begin to manufacture it as did many other astute instrument makers, and in 1862 he secured another patent for an alleged improvement.[7] We can perhaps best sum Clinton up as a strangely ambivalent personality, whose motivations may be of more interest to the psychologist than to the simple historian.

The most permanently valuable work done in the post-Boehm period was, as we can now see, that which was inspired by one or other feature of the two original Boehm designs. The transfer of much of the mechanism from the *outer* to the *inner* side of the body, the improved springs, rods and sleeves, and 'clutch' of Buffet have all been mentioned in the previous chapter, since most of these had already come into use before the instrument was generally accepted. Regarding these, Boehm wrote in 1847 that he left their value to the assessment of others for he had had no part in them himself. What the alleged improvements made by Bürger *c.* 1890 at the behest of Tillmetz (see note 1) may have been we do not know. No. 926 of the Dayton Miller Collection is one of his flutes, but nothing special is noted about it except the closed G♯. Probably Bürger's contribution was no more than some adjustment to the bore such as many other minor 'improvers' have made.

In 1850, however, something really important did occur—at the hands of Richard Carte. It will be recalled that Carte had taken up the 'Cone–Boehm' with enthusiasm on its first appearance in England *c.* 1843. For some years, while accepting the instrument as it stood for his own use, he observed the efforts of others to make a better flute on the same lines, 'intending', as he said, 'if one should be produced with the same perfection of tone and tune, but with greater facility of execution, to adopt it'. He found nothing to satisfy him as the years passed, and in 1850 embarked on the project himself. In spite of his public successes he still felt that the need to keep the left little finger and thumb on their own keys a great part of the time tended to limit his facility. To quote him again, 'As the open keys were the cause of the superior *tone* of Boehm's flute, and the closed keys the cause of the superior *facility of execution* of the old flute, the object was to free the little finger and thumb, so that facility of execution and beauty of tone might be at once secured.'[8] Carte's work was rewarded by the grant of a prize medal at the Great Exhibition of 1851, and before the end of the year a second version with some modifications appeared before the public as the '1851 Patent Flute'. The fingering of this instrument was to all intents and purposes that of the old eight-keyed flute. Plate 8c shows Carte's 1851 mechanism as originally applied to the cone-bore, and Fig. 42 the same thing as applied to the cylinder bore, with large holes, shortly afterwards.

In 1850 Carte joined Rudall and Rose as the third partner in a firm whose name was soon to be recognised throughout the world as

Fig. 42   Carte's patent flute of 1851

standing for all that was best in flute-making. About this time, too, they introduced a revised conoidal bore, to the proportions of which they made all their subsequent 1832 model flutes. Carte explained the object of the new bore in the same essay from which we have just quoted, and—without in any way withdrawing his admiration for the 1832 flute—ventured to suggest that if Boehm had to some extent failed to get all the fullness of tone in the lower notes that was desirable, this might be due to two causes: first, that the initial work had been done in Germany where sweetness rather than power was traditionally expected, and second, that by 1832 Boehm had not yet acquired all the scientific knowledge that might have enabled him to exploit the cone-bore to its fullest capacity. With the new cone-bore Carte felt that there was now little to choose between the two designs. Nevertheless, the most important subsequent experiments were nearly all based on the cylinder, as we might perhaps expect in England where the example of Nicholson had made power a primary objective.

The year 1852 saw another remarkable, though not entirely surprising, move. We have already noticed Rockstro's defection from the Cornelius Ward flute—now he too joined the ranks of the would-be improvers. With the arrival of the cylinder flute Rockstro had given that a trial but finding 'that the intonation of the open-keyed flutes [*sic*] was as false as that of the eight-keyed flute' had given it up again. Now he became impressed with the advantages of the new Rudall and Rose bore—not that he found all their flutes so constructed well tuned according to his ideas—and set himself to designing a new lay-out for the holes of the 'Cone-Boehm'. After some admittedly well conceived experiments he submitted his plan to Rudall and Rose in the April, and exactly a month later had the flute in his hands. He had, he hastens to tell us, no intention of posing as a regenerator of the flute, but merely to have for his own use an instrument correctly tuned according to equal temperament. With this personal element in mind Rockstro made some additions and modifications to the key-work also,[9] claiming among other things to have designed a crescentic touch-piece for the d'♯ key. So much for poor Ward whose patent of 1842 included just such a key. In 1858 Rockstro sold this flute and lost sight of it, as well as of the design. Should it ever come to light again it will be a rare prize for some collector.

Although Rockstro's revised cone-flute did not come into general use, his experiments had considerable influence in a rather unexpected direction. In the same year Sidney Pratten, who had adopted the Siccama flute about 1846, began to experiment with improved flutes on the strictly 'old system'. In company with a former employee of Siccama's he produced a surprising number of instruments bearing the mark 'Pratten's Perfected'. Many of these differed very little externally from the standard simple instruments of the time. The piccolo shown on Plate 10H may be regarded as typical of them. Pratten, however, became impressed with Rockstro's 1852 design, and obtained permission to copy the sizes and lay-out of the holes. These he combined with a bore widened in its lower part, at the same time introducing a closed C key for the left thumb for those who wanted it. In 1856 Pratten's associate became foreman to Messrs Boosey and Co. who then entered the flute-making business in a large way. Pratten continued his association under the new régime, carrying on with the 'Perfected' model but also seeking to apply the old fingering bodily to the cylindrical tube. Of this D. J. Blaikley[10] has said: 'Recognising the merits of Boehm's work, and yet not seeing his own way to taking up the new fingering, he increased the size of the holes of the cone-flute and added various keys, leaving the original eight-keyed flute as a seventeen-keyed instrument with holes practically as large as those of Boehm. With the cylinder flute his work was to bring it to the same fingering as his seventeen-keyed cone-flute. He worked at this, not as introducing a modification of the Boehm-fingering, but with the aim of boldly transplanting the cone-fingering to the cylinder flute.' The many players who, like Pratten, 'could not see their way to taking up the new fingering' must have been a godsend to Messrs Boosey and Co. Their list of flutes as at 1892 reads like an epitome of Pratten's musical life. They quote Pratten cone-flutes with eight and ten keys; Pratten cylinder flutes with twelve keys; the same [Large Holes] with fourteen or seventeen keys (all finger-holes were covered on these models); and all could be obtained with German silver or sterling silver keys. The most advanced models could also be supplied with gold mounts and lip-plate. In addition to this formidable array Messrs Boosey also offered 'Improved Siccama Flutes' and Boehm flutes, both in wood and metal. Of course it is not to be supposed that either Pratten as an individual, or Booseys as a firm, were the only ones to cultivate this profitable commercial field, there must have been many others whose names have escaped record. Plate 9F is a typical example of French (possibly Belgian) make imported by Lafleur and Son.

Before passing on to the next major British contribution we must turn for a moment to France. In that country comparatively little modification seems to have been made to the basic Boehm design after Buffet's improved key mechanism, and the Dorus G♯ key. When Godefroy secured the manufacturing rights to the Boehm cylinder flute it did not seem to make a great impression at first, many French players finding that the interconnected cover-plates deprived them of certain 'vented' fingerings inherited from the old system which, though unorthodox according to Boehm's ideas, could still be employed on the ring-keyed model. Godefroy, therefore, had the idea of perforating the key-plates, supplying them with annular pads. In this form he and Louis Lot made many cylinder flutes of exquisite workmanship, and indeed these remain the favourite models in France to this day. According to Constant Pierre (*La Facture*) it seems that many French players at first found the annular pads difficult to adjust without the aid of a skilled mechanic. In 1886 the Paris maker Martin Thibouville *aîné* eliminated them entirely by substituting pairs of smaller holes, one of each pair covered directly by the finger and provided with a ring which controlled a normal padded cup closing the other. The writer has never seen an example of this mechanism, which does not appear to have become at all common.

At the present time the antiquated fingerings are probably little used, but perforated plates allow holes to be 'shaded' or effectively reduced in diameter by applying the finger to the edge instead of at the centre, a device that many players find valuable in venting harmonics. In England, as ever, a 'foreign notion' was regarded with some suspicion at first—it was seriously suggested that perforated plates would be more difficult to stop cleanly than open holes, whereas in fact they impose a useful discipline on the fingers—but very shortly Rudall and Rose, with their usual fair-mindedness, were prepared to supply.

The first English experimenter to employ perforated plates, albeit to a limited extent, was Rockstro, and we must in fairness admit that, however tiresome a client he may have been to satisfy, he was never slow to try out an idea. In 1858 he concluded that Rudall, Rose, and Carte had at last produced a 'parabolic' head that was fit to use (see p. 126 above) and he determined to adopt it. The cylinder body, however, he found as ill-tuned as ever, and he repeated his experiments

L

of 1852. Again the same firm made an instrument to his specification, and to the normal mechanism he added an extra F♯ lever, as in his earlier design, and the Briccialdi B♭. The pivot of the G♯ and A♮ plates was transferred to the near side of the instrument, for which undoubted improvement Rockstro also claimed responsibility. In his account of this flute,[11] he further claimed that thereafter Rudall and Rose adhered permanently to his placing of the holes, and gave up the original Boehm measurements, though we have only his word for this. The G♯–A♮ arrangement was, of course, an adaptation of the Dorus key, and moving the pivot did not get rid of its inherent mechanical weakness (see p. 124 above). This was eliminated later by uniting the G♯ and A plates rigidly and providing a duplicate G♯ hole which alone was opened by the little finger touch. The duplicate is probably the commonest form of closed G♯ at the present day. Still later Rockstro proposed an even more complex arrangement which allowed the A hole to be used to vent the e''' without unavoidably opening the G♯ hole, but this does not seem to have come into common use (but see 'split E' below).

For some six years this instrument satisfied Rockstro in all his professional work, but in 1864 he was at it again. He still found the third octave poor in intonation, and this he attacked by yet another enlargement of the holes in general. The basic mechanism was as on his former design with some additions and the reader is referred to his *Treatise* for details.[12] J. M. Rose, who was at that time the manufacturing partner in the firm, was so impressed with the design that he marked all future flutes with the largest holes as 'Rockstro's Model' though not all conformed in every detail. The 'Rockstro's Model' still appeared in Rudall Carte and Co.'s catalogue as late as 1931. From 1864 till 1877 Rockstro continued to work at his flute, adding and modifying one or other detail. The final form had five perforated plates, which rendered the 'extra' F♯ key less important, a large 'vented D' (Fig. 43) which is much used today, and finally a very small vent-hole, 0·1 inch in diameter, immediately above the C♯ hole. This was covered by a small cup attached to the C♯. The reader will recognise this as an inversion of Cornelius Ward's arrangement of 1842 (see Plate 9A). In some quarters Rockstro's little vent has attracted supercilious smiles, but in 1966 Arthur Benade, in the course of his investigations into the flute tube, has come to the conclusion that it may indeed have been of some value.[13] Neither this nor the D vent appear on all flutes offered as the 'Rockstro's Model' and they do not figure in Rudall, Carte's latest illustrated catalogue.

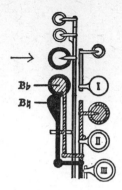

Fig. 43 The 'vented' D

After so much tinkering with what we now regard as a classic instrument which satisfies the needs of the majority of present-day flautists, it is pleasant to turn back to some work which seems to be based on admiration rather than criticism. It will be recalled that Carte's 1850 researches had been based on a sound appreciation of Boehm's original work on the flute with open holes, and his instrument embodying them had a considerable success. Nevertheless, Carte realised that in designing it he had lost certain fingerings of the Boehm instrument that in some sequences of notes were valuable. He therefore started in 1866 on a fresh design which combined the most useful fingerings of both instruments, patenting it in the following year. The most conspicuous feature was the absence of the old F key for the left little finger. The hole for this note, placed on the outer side in the 1851 model, was transferred to the top of the body beneath the F♯ finger plate, though at first the touch-piece was kept in the accustomed position. It is generally supposed that a certain Mr Spencer, an amateur flautist and engineer,[14] first suggested this idea, but Christopher Welch claims that it resulted from his own requirement for a raised F♯ touch-piece to accommodate an injured finger. His account is so circumstantial and his drawings so interesting that we reproduce them herewith in Fig. 44.

As can be seen, the raising of the touch-piece revealed that there was plenty of room for the hole on top of the tube, a point that had been missed. In the final form Carte dispensed with the left-hand touch for the F♮ entirely, replacing it with a second lying beside that for the F♯ and operating through a clutch (see Fig. 45). A duplicate F♮ hole opened by the right third finger was also provided. Thus, with the right

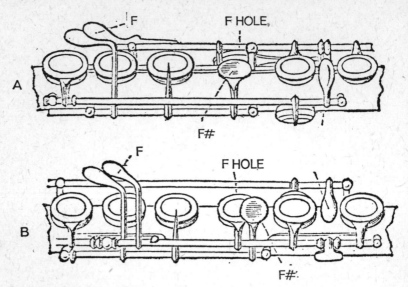

Fig. 44   Carte's 1867 flute
           A. Arrangement of alternative F♮ as on 1851
              model
           B. 1st modification. Alternative F♮ hole on
              top of tube

forefinger on the upper plate, the F and F♯ could be played as on the
simple system, but with the finger on the lower plate the Boehm fingering
operated. Since the space usually occupied by the c″♯ and d″ shake
touches had been usurped these were transferred to the right forefinger.
An 'open D' above the small C♯ key was added with a touch-piece lying
over the C♮ plate. A duplicate C hole and the B♮ were both placed in
charge of the left thumb, providing alternatives to the Boehm fingerings
for B♭ and B♮ by means of linkages with the holes on the top of the
tube. The 1867 flute was very successful and still remains the favourite
of many English players. A version of the same instrument giving C♯
'all fingers off' as with the eight-keyed flute, instead of D, and with
the d″ and d″♯ shakes in the more usual position was produced as the
'Guards'' model and is also popular (see p. 6 above).

Although the last two instruments mentioned both arose in the first
place from the needs of individual specialists, each became in the end a
recognised 'system' with many confirmed devotees. In addition there
are several minor additions to the basic Boehm key-work among which

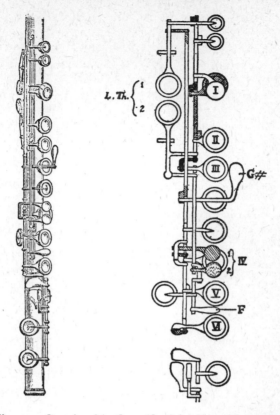

Fig. 45   Carte's 1867 flute (final form) and keywork
displayed (*after Baines*)

well-known players have selected according to their personal ideas.
The most used are probably the Rockstro F♯, to which we have already
referred; the Brossa F♯; and the so-called 'split E'. The disadvantage
of the Rockstro key is that it necessitates moving the touches of the
shake-keys one place up, which many players dislike. The Brossa key
which has a tiny touch overlapping the shank of the E plate does not
entail this shift (see Fig. 46). As regards the 'split E' we have already
noticed that G♯ arrangements that tie the G♯ and A♮ plates together
interfere with the correct venting of the e''', which is made as the 4th
harmonic of e. With this device the right second finger can keep the
G♯ plate down allowing the A hole only to function as the vent.

With the completion of the 'Rockstro's Model' and the Carte 1867

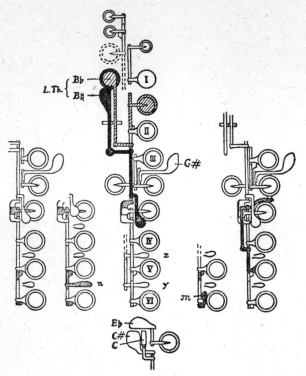

Fig. 46   Diagram of Boehm flute mechanisms. *Left:*
with open G♯; *centre:* with closed G♯; *right:* the same,
with 'split E'. *n* and *m* Rockstro and Brossa F♯ keys
(*after Baines*)

type one might perhaps think that the ultimate development of the
cylinder flute had been reached. This was quickly shown to be untrue.
Very shortly after the completion of the 1867 instrument W. L. Barret
devised a mechanism by which a pressure on the c″–d″ shake lever
could automatically throw the 'open D' hole out of action thus restoring
the old fingering of C♯, and greatly easing passages containing c″ and
c″♯ and their octaves in juxtaposition. Rockstro, too, went a stage further
by building up his tiny C♯ vent with an inserted tube standing above
the level of the body surface.

    In 1958 Alex Murray, now of the Michigan State University Music
Department, a player of the standard Boehm flute of the time, became

interested in the one departure from his theory which Boehm had felt it necessary to accept for practical reasons, i.e. the relatively small hole, too highly placed, which he used for the C♯ and as a vent to the d″ and ‴, d″♯ and ‴, etc. (see *Die Flöte und das Flötenspiel*, p. 30). Working in association with the London artist-maker Albert Cooper and a mathematician colleague and flautist, Elmer Cole, Murray has, after nine years experiment, produced a Boehm flute with a full-sized C♯ hole, and a separate d″ vent, both correctly placed. Murray has adhered to Boehm's logical disposition of the B and B♭ keys, in preference to the Briccialdi action. An account of this instrument will shortly appear in the American journal *The Instrumentalist* but in anticipation the author and editor have kindly permitted this short preview of what may possibly become the final Boehm flute.

In following chronologically the work done since Boehm's time it almost seems that the story of the cylinder flute has been a sort of 'Rake's Progress' of complexity. Admittedly the 1867 instrument, for example, is a very considerable piece of miniature engineering, but, as made by the original firm, it is extraordinarily light in the hand, sensitive, and reliable. Mechanical break-down is almost unknown. Nevertheless, there are always some flautists who feel that the advantage of a multiplicity of fingerings, some not very often used, weighs light against the cost and possible anxiety of the most advanced models. One such was John Radcliff, who in 1870 designed a model of his own which was basically a simplification of Carte's 1851 flute, retaining most of the 'old' fingering but securing full venting throughout. The paired keys for the left thumb were also adopted (see Fig. 47). This instrument, too, found a place in Rudall Carte's standard catalogue, and its capacities were sufficient to satisfy many professional flautists, notably the celebrated John Amadeo.

Finally under the present sub-heading, the reader is invited to look at the specimen shown on Plate 8J. This is an anonymous cylinder flute with 'parabolic' head, quite well made in plated brass, and with a built-up *embouchure* and finger-holes. Except for those in the foot, all holes are of the same diameter and comparatively small, and are laid out exactly as in the old eight-keyed flute. The intonation is unspeakable, and illustrates the futility of trying to apply old fingering to the new bore without a due knowledge of the acoustical principles involved. Truly a horrible example which is better left in its anonymity.

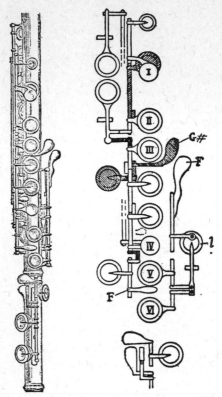

Fig. 47   Radcliff model flute and keywork displayed
(*after Baines*)

We have now to consider what happened to the traditional cone-flute.
In England, as we saw in Chapter 6, it had by 1825 acquired six or eight
keys, and the large holes of Charles Nicholson, and was being exploited
principally for power of tone. Relative intonation was still thought of as
very much the concern of the individual player, though the better
makers were regarding it as their duty to make the internal tuning as
good as they possibly could. In this matter Rudall and Rose were particularly successful with their system of chambering (see p. 35 above),
though with their revised bore of *c.* 1850 this had, according to Rockstro,
become redundant. About this time, too, we find them adding to some
of their best flutes the two rings and vent—in German *Brille* =
'spectacles'—on the upper joint for improving the c″ and c″♯, though
this is more typical of Continental than of English practice.[15]

On the Continent very different ideals prevailed. There, those players who had not been seduced away by the open-keyed system within a very few years of its appearance seem to have closed the ranks, and to have adhered even more rigidly to the traditional fingering, narrow conical bore, and relatively small holes which gave what they conceived to be true flute tone. With them the benefits of mechanisation were directed solely towards increased facility and a more even scale within the above terms. Fig. 48 illustrates an early and typical effort in this direction. This is a sketch of the instrument submitted to the Great Exhibition of 1851 by the Paris virtuoso and flute-maker Tulou. It is essentially a narrow bore cone-flute with small holes, both the long and cross Fs, and c"♯ and d" shakes. There is the usual C♮ of the time allocated to the right forefinger and a duplicate C with its own hole operated by the left ring-finger. The most unusual addition is a length-wise F♯ vent-key for the right third finger, similar to that often found on the contemporary clarinet. Most of the longer keys are mounted on axles, but curiously enough the foot-keys are of the Boehm 1832 first type.[16] A more sophisticated version of the same instrument is to be found as No. 188 in the Dayton Miller Collection and is there listed as 'Tulou Model'. Tulou was, like Boehm, one of the celebrated Continental players who visited London in the early 19th century and made a great impression on the cognoscenti, only to be eclipsed in popular esteem by the giant Nicholson. He was violently opposed to the Boehm flute, and, according to Welch, to the Siccama model also—in fact to the whole 'open-keyed' concept. Until 1853 he was in partnership with a very skilled maker, Nonon, but after that year the two men went their separate ways. Both produced typical French flutes of exquisite workmanship, the two piccolos shown in Plate 101 and J being good examples.[17] A slightly younger contemporary of Tulou was Louis Drouet. He too visited England and created a passing sensation, though critics were much divided in their opinions of his intonation, which some said he disguised by sheer technical virtuosity. For a year or two between 1815 and 1819 he attempted to set up a flute factory in London (almost exactly at the time when Tulou was starting *his* business in Paris) but he was unsuccessful; the French ideal being no more appreciated by the British public than was Nicholson's in France.

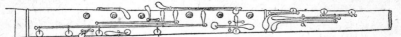

Fig. 48   Tulou's flute as at 1851

In Germany the cone-flute remained much in the same state (except for the addition of the b♮ to the foot) till *c.* 1885 when Schwedler of Leipzig designed a 'reform-flute' which was shortly put into production by himself in association with Carl Kruspe jun. In 1897 this instrument was awarded a gold medal at the Leipzig exhibition, and Kruspe secured sole manufacturing rights. These flutes had considerable popularity, and were, from time to time, improved in mechanical detail. In consequence, the student may find a number of minor varieties, with varying proportions of axle and simple lever mechanism. The foot joint was early converted to axles as the standard thing. The characteristic features were a side trill-key high up near the head for the d‴–e‴, and certain other shakes; a c″♯–d″ with a cross-wise touch for the right middle finger; the usual side C♮ key; and long and cross Fs. Schwedler also incorporated his version of the 'reform mouth-hole' with raised bosses above and below (see p. 9 above). This was the staple instrument of the 'old school' of German flautists during the Wagner–Brahms period, and we may perhaps see some mutual influence between them and the latter composer in his sombre orchestration.

By the end of the century other makers were carrying mechanisation of the 'reform-flute' even further, notably various members of the Mönnig family of Leipzig. Basically the instrument remained traditional but it varied in detail. Plates for the sake of convenience were placed over some holes, and rings to operate automatic devices surrounded others. Fig. 49, which is taken from the well-known Heckel catalogue of 1931, is typical. It shows the usual shake-keys plus an F♯ correcting device which can be cancelled at will for producing the c‴♯ in tune; an A♭–B♭ trill for the thumb; and rings and a vent on the upper part for improving the c″ and c‴. The head shows Mönnig's version of the 'reform mouth-hole' with raised cusps on either side. This type of head enjoys much favour in Germany today on the Boehm flute as well.

Fig. 49   Modern fully developed 'reform-flute'

The situation, then, at the time of writing is that the Boehm flute, with perhaps one or other of the alternative extras, meets the requirements of the majority of flautists. In France perforated plates and the closed G♯ are generally preferred, as are metal instruments in general.

These are now making their way in England too, thanks to the example of some superb French players of international repute, but a good many English professionals still seem to prefer wood, sometimes with a metal or a thinned wood head. Thinned bodies all of wood can be obtained but do not seem to be in much demand. They are of course proportionately expensive. A considerable number of British players prefer the Carte 1867 flute, and this is still to be obtained on order.

In America excellent Boehm flutes have been made almost since their first introduction, largely due to the powerful influence of several of Boehm's own pupils who settled in that country. Flute clubs and Quartet and Trio Societies have played a great part in American music making for many years, and this has had a salutary effect on the instrument industry there.[18]

In German speaking countries the Boehm flute now holds general sway, but the advanced cone models still have enthusiastic adherents.

Good flutes of all types, in all price ranges, are now made by the leading manufacturers, and there is little to choose between the best of them. Unfortunately the average cost of a good flute has, in line with woodwinds generally, risen alarmingly in the last few years, with the result that the second-hand market flourishes. Here the would-be purchaser is warned to be careful. A beautiful flute with hopelessly worn-out mechanism is not a bargain at any figure, and if the buyer is not quite sure of his own judgment he should certainly take advice. The pages of various musical journals today carry a confusing array of advertisements for flutes of all kinds, many of which originate in specialised workshops catering for agents or dealers who put their own names on them. Some of these 'trade' instruments are not at all bad, but the serious flautist will satisfy himself as to the real maker of his instrument (see also note 9, p. 213). It should be remembered that by the provisions of French copyright laws the purchase of a business carries with it the right to reproduce former trade marks, which may therefore be no guarantee of workmanship. A few names esteemed among flute players today are Alexander, Hammig, Haynes, Heckel, Lot, Marigaux, Mönnig, Powell, Selmer, U.S.A., Couesnon (which embodies a number of fine old *artiste-ouvrier* marks), and Rudall, Carte, which, though no longer an independent firm, still has an unimpeachable *cachet*.

NOTES

[1] The various social influences, facilities for easy travel, etc., which in the present century have made orchestral playing on the largest scale an *international*

rather than a national thing, have had their effect on instruments too. Hence
the almost completely uniform use of the cylinder flute. The preference for the
distinctive tone of the 'old' instrument, to which we have referred several
times in the foregoing chapters, has today its principal stronghold in Germany—
in amateur circles where the pressures that affect symphony players are not so
strongly felt. Such matters of taste are notoriously difficult to define or explain,
but one artist who has come nearer to doing so than most is Rudolf Tillmetz.
In the Preface to his *Anleitung zur Erlernung der Theobald Böhm'schen Cylinder-
und Ringklappen-Flöte, mit konischer Bohrung*, Leipzig, Fr. Kistner, 1890, this
celebrated flautist sets down his own personal testimony. The passage is too
long to quote *in extenso* here—suffice it to say that, beginning with a good
many years as a professional player on the old flute, he transferred to the
Boehm cylinder flute on becoming a pupil of the inventor. For nearly twenty
years he remained a loyal exponent of that instrument, defending it against
many objections. In the end, however, after no less than thirty-three years of
solo and orchestral experience, he came to the conclusion that some of the
criticism was indeed valid on musical grounds. He therefore reverted, not to
the eight-keyed instrument, but to the ring-keyed cone-flute of 1832, which
he found satisfactory both technically, and from the points of view of tonal
homogeneity and dynamic flexibility. The instrument was resurrected for him
by J. M. Bürger of Strasbourg, and he predicted a great future for it, in orchestral use. This, in the event, has not been realised, probably because the above
mentioned pressures were already beginning to be felt at the time. The reader
is strongly recommended to consult the original Preface for the light it sheds
on a matter of musical aesthetic.

It is perhaps only fair to point out that Clinton changed instruments the
other way as the result of an experiment conducted in the Albert Hall under
solo conditions. See Welch, *History of the Boehm Flute*, p. 12, note A.

[2] Card's name figures in the *Musical World* letters mentioned in Appendix I
where he is referred to in an anonymous verse as 'old Card'—though possibly
only for the sake of scansion. In the same letters Cornelius Ward mentions him
as one of the unsuccessful sponsors in London of the 1832 flute. As a 'designer
and manufacturer of flutes' he showed instruments at the Great Exhibition of
1851, and held a Royal Appointment. He seems latterly to have concentrated
on applying the axles instead of ordinary levers to the common flute. A very
ornate silver-plated and engraved example in the writer's collection shows foot-
keys of the earliest Boehm 1832 type. After his death in 1861 his son E. J.
Card carried on the business for another fifteen years, apparently for a time
as Card & Co.

[3] See British Patent 10553 of 13 March 1845.

[4] Many writers have drawn attention to earlier examples of the open key
applied to the fundamental scale of the flute. Why? Surely the purpose of any
key, open or closed, is to bring a remote hole under finger control, and it seems
to matter little what that hole was, once keys had been invented. It is Siccama's
third order levers *on top* of the flute that have so distinctive an appearance.

[5] Rockstro, R. J., *The Flute*, London, Rudall, Carte and Co., 1890, Article
658, p. 376. The reference is not entered in the Index, and occurs under 'Guilio
Briccialdi, 1849'. Rockstro says that Dr Burghley, *c.* 1845, made the first
suggestion of a mechanism now known as the Briccialdi B♭ lever, though he
admits that Briccialdi was probably unaware that he had been anticipated by
the Englishman.

[6] This appears to have been the model introduced in Clinton's *Treatise upon
the Mechanism and general Principles of the Flute*, London, H. Potter, 1852.

No. 342 of the Dayton Miller Collection, dated by that authority as *c.* 1850, bears the mark of Clinton and Co. and conforms to the 1848 patent.

[7] This was nothing less than a revival of the idea of graduated holes, which Boehm had decided were not sufficiently advantageous to warrant the difficulty and cost of continued commercial manufacture (see p. 126 above). Nevertheless Boehm thought it necessary to write to Louis Lot (then one of his Paris licensees) in June 1862, affirming his own priority in the idea. It seems that Clinton, having secured an English patent for graduated holes, represented himself to the jury of the 1862 London Exhibition as their sole inventor.

[8] Carte, Richard, *Sketch of the successive improvements made in The Flute, etc.*, 1st edn., London, Rudall, Rose, Carte and Co., 1851.

[9] Rockstro, *op. cit.*, Article 668, p. 384.

[10] D. J. Blaikley, a most distinguished acoustician. He was technical adviser to Messrs Boosey and Co. for over sixty years, and was the inventor of the system of 'Compensating Pistons' for brass instruments which so materially contributed to the reputation of that firm.

[11] Rockstro, *op. cit.*, Article 673, pp. 387–9.

[12] *Ibid.* Article 679 *et seq.*, pp. 392–6.

[13] Personal communication to the writer, 1966.

[14] Rockstro, *op. cit.* Article 684, p. 398. *But* see also Welch, *History of the Boehm Flute*, 2nd edn., London, Rudall, Carte and Co., 1892, p. lxxvi. Spencer also interested himself in the clarinet and his model with 'Barret Action' but no 'patent C♯' was produced by Boosey and Co. In 1858 Carte also applied himself to reforming the clarinet and applying Boehm acoustic principles, which he felt had not been fully exploited by Klosé and Buffet in the so-called 'Boehm Clarinet'. He was less successful than with the flute.

[15] The writer recently acquired an example in *box-wood* (surely unusual at its date, with the largest Nicholson holes, and two heads, one standard, the other with the patent screw tuning-slide and stopper. The whole is in a fitted case specially designed. Another example has the Continental *Brille*. These are typical evidence of Rudall and Rose's willingness to fulfil special commissions.

[16] According to Welch, *op. cit.* p. 221, and note 61, Tulou called this instrument an 'improved Boehm Flute'. It is difficult to see why, since even the narrow traditional bore employed differed from Boehm's version of the cone, and the closed-key system was fitted.

[17] Most French instruments of this period are remarkable for the elegant shaping of the key touches, just as the English appeared utilitarian (on the old style flutes), and the German rather heavy but eminently practical.

[18] For a full account of these activities, and biographies of a great number of American flautists, the reader is referred to L. de Lorenzo, *My Complete Story of the Flute*, New York, Crescendo Publishing Co., 1952.

CHAPTER 9

The Transverse Flute in the Orchestra

IN PREVIOUS sections we have seen something of the long and honourable history of the transverse flute, its development in Europe, and the various uses to which it has been put. The small selection we have made from a wealth of references in contemporary pictorial art and literature shows that, in addition to doing organised military, ceremonial, and municipal duties, it has held an important place in social, even domestic, music making from the time of the Minnesingers onwards. In one field, however, the transverse flute did not at first find general acceptance, and this was the early, and often experimental, instrumental ensemble which in time grew into the symphony orchestra. At first sight this may seem surprising, and in this chapter we shall attempt to survey the reasons and circumstances. In what follows it should be understood that in many cases composers are named more as convenient landmarks in musical history than as the sole originators of any specific trend or technique.

The standardised musical body we recognise as 'The Orchestra' assumed its present form only in the course of the late 19th century, though the story of *orchestration* can be traced back some three hundred years earlier. By the latter part of the 16th century polyphonic vocal music had reached its culmination in the Mass and motet for the Church, and in the madrigal for secular entertainment. Educated musicians then began to explore the possibilities of music written for combinations of string, wind, and keyboard instruments in their own right. They also experimented particularly with the single-voice line with *harmonic* support or contrast supplied by variable groups of instruments as a dramatic method of expression, and so created the first primitive forms of opera, oratorio, and ballet. 'The birth of the orchestra', says Adam Carse, 'is connascent with the creation of secular instrumental music as a cultured form of art, and largely arises out of the transition from modal polyphony to monody.'[1] From these unorganised beginnings there finally developed the modern symphony orchestra with its vast expressive ability; but we must not suppose that the process was uninterrupted or that it was equally advanced in all parts of Europe at any one time.

Looked at broadly, orchestral development divides itself into two main eras; the first ending with the deaths of Bach and Handel, the two great masters of *harmonic* polyphony; the second covering the rise of what we may call 'present-day' orchestration as initiated by Haydn and Mozart and incorporating the successive periods generally labelled 'classical', 'romantic', and 'modern'. The transition is not, of course, in any way rigidly marked, but it corresponds roughly to the life of Gluck (1714–87) and some less important composers of whom C. P. E. Bach is probably the best known. During the initial phases the influences that affected orchestral organisation were many and varied. Some were concerned with the advent of new or improved instruments, as for example the violin family, which offered the composer greater brilliance and attack than did the older viols, and in turn stimulated him to make even greater demands on his string players. Others were connected with the conditions, social or geographical, in which composers worked. The absence of cheap and easy methods of reproducing pages of written music, as well as the lack of ready communication between countries, must have restricted many important innovations to purely local significance for a long time.[2] For example, we need only think of the very small public who heard the music of Bach the church cantor during his lifetime, and compare this with the opportunities which fell naturally to Lulli the favoured Court musician of Louis XIV of France. Bach also provides an illustration of another sort. A look at his scores at different periods of his career reveals clearly the limited resources furnished by his different employers, and the use he made of them is a measure of his genius. Bach's surviving records contain many pleas to authorities for new instruments, even repairs to existing ones. Compare this situation with that of Haydn as a servant in a princely household—even if the implications of the Court livery were at times irksome to him. Those minor nobility of the 18th century who were music patrons at all vied with each other in the establishments they could afford their *kapellmeisters*—and Haydn was one of the relatively fortunate ones. Still other influential factors are illustrated by such a comparison as that of Handel with Schubert. The one was the true cosmopolitan of the 18th century, and he always wrote music adapted in style and instrumental demands to the towns in which he had for the time settled—were it in Germany, England, or Italy. The other, though born over a century later (he survived just into the age of railway transport), lived in so confined a circle that little, if any, of his major orchestral music was published during his lifetime. His marvellous melodic use of the full classical orchestra had therefore little influence on the main stream of progress until virtually rediscovered after his death. It is against this very varied background that we must look at the flute as an element in the developing concert orchestra.

Although between Roman times and the Middle Ages there is a long gap during which we have no information about any flute-type instrument in Europe, from the 12th century on, there is abundant evidence regarding both cross-blown and fipple instruments. Well before the year 1500 in Germany the slender fife (at first a purely military instrument) and small drum had become the favourite accompaniment for dancing, while in England the vertical pipe and tabor were preferred. By the early 16th century instrumental music, following the vocal pattern, had entered fully on the period of the *whole consort*, and with the demand that implied for homogeneous groups of instruments at different pitches, both types of flute advanced greatly.

This is the age of the great musical writers—Virdung (1511), Agricola (1528 and 1545), Praetorius (1619 and 1620), and Mersenne (1636), on whom we have already drawn for descriptive matter in Chapter 4, and it will be useful now to compare their accounts for the insight they afford regarding musical practice in their times. First, in the matter of transverse flutes: Virdung mentions only a slender fife which he calls *Zwerchpfeiff* and which he associates with the small drum as a soldier's instrument. Agricola has four transverse flutes of different sizes which he labels *Schweitzerpfeiffen*, i.e. 'Swiss pipes', and again we note the military derivation, though with this group the civilian *whole consort* would be complete. Praetorius is more specific and he distinguishes between the slender military fife and a family of three sizes of larger bored instruments more fitted for Art music which he calls *Querflöten*. This is in fact the same as Agricola's group, for in four-part harmony the middle sized instrument would be duplicated and serve for both the *altus* and the *tenor* parts. Finally Mersenne cites two sizes of transverse flutes which he names *flûtes d'allemands*. That national feeling in these matters was already to the fore is shown by the writings of the Frenchman, Vincent Carloix, who, in the 16th century, had stated that it was wrong to call the transverse flute *flauste d'Allemand* for, said he, the French played it better and in a more musical way than any other nation; moreover, flute quartets were then customary in France and unknown in Germany. Alas for Carloix, he

evidently did not know the work of Urs Graf (1485–1527). A drawing
by that artist now in the Kunstmuseum, Basel, depicts just such a
quartet played by four typical *Landsknechts*, and this is of particular
value as it shows the relative sizes of the instruments and emphasises
the awkwardness of the very long bass[3] (see Plate 1).

As regards fipple-flutes the situation appears to have been consolidated rather earlier, since Virdung depicts a group of four (or rather
three, as the middle ones appear to be of the same size), the *bass*
being provided with an open-standing key to the lowest hole. Agricola
illustrates four distinct sizes, and gives similar fingering charts to
Virdung's. By Praetorius's time, however, no less than eight instruments made up the family, as follows:

1. *Exilent* or *klein flötlein*   Lowest note g″
2. *Discant flöt*   „   „ d″
3. *Discant flöt*   „   „ c″
4. *Altflöt*   „   „ g′
5. *Tenorflöt*   „   „ c′
6. *Bassetflöt*   „   „ f
7. *Bassflöt*   „   „ B♭
8. *Grossbassflöt*   „   „ F

Of these numbers 4, 5, and 6 correspond to the group that Virdung
knew just a century earlier. We note that the general name *Flöt* was
applied to all these instruments, and this custom was to continue at
least until Bach's day. From Mersenne it appears that, in France at
least, by the early mid-century the whole family of *flûtes douces* had
been again sub-divided into a *grand jeu* and a *petit jeu*, the latter comprising the *altus*, *tenor*, and *basset* of Praetorius.

In addition to the works of Virdung and Agricola, we have from the
16th century a number of musical instrument inventories, large and
small, which are of great value to the scholar. Among the most important is the list of instruments belonging to King Henry VIII compiled
in 1547, and now preserved in the British Museum (Harleian MSS.
1419). Here we find among many similar items 'v Cases with fflutes
and in euerie of iiii of the said Cases iiii flutes, and in the vth three
flutes'; 'Foure fflutes of Ivorie tipped with golde in a Case covered
with greene vellat'; 'viii Recorders greate and smale in a Case couered
with blacke Leather and lined with clothe'; 'Twoo base Recorders of
waulnuttre, one of them tipped with Siluer; the same are butt redde
woodde.' It would seem that in Tudor times, as today, materials

M

supplied were not always up to specification! We note particularly that in this inventory distinction is made between 'recorders' and 'flutes' and this certainly suggests that England was perhaps the first country to attach the unqualified title to the cross-blown instrument exclusively. In a list of instruments belonging to the *Accademia Filarmonica* of Verona in 1569 a similar nomenclature is adopted, but in an inventory of the *Berlin Hofkapelle* instruments made in 1582 seven fipple-flutes are entered as *Handt-flöten* and nine others as *Brauhne-flöten*. Nine transverse flutes appear under the usual German appellation of *Querflöten*.[4]

From such evidence as the foregoing it seems pretty clear that the conservative musical thinking innate in the concept of the *whole consort* had a beneficial effect on the craft of instrument making in Europe. It provided a period of stability both in the use and construction of instruments during which successful forms became consolidated, and less satisfactory ones revealed their weaknesses. This, however, could not long continue. Solid polyphony in but one tone colour, however ingeniously its threads were interwoven, could not satisfy indefinitely and the 'broken' or 'mixed' consort came into being. No doubt the combination of instruments was often dictated frankly by what was available, or could play a part at the required pitch—especially in a society where at least amateur musical ability was expected in any person of reasonable education or breeding—but these were just the circumstances which would reveal which instruments sounded agreeable together, and which did not. Thus, perhaps, the way was pointed for experiments yet to come.[5]

The beginning of the 17th century saw the first ventures in opera and oratorio, with instrumental groups supporting the voice parts and dividing them into dramatic sections with formal *sinfonie* and *ritornelli*. In the earliest scores, however, there is often little or no indication of the instruments desired. Broadly speaking the strings, as today, made the basis of opera instrumentation (though *they* did not really settle down into a coherent body till about 1660) while other instruments were introduced in a rather tentative way for tonal variety. The conservatism of the previous age was to some extent encroached on but by no means swept away. This was not to happen for nearly another hundred years, and even as late as the time of Bach when a full appreciation of tonal colour had developed, many composers (especially in Church music) were content to go no further than to contrast strings with homogeneous blocks of flutes, reeds, or brass instruments. At first sight this would appear to show little or no advance on what was being done *c.* 1570,[6] but in fact great progress had been made, for now instrumentation, though still often 'blocky', was being related to the emotional content of scenes and had become a dramatic element.

We must also remember in trying to interpret these early works that many, if not all, were *pièces d'occasion* where the composer himself was the director at production. He could therefore deploy his resources and instruct his players at first hand, and there would be little need for detailed writing down.

Turning now to the flute in particular, it must be admitted that the bulk of early operatic and oratorio scores do not tell us very much. It is therefore interesting, if no more than coincidental, that two out of the three oldest surviving *do* mention flutes though they give no other clue to intended instrumentation. In Cavalieri's oratorio *Rappresentazione di Anima e di Corpo* of 1600 there is a 'sonata' for two flutes which apart from two *sinfonie* and several *ritornelli*, is the only piece of characteristically 'instrumental' writing in the work. The remainder appears as vocal score with *basso continuo*, and even the *sinfonie* which are written out in five-part harmony bear no more instructions than that they are to be played by 'a large number of instruments'. The second of these early specific references to flutes is found in an opera, so we have some assurance that the instrument found its way into both forms of dramatic music right at the start. In 1600 also, both Peri and Caccini set the *Euridice* story in operatic form, and it is the former version that is of particular interest to us here. Peri left even less in the way of instrumental directions than did Cavalieri, but he did score a single *sinfonia* for three flutes. It was supposed to represent the actual sound of a 'property' triple flute played on stage by one of the characters, and accordingly the three parts are written close together—in what we might today call 'close harmony'. Generally regarded as a musical curiosity, this little piece of Peri's may in fact be of some importance to the student of woodwind for it represents one way by which particular instruments sometimes found their way into the early orchestras— either as direct picture-painting, or for the sake of their characteristic associations. For example, we know that with Monteverde and his successors trumpets and their allied drums began to be admitted into the body of operatic works to colour martial or jubilant episodes in the classical stories that so often furnished the libretti; and this quite apart from the fanfares which by custom heralded any dramatic performance. The combination of trombones and cornetts which, because of their special fitness for vocal support, had long been accepted by the Church, were now also brought into the field of opera for episodes of special solemnity or grandeur. It is suggested that perhaps the transverse flutes, with their more outdoor and martial associations, entered the operatic force in some such way, for the more gentle recorders were certainly the prior group to be accepted into formally organised music. The greater power and general superiority of the *traversi* only became evident gradually as the orchestra itself developed.

Although both fipple and transverse flutes were cultivated side by side in Europe throughout the 17th century,[7] after the initial experiments we have mentioned, and in some made by Cesti and by Monteverde in his early period, neither seems to have played a very distinguished part in orchestral development before about 1660. Both instruments were of course still of the one-piece type known from medieval times and neither had a very extensive scale, two or three notes beyond the second octave being the limit. The compass of the recorder was extended downwards by one tone, and the extra hole was stopped by the lowermost little finger (in the bass instrument assisted by an open-standing key), but the transverse flute remained keyless and confined to the natural six-finger scale. Except for occasional special effects we may suppose that the unobtrusive tone of the recorder kept it mainly to the humdrum duty of thickening up the general texture in unison with the strings, while in contrast the more assertive trumpet was taking the first steps towards real emancipation.

The activities we have considered so far were, of course, centred in Italy, but by the third quarter of the century a movement had begun in France which was to have a profound effect on orchestral growth generally. While in Italy the first seeds of opera and oratorio were sprouting, in France instrumental music began to be organised for other and particular purposes. Before 1625 the outdoor music of Louis XIII consisted of two treble shawms, two cornetts, four tenor shawms, two trombones, and two bass shawms, while about the same time, in London, James I had a similar though smaller band. At the opulent Court of Louis XIV—'le Roi Soleil'—(1643–1715) musical organisation reached a higher state than ever before and musicians could find employment in several different spheres: the Chapel, the Chamber Music, and above all in the *Grande Ecurie*—the large band administered by the Master of the Great Stables of the King. Nowhere else in Europe was there so large a body of musicians whose service was so secure, so remunerative, or carried such social advantages.

Appointments were eagerly sought and, when granted, were hereditary and could be bequeathed by will. With such rewards in view the highest standard of contemporary musicianship was expected and secured. The period is so well documented that we know a great deal about the Philidors, the Hotteterres, and the Chedevilles, and many other celebrated musical families who served French royalty in the 17th and 18th centuries.

The music of the *Grande Ecurie* itself was divided into five corps: (1) the Trumpets; (2) the Fifes and Drums; (3) the Violins, Shawms, Sackbuts, and Cornetts; (4) the Krumhorns and Trumpets Marine; (5) the Hautbois and Musettes de Poitou. Such an organisation could obviously provide both the rigidly traditional music required by certain aspects of Court ceremonial and the more ephemeral entertainment music, as well as being at the same time a nursery for up-to-date experiment. In three of its departments woodwind virtuosi were sure of a welcome, and it was upon these men that Lulli was to draw for the wind players required in his entertainments in the years following 1654. Lulli's practical experience began as a violinist and director of the *petits violons du Roi* but his subsequent appointment to the supervision of military music gave him great experience in composing and arranging for the shawms, and these he brought into the more refined field of entertainment music. There seems little doubt also that this irascible and scheming innovator provided the stimulus which about this time gave birth to a new voice, the true oboe.[8] This would have been a year or two before 1660, a date which accords well with a note in the celebrated Talbot manuscript of *c.* 1686, now in the library of Christ Church, Oxford (Music MS. 1187). The next ten years or so we can well imagine as a period of research and practical improvement in the hands of the French Court instrument makers, and then we arrive at a most significant date, 1671. This was the year of Cambert's opera *Pomone*, which is usually cited as the first work in which oboes as such are specifically demanded. In fact it seems likely that Lulli gave his men opportunities to present the new instrument in public before this time, and 1657 has been suggested as a probable date.[9] Certainly after *Pomone* we find few scores calling for woodwinds at all that do not include parts for oboe, and the attention the instrument received overshadowed both the flute and the bassoon for quite a long time. Only the trumpet seems to have rivalled the new oboe in its early years.

Among the men of the *Grande Ecurie* were some notable instrument makers, in particular the Hotteterre family, who have sometimes even been credited with introducing the transverse flute into France. This attribution will not, of course, stand up to scrutiny, though we may perhaps understand how it arose if we turn back to Chapter 4, p. 80. The innovations of the Hotteterre group of workers did not stop, however, at mere advances in manufacture. In the course of their work they changed the musical character of some instruments quite markedly. For example, while seeking to improve the intonation of the recorder they introduced a new bore, with a cylindrical head joint, a more pronounced taper to the body-tube, and occasionally even a very slight reverse taper in the foot. The combined result of their modifications was an instrument rather less brilliant and reedy in tone than the old model, but more adaptable to the mixed ensemble of their time. This very distinctive tone quality is also excellent in the 'whole consort' but is perhaps a little uninteresting in the solo *concerti*, etc., that were to come in with the 18th century, and this may have had some influence at that time in favour of the more arresting transverse flute. By subtle adjustments of bore and finger-holes the Hotteterres made most semi-tones as good notes as the primary scale, so that cross-fingering, from being a *faut-de-mieux* expedient, became part of the essential technique and *ethos* of the recorder. Alternative fingerings with slightly varying intonation became possible, and by these means the virtuoso player could to some extent compensate for the unavoidable rise of pitch which goes with the changes of blowing pressure that are necessary to produce musical dynamics with the fipple-flute (see also 'Generation of Edge Tones', Chapter 2, p. 26 above). In this one respect it seems that the advantage must always be with the free *embouchure* transverse flute.

Although as late as 1938 Adam Carse, describing the one-keyed conical flute, was to write, 'The new type appeared during the second half of the 17th century. It is not known by whom or where it was first made', present-day scholars tend, as we have seen, to attribute the instrument to the same sources as the true oboe and the Baroque recorder. It must be admitted, however, that of the four new designs that appeared in the latter part of the century, this was the least successful. Although the instrument found a new and appealing voice with a hitherto undreamed of dynamic range, the fork-fingerings were not improved to anything like the degree achieved with the recorder, and much correction by lip was still called for. It is interesting to note that even at this early stage *enharmonic* distinctions were recognised and catered for to some extent by alternative fingering where possible (see fingering chart, Appendix III, p. 244). In constructing the new flute the pitch of the favourite alto/tenor instrument of the old group was kept (lowest note d') and a d♯ key was added. Although a good player *could* keep in tune in all the most used keys, as has been demonstrated by present-day specialists, the one-keyed flute remained most at home in G and D which avoided in general the worst of the defective notes—just as the treble recorder was still best off in F and B♭. This natural preference for particular keys is sometimes a useful guide to composers' intentions—transverse flute or recorder—when an old score contains no special directions.

————

At this point the reader may perhaps feel that we have digressed rather far from the main theme of the chapter. In fact the marked changes in character—whoever may have been responsible technically—which overtook most of the woodwind in the last quarter of the 17th century were soon to be reflected in a very different approach to their use in the growing orchestra, and it is important for us to understand the nature of these changes.

As we have already observed, the re-birth of the woodwind took place during the years of Lulli's reign in Paris and it therefore seems a little strange to find his use of them rather unenterprising. Often there is little to distinguish his wind parts from his strings, except a perfunctory naming of *flûtes* or *hautbois* on the violin staves. It seems that he expected his woodwind to play the same parts in unison with the strings, allowing them an occasional few bars to themselves in a manner which rather anticipated Handel, but without the latter's degree of purposeful formality and balance. Much more rarely Lulli wrote for an independent woodwind group as in the 'Prélude pour l'amour' in his opera *Le Triomphe de l'Amour* of 1681. The specification here is for four flutes thus:

Tailles ou Flûtes d'Allemagne	(G clef on 2nd line)
Quinte de Flûtes	(C clef on 1st line)
Petite basse de Flûtes	(C clef on 2nd line)
Grande basse de Flûtes et B. cont.	(Bass clef)

and we note particularly *Flûte d'Allemagne* from which we may conclude that the recorder was still the common flute in Lulli's mind. The same opera contains some three-part writing for oboes and bassoons, but in general Lulli seems to have been satisfied with woodwind in pairs. In this respect both A. Scarlatti in Italy and Purcell in England, though younger men by no more than twenty years, showed more imagination in their use of independent parts, and both adopted the four-part layout for their strings which was not to become standardised for quite some time.

Following the death of Lulli in 1687 relatively little progress seems to have been made in France for nearly a generation, his pupils and immediate followers being for the most part content to adhere to the formulae he had used during his most influential period. In the meantime, however, things were moving in Germany, particularly in Munich between 1681 and 1688, and thereafter in Hanover, where the Italian-born Steffani had become famous as a composer of opera in addition to his other occupations as statesman and a dignitary of the Catholic Church. Many judge him to have been the peer of Scarlatti and Purcell, and in one respect he may even have surpassed them—his imaginative and untramelled use of trumpets. In Hanover he seems to have found an ample supply of wind players and he used them very freely both to alternate with, and to double, the strings. Under the influence of Steffani and his like, the main centres of orchestral progress now began to shift from Italy towards Germany, where there was already an enduring tradition of Protestant Church music that was before long to flower unsurpassedly in the work of J. S. Bach. Pre-eminent among the Lutheran Church musicians was Dietrich Buxtehude (1637–1707), the organist of Lübeck whom the young Bach so much admired. His instrumental scoring develops naturally via Schütz out of the pattern established at St Mark's, Venice, in the latter part of the 16th century by G. Gabrielli. His position is important in orchestral history, mainly for his conservative use of strings in five parts when this was already on the way out, and we learn little from him in respect of the flute. To summarise the state of the orchestra at the end of the 17th century we may say broadly that the strings had settled down into an organised group of voices at *four* different pitches, the second tenor line of the older composers being found unnecessary. The woodwind were showing signs of becoming a family group with a life of their own; and the brass, from being purely 'special effects', showed also the germ of group organisation.

The first phase of orchestral development ends, as we have said, with the years dominated by Bach and Handel—roughly the first half of the 18th century—and for this period we are fortunate in having a contemporary account of musical instruments, at least as known in German orchestras. In 1713 Johann Mattheson (1681–1746), a prolific north German composer, published his book *Das neu-eröffnete Orchester* which, for its bearing on 18th-century music, is nearly as valuable to the historian as are Virdung and Praetorius in respect of their periods. He lists three sizes of the fipple-flute:

Discant	f′ to f‴
Alto	c′ to c‴
Bass	f to f″

The favourite of these among amateurs in the early 18th century was the discant or soprano of the group, and a considerable number of instruction books for it were published between 1683 and 1798. By this time the term 'recorder' was falling out of use in England and the instrument was then becoming known as the 'common flute' or 'flute' *tout court*.[10] It is, however, the transverse flute that receives Mattheson's principal commendation, and he insists that it is the finer instrument. He calls it *flûte allemande, traversière*, and 'teutche oder Quer-flöte', and states that the compass is 'as on the oboe' but lacking the low C. The instrument as he describes it is evidently pitched in D and is not usually employed above the second octave. Mattheson also tells us that the favourite keys for the *traversière* are G, A, D major, and E minor. This appears to be the first printed indication that, in orchestral circles, the transverse flute was beginning to overtake the recorder, and we note that in 1707 it was placed first in Hotteterre's *Principes de la flûte*, which is the earliest instruction book to mention it.[11]

The early years of the new century were the birth period of the string *concerto*, often regarded as the invention of Torelli (d. 1708), with the string body divided unequally into *solo* and *ripieno* sections, and which led to the solo instrumental concerto on the one hand, and to the classical symphony on the other. Orchestral music was now beginning to become an expressive art in its own right, and was no longer to be associated only with opera and oratorio. The principal composers who were working at this time fall roughly into a 'conservative' and a 'progressive' group, a division which today suggests political rather than musical associations. Bach and Handel by their musical lineage were both conservatives, and the distinction of their work lies mainly in their brilliant individual use of accepted formulae. Both adhered to the established practice of imposing string-type figuration on their wind instruments, but Handel at times divided his orchestra into

three contrasted masses, strings, woodwind, and trumpets with drums,
though of course the last could hardly be a full melodic section. By
different combinations of these groups with each other and with chorus
voices in as many as five parts Handel secured great variety and some
of his grandest effects.

Curiously enough Handel does not seem to have written any really
difficult flute parts, at least in the eyes of a modern player, and his
required compass is almost always entirely confined to the two octaves
d'–d''', approximately the range of the older *flûtes-à-bec*. Further, there
are many of his major works in which he did not employ the instrument at all. *Messiah*, for instance, as written contained no flute; the
flute and piccolo parts we now know were added by Mozart. Much of
Handel's music sheds interesting light on the relations between the
vertical and transverse flutes at the beginning of the 18th century. For
example he is known to have introduced a *traverso* in a work as early
as 1705, but he continued to employ the *flûte-à-bec* till the end of his
life. Handel was notable for revising and re-using his own earlier
material and thus we get a number of curiosities. The last of all his
works, *The Triumph of Time and Truth* (1757), was in fact mainly a
version of an earlier piece of 1708, and it is interesting to see that
although in some numbers the *flûte-à-bec* is retained, in others the
traverso has been substituted. Again, in *La Resurrezzione*, also of 1708,
we find two vertical flutes and one transverse specified together in the
original score.[12] It is noticeable, too, that Handel often tended to use
his flutes pictorially rather than structurally, as in the accompaniment
to 'Hush, ye pretty warbling choir' in *Acis and Galatea*. Typical of
his period, we may think, and not the most imaginative approach, but
certainly he did it supremely well.

It is, however, when we turn to Bach that we find something that is
little less than marvellous. His basic formulae were largely those of his
time, but in his use of individual instruments the master seems somehow to have penetrated the very soul of each one and to have used
them, not only to depict or underline the *emotions* of his text, but to
inspire these emotions in his hearers. This is the more wonderful when
we remember that at no time were his resources large; often he had to
fill up his orchestra with student or amateur players whose performing
abilities were uncertain, and there are places in his scores where the
desirable instrument as well as the next best substitute are indicated.
This aspect of Bach's work, especially in his Church music, finds its
roots in the imagination and simple piety of the man, and has proved a

lifelong study for many great scholars. Here we can do no more than refer the reader to them.[13] During his working life Bach knew both types of flute and he recognised a peculiar emotional genius in each of them. To him, as to Mersenne, the *flûte-à-bec* expressed 'le charme et la douceur des voix' and, to quote Sanford Terry, 'It voices his tenderness for his Saviour, his serene contemplation of death as the portal of bliss eternal. Only rarely . . . it intrudes into a score of pomp and circumstance. Elsewhere . . . it is the vehicle of the mysticism so deeprooted in Bach's nature.' In relation to his vast output Bach uses the *flûte-à-bec* sparingly, partly we may suppose, because of this special emotional connotation, but often also for lack of competent players. We know, for instance, that the ducal *Kapelle* at Weimar was not provided with flautists, so during his service there Bach was obliged to look outside for the instrument. A general survey of Bach's scores shows that he seldom employed flutes other than the trebles pitched in a', g', or f', though there are one or two calls for the *flauto piccolo* in d″ and f″, and possibly an alto in those cantatas where three flutes are specified. It is not always easy to determine from internal evidence which flute was the most appropriate for any given part, and in compositions involving the organ transpositions were no doubt sometimes called for. In 18th-century Germany organs were usually tuned to 'chorton' or 'cornett-ton', a whole tone or a minor third respectively above the 'hoher-cammerton' which—whatever its absolute value—was the customary pitch for concerted music. Unless we remember this we are likely to get very confused over the transpositions for other instruments which sometimes appear in old scores.

According to Sanford Terry's meticulous tables, 1721, the year of the Brandenburg Concertos, is the earliest date at which the transverse flute appears prominently in Bach's scores, though he did prescribe 'due Traversieri' in the secular cantata *Durchlaucht'ster Leopold* which is questionably ascribed to 1718. Following his appointment to the Thomasschule in Leipzig in 1723 the instrument finds a regular place in his concerted music, but even so his use of it seems somewhat experimental. It is evident that Bach felt some disinclination to use the *traverso* in purely instrumental movements, and among all the cantatas, both sacred and secular, there is only one example. In the 'pastoral' Sinfonia of the *Christmas Oratorio* the *traverso* is admitted and with evident special pictorial intention. Otherwise, the instrument is found only in three of his large-scale orchestral works—the Brandenburg in D major, the Clavier Concerto in A minor, and the Overture in B

minor; and all of these have a characteristic in common with the
'pastoral'—in none of them are there any horns or trumpets. This
suggests that Bach's transverse flute may have been a pretty assertive
voice in the ensemble, and of course we must not forget that his
trumpets played in the 'clarino' manner, were not as weighty as today.
In considering Bach's orchestral writing we must always keep in mind
the smallness of his total orchestra and his care for internal balance—a
point sometimes neglected in present-day 'festival' size performances,
however well intentioned. Although Bach's employment of the transverse flute is obviously most carefully considered, the music he wrote
for it is not always easy technically, and the Flute Sonatas, and the
two Trios for flute, violin, and bass, show that he regarded it as a
worthy soloist when he had competent players available.

The characteristics which marked the 'progressive' composers of
the mid-18th century are rather difficult to define, since they consist
more in the non-observance or bending of the accepted formulae than
in any radical innovation. The importance of their work does not
become really evident till we look at it beside the mature productions of
the next generation who used tone colour, harmony, and rhythm for
their own sake and gave up pure contrapuntal writing as their sole
means of expression. Time has shown these composers to have been
mostly minor talents, yet to them we owe a debt of gratitude, for by
their persistence they kept open a path without which orchestral
composition might well have died of sheer stagnation after the passing
of the two Giants. Among the better known we find Hasse, Wagenseil,
C. P. E. Bach, and, of considerably greater stature, Telemann, all, be
it noted, north German composers.

Modern orchestration, as we may call it, really began in the last
years of the 18th century, the period dominated by Haydn and Mozart
as orchestral composers, but we must not suppose that the new system
burst suddenly on a waiting world. There was, as we have seen, a
transition, and this, though pivoted about 1750, really covered most of
the century, becoming more evident sometimes in one musical centre
and sometimes in another. The working period of Gluck coincided
almost exactly with the last years of the transition. During a long life
he travelled all over the musical centres of Europe, and even before the
death of Bach had made an international reputation as an operatic
composer. His most important years in the present connection were
1760–80 (*Orfeo* to *Iphigénie en Tauride*) in which he demonstrated his
conviction that 'the instruments ought to be introduced in proportion

to the degree of interest and passion in the words' and 'instruments are to be employed not according to the dexterity of the players, but according to the dramatic propriety of their tone'. These dicta were perhaps to some ears new, but what, in fact, had Bach been doing all those years earlier? It is not intended here in any way to belittle Gluck who was himself an important innovator (witness his use of the lowest register of the flute); what he had to say required saying, and forcibly, but the comparison between his international *réclame* and the relative obscurity of Bach in his own time illustrates just once more how often progress in the arts has been held up for lack of communication.

In the time of Haydn, Mozart, and their contemporaries[14] we find the concert orchestra fully established, notably at Mannheim, Dresden, Berlin, and Paris, in addition to specialised opera orchestras in Paris, Naples, and some lesser centres. Their strength had been filled out by acceptance of the clarinet, which had been the subject of experiment and technical development for nearly eighty years.[15] In such surroundings the gentle and somewhat expressionless tone of the recorder could not possibly hold its own and from now on it quietly yielded up to its more lively rival. The inevitable transfer of attention to the transverse flute which followed among composers may well have emphasised its remaining defects. Before 1775 the only marked improvement since the Hotteterres had been the further division of the body-tube between the two groups of finger-holes. This permitted the use of shorter or longer upper joints (*corps de réchange*) which helped in the matter of general pitch adjustment, but Burney in 1772 was still able to write that it was 'natural to those instruments to be out of tune'. A growing awareness of this problem soon led to the introduction of three new keys providing semitones that were before only available as 'forked' notes, and the flute thus became the pioneer among woodwinds in the admission of chromatic keys in the primary scale. This improvement may in fact have had little effect on the orchestral use of the instrument, but when the two additional keys for c′ and c′♯ on an extended foot joint had been proved reasonably reliable, composers began to write for the flute as for the oboe. Once again, however, conservatism made itself felt, and a full compass from c′ upwards could not be relied on before about 1820. Some experiments with c′ and c′♯ keys had indeed been made as early as 1722 and Bach's very occasional demands for these notes have been adduced as evidence that some of his flautists possessed them. The argument will not, however, really stand up to scrutiny, as Sanford Terry has pointed out.[16]

In the hands of Haydn the transverse flute seems to lose something of the specialised emotional association that it had had with Bach, and to become more of an orchestral voice pure and simple. With him, especially in his later years,[17] wind instruments generally began to have status in the orchestra equal to that of the strings, and he wrote for them more freely than did any of his predecessors. In the band at Esterhaz Haydn could call on only one flute—the player was one Hirsch—and this is reflected in his scoring at that time. Later, however, he used two or three flutes, as, for instance, in the Introduction to part III of the *Creation*, where the third flute is written into an oboe part, suggesting the availability of a 'double-handed' player. Altogether we may say that Haydn's scoring for the flute clearly foreshadows its future place in the symphony orchestra, although he remained wary of the extremes of its compass and commonly confined its important passages to the middle register—usually f' to f".

With Mozart the picture of the flute is somewhat different. In his travels the young virtuoso must frequently have heard the woodwind of the Mannheim orchestra who in their day had a reputation for delicacy and dynamic subtlety that was envied, but seldom matched, throughout Europe. When in Mannheim Mozart frequently stayed at the house of J. B. Wendling who was then principal flute in the orchestra, and we may perhaps detect in this experience an influence on his later orchestral scoring. It has been said that Mozart had no great taste for the flute as soloist and that he only wrote 'pot-boilers' for it in that capacity. Be that as it may, his complete works contain no less than nine solo flute pieces of different sorts, and their particular interest for us here lies in the fact that in them the composer adhered to the comparatively 'safe' keys of C, D, G, and A.[18] Mozart's sensitivity to intonation is well documented and his choice of keys clearly indicates the limitations of the flute, at least in average hands, during his lifetime (1756–91).[19] Mozart's early acquaintance with Wendling, who was undoubtedly a fine artist, may well have engendered some impatience with inferior players which in turn would account for his rather sparing use of the flute in his symphonies. In the serenades, however, the flute is much more prominent, possibly because in these *pièces d'occasion* he was more certain of the performance he could expect from players who were known to him. In the operas Mozart's use of the flute is extremely skilful in spite of his supposed prejudice, and he wrote quite florid passages for it in the middle and upper registers— passages which, however, suggest some return to the 'special effects' approach as distinct from his more formal symphonic writing.

At the beginning of the 19th century we find Beethoven using the entire woodwind with complete freedom and mastery—except the clarinet—and to that instrument too he gave solo status with essential thematic material in the 'Eroica' (1804). As regards the flute in particular Beethoven seems to have had few misgivings, and he wrote important passages throughout its compass. Occasionally the lowest octave is not well heard owing to its relative weakness, as in the well known first flute passage in 'Leonora No. 3' but there is not one of Beethoven's

BEETHOVEN, Overture, *Leonora, No. 3.*
SOLO FLUTE.

symphonies that does not contain important matter for the flutes. Much has been written about the famous 'bird' passage at the end of the slow movement in the 'Pastoral' Symphony, but whether Beethoven intended his quail, cuckoo, and nightingale as a joke or as deliberate (incidentally quite inaccurate) tone painting does not matter. The nightingale phrase in itself though very simple is completely evocative, and by its juxtaposition with a solo violin is perfectly related to what follows.[20] In spite of its manifest unrealism it is a great deal more acceptable than many 'bird' *obbligati* composed later in the century as display pieces for flautists and ambitious sopranos. It illustrates one pole of Beethoven's attitude to the woodwind just as surely as the sombre chording in, say, the Fifth Symphony represents the other.[21]

To summarise thus far, then, we may say that by the end of Beethoven's life the place and scope of the woodwind in the orchestra had been established definitively.

In a limited book such as the present it is quite impossible to comment individually on the many composers who since Beethoven have contributed one or other new device to the sum total of orchestration as it stands today, and we can only refer the enquiring reader to the excellent books on the subject, some of which are noted in the bibliography, and leave it at that. Before doing so, however, we must just mention one other early 19th-century composer because of a characteristic in his work which appears strangely to anticipate one trend in modern scoring. This is C. M. von Weber (1786–1826) who alone among his contemporaries seems to have appreciated at all fully the peculiar effectiveness of the extreme low register of the flute when not masked by other instruments. In *Der Freischütz*, for example, the sustained low notes of two flutes *pp* in the accompaniment to 'Softly sighs' have an extraordinary tenderness, while in the 'Wolf's Glen' scene two flutes in the low octave in unison with the second violins produce a remarkable effect of gloom. Again, at the casting of the magic bullets, long sustained chords for flutes on e'♭ with g'♭, and f'♯ with a', are incredibly sinister, an effect that Wagner was to use many years later.

———

From the lower register of the normal flute we turn naturally to the lower pitched flutes themselves. Their use in the orchestra is in the main a modern phase which ties up with a limited revival of the 'whole consort' concept though with a different basic motive. No longer is the instrumental group modelled on the human voice—the new idea, of which Wagner was the great protagonist, is to extend the available compass of characteristic tone colours. If the complete families of instruments we now possess allow of neo-consort style writing this is quite incidental. The composer can today call on such resources as the bass (baritone) oboe, alto, bass, and contrabass clarinets, the alto flute, and the true bass flute one octave below the concert instrument. But if he does so he may seriously limit the chances of having his music performed, for none of these instruments, except perhaps the bass clarinet, are at all common. The incredible rise in the cost of instruments in the last ten years or so has done nothing to ease the situation and, in England at least, the fortunate possessors of specimens do good business today in hiring them out to colleagues who may require them for special engagements. At the time of writing the principal call for unusual instruments seems to come from the composers of specially commissioned scores for films or radio and television programmes. Of course it is not intended to imply that wind instruments built to other than normal pitches are in themselves an innovation—the only novelty lies in their addition to the accepted standard complement of the orchestra.

As regards the flutes this might well have happened a good deal earlier than it did, but for the practical difficulty of making relatively large instruments that would be both reliable and capable of fingering with the agility that was being increasingly required by composers. Some attempts to produce such instruments have been noticed in our historical chapters, but real success proved elusive until the introduction of Boehm's mechanism pointed the way. Soon after the *mean* of the old consort group had shown itself to be the most useful size of flute in the developing mixed orchestra, other sizes began occasionally to be called for, but until the early 20th century these have remained principally solo instruments specially studied by individual players. We are not, of course, referring here to the various intermediate pitched instruments which fill in the harmonies in the modern flute band.

In Bach's day the *flûte d'amour* in A was well known, and quite a number of 18th- and early 19th-century examples have been preserved; likewise flutes in G. Theobald Boehm gives details of one such in his treatise, and following his model many excellent instruments have been built. These are still often erroneously called *bass* flutes, but properly the bass is pitched in C. A description of the true bass flute in its completely satisfactory modern form is given in Chapter 10.

Of the larger flutes, that in G is probably the most employed in modern orchestral music, but it is interesting to note that in 1871 Verdi originally intended the *Sacred Dance* finale to Act I of *Aïda* to be played on three flutes in A. Instruments were actually made in Milan for the first performance but they did not prove effective and were abandoned. The student who may be anxious to know how notable composers have written for the deeper flutes is recommended to look at such scores as Rimsky-Korsakov's *Mlada*, Ravel's *Daphnis and Chloe*, or Holst's *Suite Phantastique*. In modern operas both Mascagni and Puccini have used the bass flute (*Albisiphon*, see p. 189), the latter notably in *The Girl of the Golden West*. Others who have used alto or

N

bass flutes effectively are Bax, Richard Strauss, Mahler, Glazounov, Stravinsky, and Holbrooke, all men noted for their orchestral colouring; while Bliss has introduced them into chamber music. In the mid-19th century Berlioz, perhaps the greatest orchestral colourist of all, is known to have expressed regret that the alto flute was not then more frequently employed.[22]

Next, under the heading of orchestral use we must look briefly at flutes pitched higher than the concert instrument. There is only one of importance today, the *piccolo* or octave flute, and no doubt, subject to the reservation made on p. 184 below, its antetype was the *klein diskant* of the consort group. In general its history is little different from that of the C flute, save that modern mechanism was applied rather later, and that even today the extended foot joint with c″ and c″♯ keys is so rare as to be almost non-existent. The occasional demand for these notes in modern scores suggests a lapse on the part of the composer rather than the availability of an extremely unusual instrument. The upward compass of the piccolo is said to reach C *in altissimo* but it is

rarely employed above the A or perhaps a very occasional B.

The piccolo is not an easy instrument to play softly and with much refinement, though there have been notable artists who have mastered it completely and have subdued its inherent shrillness. The usual orchestral practice of making the piccolo a 'double' for the second flute player—though it does bring in an additional fee—has often been called in question. Many think that the very different embouchure demanded can be injurious to a player's tone on the normal flute, and indeed it seems that some of the most esteemed piccolo players in modern times have been rather less distinguished as flautists.

'Piccolo' parts appear in orchestral scores from about 1700, but, as with the other flutes, there is often doubt as to whether the recorder was not the actual instrument intended. Indeed, the indication *flauto piccolo* at this period is often more likely to have meant a small *flûte-à-bec* than a *traverso*. There is, for instance, an elaborate cadenza marked *flauto piccolo* in Handel's *Rinaldo* and other passages in *Riccardo Primo* and the *Water Music*, but there is doubt about the authenticity of the instrumental specifications. It seems most likely that Handel intended vertical flutes here, in which case he probably never employed the transverse piccolo at all. On the other hand, it is to be noted that in some cases the parts are written in the same key as the non-transposing instruments; and the recorders, we remember, were characteristically transposers. The famous *obbligato* to 'Oh, ruddier than the cherry' that is now usually played on the piccolo has had interesting vicissitudes. In the first (Italian) version of *Acis and Galatea* the song is not included at all, but in the English version (*c.* 1720) where it does appear, the accompaniment is just marked *flauto*, i.e. *flûte-à-bec*. Mozart re-scored the piece giving the *obbligato* to a transverse flute, and later Mendelssohn gave it to *two* flutes. At the London Ancient Concerts the part used traditionally to be played on a flageolet as a fair substitute for the small discant recorder—and it is perhaps this substitution which has led Curt Sachs into one of his very rare errors in terminology. Writing of the *flauto piccolo* of Handel's time he describes the instrument as a 'French flageolet', a term which implies a very different thing from any true recorder.

Further evidence that some early 18th-century composers of substance did employ the transverse piccolo is afforded by three Vivaldi *concerti* for *flautino*. Dale Higbee has examined the solo parts in these and compared them with the possible compass of the flageolet and the discant and *sopranino* recorders. His conclusion is that some passages as written were impossible on any of these instruments, but possible (with difficulty) on the one-keyed transverse piccolo. In support he quotes Corette, who says in his *Méthode* (*c.* 1730), 'On fait présentement à Paris des petites Flûtes Traversières à l'Octave qui font un effet charmant ... dans les Concerto faits exprès pour la Flûte.'[23] Higbee does suggest, however, that these *concerti* may reflect Vivaldi's enthusiasm for novel effects in music.

With Gluck we come on to less debatable ground and there seems no doubt that the double trills for two piccolos in *Iphigénie en Tauride* were played on *traversi*. This highly dramatic effect was later used by both Weber and Meyerbeer, and through their example became something of a stock device with operatic composers in the 19th century. Both Haydn and Mozart employed the piccolo somewhat sparingly, and both mainly for pictorial purposes. Examples that come to mind are Haydn's 'husbandman whistling at his work' in the *Seasons*, and Mozart's 'Turkish' music in *Die Entführung* and the storm scene in *Idomeneo*. Beethoven gave to the piccolo, as he did to the concert flute, a more solid and dignified status. Appreciating its capacity for 'floating' above the *tutti* and imparting a glitter to the general texture, he used it in his *Egmont*, *King Stephen*, and *Ruins of Athens* overtures, as well as in his Fifth and Ninth Symphonies. In Beethoven's hands the piccolo may be said to have come to orchestral maturity, ready to take its place in the standard symphony orchestra.

Before closing this section we should for the sake of completeness mention one other high-pitched flute which has occasionally been called into the orchestra and which might perhaps be used more often with advantage. This is the F flute which can cover much of the piccolo compass, but with a more solid and less shrill tone. There are not very many examples to quote from the standard orchestral repertoire— Spohr's *Jessonda* is probably the most familiar—but the idea might be recommended. A flute in G was used by Sullivan in *Ivanhoe* with the same idea in mind, but for general orchestral work F would surely be the more satisfactory pitch. The value of the instrument was illustrated by the Australian John Amadeo who used it extensively in recital work, and we note that Bishop's famous *obbligato* to 'Lo, hear the gentle Lark' was originally written for it.

Finally, as an illustration of the present scope of orchestral flutes the reader is recommended to look again at a score of Ravel's *Daphnis and Chloe*. Here he will find a descending run from top A on the piccolo, through the concert flute, to the lowest notes of the bass flute, a *tour de force* and a veritable epitome in one.

NOTES

[1] Carse, Adam, *The History of Orchestration*, London, Kegan Paul, Trench, Trubner and Co. Ltd., 1925, Introduction.

[2] The operative factors here were undoubtedly the difficulty and hence expense of the processes. The actual printing of music from movable type followed very soon after the discovery of letterpress typography, and some of the earliest examples are attributed with some certainty to Wynkyn de Worde. Music engraving on copper plates seems to have been very general by about 1680, and the process of stamping on pewter plates by about 1710, but the cost of such printing on the scale required by a score and set of parts for even a small symphony must have been prohibitive unless the market was assured. See the introduction to Kidson's *British Music Publishers*, London, W. E. Hill and Sons, 1900. Before the 19th century the circulation of large orchestral works depended almost entirely on the transport of sets of manuscript parts, and there

is evidence that composers would sometimes even add a specially effective part for the benefit of a known brilliant performer in one centre or another.

[3] Evidence of the use of the flute *façon d'allement* and its manufacture in Paris in 1542 is found in documents preserved in the *Minutier central de Paris aux Archives nationales*. See François Lesure, 'La Facture Instrumentale à Paris au Seizième Siècle', *Galpin Society Journal*, Vol. VII, 1954. Albert Cohen, *ibid.* Vol. XV, p. 5.

[4] For detailed consideration of both these documents, and the instruments of all types recorded therein, the reader is referred to A. C. Baines, *Woodwind Instruments and Their History*, London, Faber and Faber, 1957, Chapter X.

[5] Bacon in his *Sylva Sylvarum* says: 'In that music which we call broken music or consort music, some consorts of instruments are sweeter than others— But for the melioration of music there is yet much left (in this point of exquisite consorts) to try and enquire'.

[6] Baines, A. C., *op. cit.* Chapter X.

[7] Carse, Adam, *op. cit.* Chapter I.

[8] Bate, Philip, *The Oboe*, London, Ernest Benn Ltd., 1956, 1962, p. 34.

[9] This would, of course, have been during the experimental period.

[10] Although some form of the appellation 'German flute' for the transverse instrument is found in most European countries from the mid-16th century it does not seem to have become current in England before the 18th (see pp. 67–8 above). Galpin, *Old English Instruments of Music*, London, Methuen and Co. Ltd., 1910, p. 154, suggests that the term may have been popularised in this country as a result of the Hanoverian succession, but there appears to be little proof of this.

[11] Hotteterre-le-Romain, *Principes de la Flûte Traversière, etc.*, Paris, Christophe Ballard, 1707.

[12] Fitzgibbon, in his *The Story of the Flute*, 2nd edn., London, William Reeves, 1929, pp. 123 *et seq.*, quotes several interesting curiosities among Handel's scores, and variations between successive versions.

A commentary on the relative positions of the transverse flute and the recorder about the end of the first quarter of the 18th century in fashionable amateur music is afforded by *The Musical Entertainer* published in 1737. This is a volume of songs from many sources beautifully engraved by George Brickham jnr. (better known perhaps for his models of calligraphy in *The Universal Penman*), and of eighty-nine numbers only seven are without flute parts added. On analysis we find that seventy-seven simply specify 'Flute', but five titles are more specific and are worth quoting, *viz.*

'Achilles brought by Thetis to his Tutor Chiron'
The Music by Mr. Purcell
(With ye compass of ye flute).

'In Praise of Bacchus'
Music by Corelli
For two voices and other instruments (1st and 2nd flute parts printed)

'The Address to Sylvia'
Set by Mr. Handel

'The Lover's Protestation'
Set by Mr. Popely

'To Amanda'
Set by Mr. Howard

The last three have the flute part at the bottom of the page marked 'For the German and Common Flutes'. This very fine volume has recently been reproduced in facsimile.

[13] First among them C. Sanford Terry with his studies *Bach's Orchestra* and *Life of Bach*, London, Oxford University Press, 1923 and 1933 respectively.

Parry, Sir Hubert, *The Art of J. S. Bach*, London, Putnam, 1909.

David, H. T., and Mendel, Arthur, *The Bach Reader*, London, J. M. Dent and Son, 1946.

The standard Bach textbook by Spitta is also available in English translation, London, Novello and Co., 1899.

[14] The best known today, and their spheres of influence are:

Piccini—Italy, St Petersburg, London.

Sacchini—Italy, Paris, London, Germany.

Paisiello—Italy, St Petersburg, Paris.

Cimarosa—Italy, St Petersburg, Vienna.

Cannabich—Mannheim, Munich.

Dittersdorf—Vienna, South Germany.

Stamitz (the younger)—Mannheim, Paris, London, St Petersburg.

Gossec—Paris.

Grétry—Paris.

[15] See 'Handel and the Clarinet', R. B. Chatwin in *Galpin Society Journal*, Vol. III, London, March 1950, pp. 3 *et seq.*

[16] Terry, C. Sanford, *op. cit.* p. 75.

[17] Fitzgibbon, *op. cit.* p. 132, quotes Haydn's remark to Kalkbrenner: 'I have only just learned in my old age how to use wind instruments, and now that I do understand them I must leave them.'

[18] Two *concerti* for flute: one first performed by Cosel in 1774, the other composed in 1778 for Deschamps, a rich amateur. A concerto for flute and harp written at the request of the Duc de Guines, an amateur flautist whose daughter played the harp. These are Mozart's major works for solo flute. For comment see Fitzgibbon, *op. cit.* p. 138, also Rockstro, p. 524.

[19] Fitzgibbon, *op. cit.* p. 135, quotes Mozart on the subject of Wendling: 'He is not a piper (the French would use the word *fluteur*) and one need not always be in terror for fear the next note should be too high or too low; *he* is always right—he does not imagine that blowing and making faces is all that is needed; he knows too what Adagio means.' I have been unable to trace the source of the quotation, but it illustrates well Mozart's views on some of his contemporaries—even if, as some suspect, it is not authentic.

[20] For contrasted opinions see again Fitzgibbon, *op. cit.* p. 140.

[21] The characteristics in which we recognise the essential man in great composers are often most difficult to express in words. As regards Beethoven the reader cannot do better than see Adam Carse, *op. cit.* pp. 234–5.

[22] See also Dayton C. Miller, 'Modern Alto, Tenor, and Bass Flutes' in *Proceedings of the Music Teachers National Association* for 1938, New York.

[23] Higbee, Dale, in *Galpin Society Journal*, Vol. XVII, 1946, p. 115.

CHAPTER 10

Larger and Smaller Flutes—Modern Aspects

IN THE foregoing pages, right from Chapter 1, we have had occasion to refer from various standpoints to instruments both larger and smaller than the standard C (six-finger d') flute. This is but natural since the story of these instruments also is part of general flute lore, but in the course of time certain types have developed which must be regarded as somewhat 'non-standard', and these require some consideration in their own right. Because most of the non-standard flutes owe their present-day form mainly to orchestral demands, I have placed this section *after* the general chapter on 'The Flute in the Orchestra', in the hope that this will have supplied something of the necessary background.[1]

In the first place it seems that the French reformers of the late 17th century, whom we believe to have created the cone-flute, concentrated their work on the 'mean' instrument of the old consort group, and did not attempt to perpetuate the other sizes. At first sight this may appear a little strange as the Baroque *recorder*, which we trace to the same source, continued to be made in sets or 'chests' of different sizes, at least during the first thirty years of the 18th century.[2] The explanation seems to be that the *flûte-à-bec* had long been, and was still, the accepted flute of cultured music, while the cross-flute, with its more plebeian associations, was at the time being admitted to the polite circles of the opera, etc., primarily as a 'special effects' instrument. It was only *after* its reorganisation that the transverse flute became fashion-able—though how quickly it did so—and by that time the 'consort' had given place to a developing mixed orchestra. Even so, as we have seen, the higher orchestral wind parts remained for some time in the hands of the recorder player rather than in those of the flautist.

We begin the 18th century, then, with the new flute well established and on its way to supremacy, but still at one pitch only. Very soon, however, we find evidence that some solo players were beginning to desire its qualities over an enlarged range, and there are signs of some experiment with an extended foot (p. 94 above). Some distinguished players, among them Quantz, raised objections that were at the time no doubt valid, but by about 1730 the foot joint down to c' had arrived, and the compass matched that of the contemporary oboe. This was to take another fifty years to be accepted fully, but by the beginning of the next century certain Viennese makers had carried matters even further and were producing a long foot down to b♭ or even a♮. There were, however, two very serious objections to extending the compass of the cone-flute down more than a semitone or two by these means. One was that a natural geometrical extension of the bore rendered it increasingly narrow and so reduced the fullness of the lower notes, as well as making blowing difficult. In fact the air column was getting away from the optimum acoustical proportions (see Chapter 2, p. 21). The second objection was that lever mechanism of the necessary length, even with the tube folded back on itself for some distance (p. 112 above), was unreliable in operation.

The enfeebling effect of over-narrowing the lower part of the tube had evidently been observed quite early, for there are preserved both recorders and flutes of the Hotteterre period, and immediately after, in which the foot joint does not exactly continue the general taper of the body, but has a cylindrical bore, or even a slight reverse cone. Elongation of the standard flute, whatever it may have done for the performance of certain individuals, was obviously not the right approach to extending the overall availability of flute tone, and even before the extended foot had passed the experimental stage deeper toned normal flutes with a bore proportionate to their length had begun to appear. These larger 18th-century flutes cannot, however, be regarded as *direct* descendants of the corresponding consort sizes. There is no evidence that the latter ever passed through the hands of the reformers, and at present there seem to be no recorded specimens that are homologous with the Hotteterre type of C flute. Rather do they appear to be carefully calculated enlargements of the immediate *post*-Hotteterre type, called into being by special demand.

From the relatively small number of these instruments which have survived it would appear that they were never very common, and, of them all, that pitched in A and sometimes termed *flûte d'amour*[3] seems to have been the best known. At a time when the intonation of the one-keyed C flute was such that only some four or five key-signatures were really acceptable to a fastidious ear, the appearance of another a minor third lower must have been a boon to composers. There is, however, an important point to remember here. As the *flûte d'amour* and other deep toned flutes were constructed to appropriate scales (in the organ-builder's sense) their tone was not quite identical with that of the C instrument, even in those parts of their compass which overlapped. The larger instruments tended to have a more sombre tone-colour the deeper they were pitched, and perceptive composers were not slow to turn this to advantage. It seems likely that Bach, for example, used his *flûte d'amour* quite as much for the emotional quality of its sound as for convenience in respect of key-signature.[4] A century later, when writing of the G flute which he designed in 1854, Boehm was most careful to point out that his intention had been to create an entirely new voice of the flute kind, and not to extend the existing instrument.

As the 18th century went on, further large flutes were introduced; an *alto* in G, a *tenor* in F (both often still unjustly called *bass*), and even a true *bass* in C. Plate 11A and B show two typical altos, the first by Scherer of Paris (*c.* 1770) which retains the typical high-placed mouth-hole of the 18th century and a rather long foot joint; the other by Clementi, London, about 1830. Although both instruments are nominally in the same key, the sounding length of the earlier one is evidently rather greater due to a lower prevailing pitch standard. Placed side by side, they afford an interesting illustration of the subtle but quite appreciable change in appearance which the one-keyed flute had undergone between, say, 1750 and 1830. The Clementi alto, of course, belongs to the time when key-work was getting quite advanced—four or six keys were the common equipment of most better class flutes by then—and one wonders why so important and unusual an instrument should retain the more primitive construction.

Mention of key-work brings us to our next point. The reader will by now be familiar—though not, it is hoped, to the point of boredom—with the ever present problem of reconciling the required siting of finger-holes with the span of the hand. We have to return to it once again here because in the larger 18th- and early 19th-century flutes it gave rise to certain interesting features of construction, some of which have survived into modern times. With the flute in A, only some 7 cm. longer than the concert instrument, the difficulty was not too great, and oblique boring of the A and E holes proved almost sufficient, as witness a specimen by Oberlender (*post*-1750) formerly in the Galpin Collection, now Boston No. 47, and reputedly once the property of Kraft, the celebrated 'cellist in Haydn's band. The longer alto and tenor flutes were a different matter, and many makers seem to have had no better solution to offer than a return to the old system of bunching the holes in two widely separated groups, and compensating for the inevitable poor intonation as best they might. By about the mid-century, however, something a good deal better had appeared, at least in France, for in the 'Luthérie' section of Diderot's and d'Alembert's celebrated *Encyclopédie*, published in parts from 1751 onwards, we find the drawing reproduced in Fig. 50. This shows a large flute with the finger-

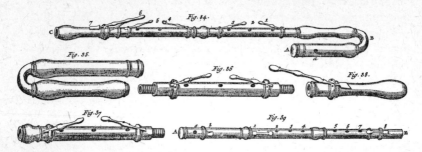

Fig. 50   Large flutes *c.* 1750, from Diderot and
d'Alembert
A. Flageolet—flute (*see p.* 198)

holes distributed more or less rationally, Nos. 1, 3, 4, and 6 being governed by open-standing keys with the touches placed comfortably on either side of the other two holes. This mechanism may perhaps have reduced agility of performance a little—the second order levers used inevitably stand rather far from the surface of the tube when the holes are sufficiently uncovered—but it was evidently practical. A specimen of this construction by Delusse of Paris may possibly be of 18th-century date (Paris Conservatoire Collection E. 1079, C. 1108), and several examples by Wigley and MacGregor of London are known. MacGregor obtained an English patent for the idea in 1810, and his firm made such instruments in both alto and bass sizes between 1811 and 1816. Specimens are to be seen in Boston (ex-Galpin) and in the Brussels Conservatoire Collection.[5] A similar arrangement was employed by Boehm in his first redesigned flute of 1831, and later by Abel Siccama, though both these men made use of a lever of the *third* order in which the touch-plate was placed between the hinge and the cover-plate, thus reducing the height to which the finger had to be lifted to secure adequate opening (see Plate 9E). A very interesting specimen is a bass flute by J. Beuker (Paris Conservatoire E. 248, C. 453) which may well be dated pre-1750. In this case the remote holes are closed by jointed keys with two linked levers each, similar to those found on early oboes. The open keys have the 'fishtail' type of touch for right- or left-handed playing, and this feature suggests a fairly early date, although it is not an infallible proof. The 'fishtail' survived on the oboe as a convention for some years after 'left above right' had become the accepted way of holding that instrument and other keys had been added in conformity therewith.

Comparison of Fig. 50 and Plate 7 emphasises another problem of these large flutes, i.e. the unavoidably long distance between the *embouchure* and the highest finger-hole which makes some of them extremely uncomfortable to hold in playing position. The *Encyclopédie* figure shows an early and practical solution. The head is bent back on itself so as to bring the mouth-hole to a more convenient position. This arrangement was adopted by MacGregor who devised head joints, either in two parts united by a metal U tube, or with two parallel bores in a single piece of wood of oval section. Almost all modern flutes larger than the alto are shortened in this way with one or two U bends (see Plate 12).

The arrival of Boehm's mechanism, and the improved clutches of the contemporary French makers, really solved the difficulty of the over-long flute once and for all, for by suitable modification convenient touch-pieces for all the fingers could be connected to cover-plates in virtually any position. Fig. 51, taken from *Die Flöte und das Flötenspiel*, is part of Boehm's own adaptation for his alto flute in G.

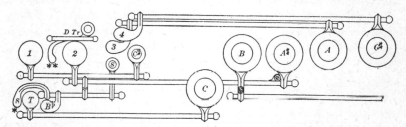

Fig. 51   Boehm's mechanism adapted to the G flute

It is fairly obvious that the various structural difficulties inherent in the larger flutes become more formidable with overall increase in size, and in fact the true bass flute in C has become fully reliable only in quite recent years. The instrument illustrated in Plate 12, formerly in the writer's collection, is a straightforward enlargement of the concert flute with Boehm mechanism arranged to place the two hands in a comfortable position about the point of balance of the tube. Mechanically it is quite satisfactory but unfortunately it is heavy, and no attempt has been made to reduce the distance between *embouchure* and touch-plates. In consequence it is very tiring to hold for long, although the blowing is not difficult. This instrument has been accepted by some authorities as a genuine product of the Boehm workshop on the evidence of an engraved mark 'Theobald Boehm, Munich', but I think that some considerable doubt exists. There are many details of construction which suggest French workmanship of a decidedly *post*-Boehm date, and the English form of the mark invites suspicion, although the late Professor Miller once told the writer that he had seen examples similar. There is, as far as I am aware, no evidence that Boehm himself ever envisaged building a C bass, but his name has been so esteemed that it has found its way, both legally and otherwise, on to instruments that he never saw (see p. 133, note 20).

It is interesting to observe that none of the 'systems'—Card, Siccama, etc.—that appeared in London in rivalry to Boehm's 1832 instrument seem to have been applied to the larger flutes, though Ward, to be sure, did use his tracker wire arrangement on a super-extended foot joint. The Carte 1867 system was, however, another matter. As this, like Boehm's own design, was based on rod, sleeve, and clutch mechanism, there was nothing to prevent it being applied in any size, and many excellent alto flutes have been built on this model. In 1898 G. W. Haynes (Los Angeles) produced a very fine bass (tenor) flute in F on the Boehm system. This instrument was on the straight model, and had all the refinement and efficiency which have made the family name of Haynes one of the most respected in the flute world. Indeed it was probably the last word in deep toned flutes for some forty years, until Rudall, Carte and Co. introduced their altos and basses on the Boehm or 1867 model with the upper part of the tube coiled on itself just below the head socket. Then at last the discomfort of too great a distance between mouth-hole and left-hand keys had been removed, and by careful placing of the two groups of touch-plates in relation to the total length of the tube these instruments became no more un-wieldy than the concert flute, and not much heavier.

It was indicated in the last paragraph that the innovators of the mid-19th century do not seem to have turned their attention to the larger flutes, but to this we must note one exception—the indefatigable Dr Burghley. Plate 11E shows one of two known examples of the C bass flute by that experimenter. Like his other flutes already mentioned (p. 139 above) the instrument is made of mahogany, French polished, and ornamented with ivory and fancy turned work. Burghley based all his work rigidly on the 'open-hole' principle with as few keys as possible, and, in consequence, was obliged here to revert to the centuries old expedient of bunching his six principal finger-holes in two groups. Unfortunately the specimen is in poor order and it has been impossible to assess how far he was successful in bringing them into tune. The head is reflected at an acute angle, with a fixed cork at the end, another closing the body-tube above the point where the head communicates with it. Burghley's confirmed habit of using only wood as a material has resulted in another interesting feature. The tube has been extended beyond the necessary sounding length in order to provide anchorage for the long springy strips which form the levers for the foot-keys, and the air column is terminated by two large holes with ebony bushes. Below these the tube is belled out to reduce further the flattening effect of the extra length. An ivory screw limits the rise of these keys, and another which can be turned out of the way, locks them open permanently if desired. The body-tube is all in one piece and represents what must have been a formidable exercise in boring, for the inner surface is remarkably smooth.

It remains only to record here three modern versions of the C bass flute, all highly mechanised, and each with individual features of much interest. The first of these instruments is the *Albisiphon*, brought out *c.* 1911 by Professor Abelardo Albisi of Milan. It is a bass flute with a relatively wide bore (39 mm. in the original model) and a compass extending to the low B♮, fingered basically on the Boehm system. The excessive length of the tube has been ingeniously dealt with by coiling the head tube, and the mouth-hole is placed in a transverse section so that the top of the instrument resembles a letter T. The playing position thus becomes vertical, as in oboes and clarinets, and any twisting of the body is obviated (see Plate 12). Considerable interest was aroused by the first appearance of the instrument and contemporary Italian opera composers, notably Mascagni and Puccini, wrote effective parts for it. In his opera *La Parisina* the former employed the Albisiphon both in C and in F, as well as a flute in G. These instruments were specially constructed, and are now in the Dayton Miller Collection. The Albisiphon does not, however, seem to have commended itself to flautists in general, possibly because it was thought to be fatiguing to blow for long. An observation in Curt Sachs's *History of Musical Instruments* suggests that recognition of this difficulty led to the production of a later model with a reduced bore. [6]

About 1925 Gino Bartoli, also of Milan, introduced what was called a 'contra bass' flute in C. As will be seen from Plate 12 this was in fact a true bass flute on the Boehm system with a reflected head of U shape. Dayton Miller, who secured a specimen, is non-committal about its qualities.

Thirdly we come to the C bass flute introduced by Rudall, Carte and Co. in the '30s of the present century, and with this we may say that the true bass flute reached complete practicality (see Plate 12). This instrument is in fact a straightforward Boehm system flute carefully enlarged to the requisite size, with all its proportions appropriately adjusted—and it may be well to repeat here that doubling the length of a resonant tube does not necessarily imply doubling its diameter also. The upper part of the tube in this instrument is coiled below the head, as in the same maker's altos, but an additional obtuse bend is introduced so that the main tube lies across the player's body to the right. An adjustable bracket of light metal allows the player to take most of the weight on his right thigh when sitting down. The combined result is a comfortable playing position for both head and hands. For its size the instrument is not difficult to 'fill', and its tone is warm and distinctive. Unfortunately the cost of such flutes at the present time is high, and comparatively few have been made—otherwise there appears no longer to be any reason for composers to limit their demands for flute tone in all ranges.[7]

The history of the smaller flutes is much the same as that of the normal C instrument, save that in general each phase seems to have come just a little later. In the first decades of the 18th century there is evidence that flutes a minor third (E♭) and a fourth (F) above the concert instrument were beginning to be called for, mainly, one supposes, as a convenience to the composer; and after about 1750 the appearance of quasi-military bands based on clarinets started a considerable demand for E♭ flutes, as more convenient in the flat tonalities that were favourable to the transposing reed instruments. On the basis of size it is not always easy to distinguish English E♭ instruments from Continental examples in F owing to the difference in contemporary pitch standards.

In orchestral work the piccolo in C is the one important small flute, but even so, for reasons touched on in Chapter 9, early specimens are by no means common these days. A larger piccolo in A♭ which has occasionally appeared in the orchestra is excessively rare. In respect of the lay-out and control of note-holes the piccolo has never presented the mechanical problems of the larger flutes, and indeed the only difficulty with its closely situated holes seems to be that sometimes experienced by players with large hands! All the same, the various acoustical modifications that have appeared in the concert flute have been repeated in the piccolo, and similar fingering systems have been applied. Thus the Boehm 1847 flute (but curiously enough not the 1832 model) soon had its octave counterpart, a few of these being actually produced in the Boehm and Mendler workshop in the 1860s. In more recent times there has been a reversion (in some quarters) to the cone-bore combined with 1847 key-work. This appears to be peculiar to the piccolo only, and is held by some players to mitigate the shrillness of the instrument.

In the course of the later 19th century most of the rival 'systems' which followed on Boehm's innovations appeared in octave form and so we have Card and Clinton 'Equisonant' piccolos, as well as the more orthodox Briccialdi, Carte, Radcliff, and 'Guards' ' models. In addition the stamp 'Pratten's Perfected' is to be found on piccolos which appear externally to be ordinary 'old system' instruments. The 'perfection' must therefore consist only in adjustments to the bore, and the instruments belong to the earlier years of Pratten's association with the firm of Boosey (see Plate 10H). Occasionally collectors find what appear to be 'old system' piccolos with covered holes, and these, it is thought, may represent attempts to assist players who have had difficulty in stopping the close-set holes.

In most musical collections today piccolos smaller than the standard C size are the commonest, and these are usually the high D, E♭, or F instruments made expressly for the 'fife and drum' band, the old keyless *fife* being represented by a five- or six-keyed descendant in B♭ (see p. 6 above). Although C has long been standardised as the most useful key for the principal orchestral flutes, there are still times when a slightly higher pitch might be more convenient and, recognising this, in 1914 Nicholas Alberti of Chicago secured a British patent for a transposable piccolo in C and D♭. Externally the Alberti instrument appears little different from any ordinary Boehm flute or piccolo—the idea was originally conceived for the former—save that the cover-plates are oblong instead of circular. The secret lies inside. A tube of thin metal is permanently attached to the head, and slides accurately inside the body, which is in fact no more than a wooden or ebonite shell carrying the key-work. In this tube, which is slightly longer than the body, are cut all the holes required for a normal Boehm flute, plus one more. Under the cover-plates the shell is perforated with a series of oval slots or 'windows' through which the holes in the inner tube appear. Thus when the head and tube are pulled out the instrument behaves simply as a piccolo in C, but when the head is pushed in the whole mechanism 'moves up one' as it were, raising the pitch by a semitone and preserving the proper spacing of the holes. Hence the need for slots in the outer shell. The small holes for the c″♯ and d″♮ shakes are duplicated since their small size and relatively wide spacing allow this.

It is evident that Alberti's idea is applicable to any woodwind having a mainly cylindrical bore, and his specification makes a point of this. So far the writer has not, however, seen any practical example in instruments other than the flute. The same patent covers another extremely ingenious application of the sliding perforated tube principle, designed to afford continuous pitch adjustment over a fixed range, say between 'Old' and 'New' Philharmonic pitches. In this case the perforations in the lining tube take the form of helical slots, each of which crosses a corresponding vertical 'window' slot in the outer tube. The openings formed by the crossing of the two sets of slots act as note-holes, and when the inner tube slides up or down, at the same time turning under the guidance of a very coarse screw thread and pin, these all move together towards or away from the mouth-hole. At the same time, by careful design of the inner helical slots, the relative spacing of the 'note-holes' is automatically adjusted so as to preserve intonation. As in the straightforward transposing scheme, the outer tube carries normal Boehm type key-work with oblong plates which cover each window completely.

Alberti's instrument is not the only attempt that has been made to produce a transposable flute, and an even bolder arrangement was proposed some time before the war and actually realised c. 1953 by T. W. Moore. This was nothing less than a concert flute which should include in its compass all the notes of the piccolo as well. The aim was achieved by adding a supplementary tube of small bore to the top of an ordinary Boehm flute, and replacing the usual cork with a sliding plug operated by a tracker for the right thumb. At rest this plug acts as the normal stopper, but when the piccolo range is required it slides down-ward cutting off the flute tube, and connecting the mouth-hole to the piccolo section. As the notes from a″ down to d″ can be well sounded on the concert flute it was thought best to limit the piccolo tube to the length necessary to produce the notes from the a″ upwards, and to adjust the bore accordingly. In practice a slightly coned tube proved the best tonally. Two systems of controlling the piccolo holes were envisaged; in the first the cover-plates were connected with the corresponding touches on the flute section by long axles so that no displacement of the fingers was required; in the other the axles carried independent touch-pieces placed close to, but separate from, the flute-keys. Although this implied a slight shift of the fingers between 'flute' and 'piccolo' registers, it made for a lighter action as each finger had then to overcome only one spring instead of two in parallel.[8] As far as I am aware this instrument has not yet been put into commercial production.

The idea of transferring control of remote note-holes to more convenient situations is, as we have seen, the *raison d'être* of nearly all modern key-work, and in most cases it has been used to overcome the difficulty of holes that are for acoustic reasons spaced too widely for the fingers. There is, however, no reason why it should not be used in the reverse way, and one example occurred in the mid-19th century. The specimen is an anonymous *octave* piccolo, No. 610 of the Dayton Miller Collection, and it is, as far as we know, unique. The following is Miller's own description: 'Block of hard wood partly stained brown, with a "tube" formed in the interior, speaking length, 132 mm. [the writer's eight fingers placed close together measure 145 mm. across] with six "finger" holes and D-sharp hole. All holes are covered with flat brass keys, each having an extension lever-system so that the "touch" pieces are spread out over 140 mm. below the "lower end" of the tube.' We may perhaps question the value of adding so high pitched an instrument to the orchestra. If it conformed to the normal behaviour of the piccolo it would carry the range up to c"""", more than an octave above the top note of the piano. This note, on modern standards (A = 440), has a frequency of 8,368 cycles per second approximately, which is well within the hearing range of a normal healthy human ear, but is getting into a frequency area where the ability to differentiate adjacent notes begins to fall off appreciably. Probably an octave piccolo might add something to the brilliance of the *ensemble* by reinforcing upper partials already present; in its own right it would seem to have little to offer. The one example remains a tribute to the ingenuity of its unknown maker.

As this goes to press the discovery of a unique piccolo in high G in the Birmingham School of Music has just been reported.

NOTES
[1] It will be appreciated that in this chapter we are not considering the seven sizes of cone-flute which make up the complement of the modern 'flute and

o

drum band' (see p. 6 above), but we may note that without sacrificing the characteristics of the simple five- or six-keyed instrument, the larger sizes of these are today made with reflected heads, and sometimes axles to the key-work.

[2] The word refers to the box or case in which sets of instruments of different sizes, both wind and string, were customarily kept in the 'consort' period, and so by transference to the instruments themselves. Flute and recorder 'chests' were often very handsome and assumed curious shapes. Recorder chests shaped rather like a gigantic pan-pipe are well known, for example a 16th-century specimen in the Historisches Museum, Frankfurt-am-Main, illustrated in Baines's *European and American Musical Instruments*, N. 418, or in the foreground of Hans Holbein's *The Ambassadors* (see also Plate 1).

Dr. H. Fitzpatrick of Oxford has recently expressed the opinion, based on his study of early 18th-century makers' accounts and record books, that the survival of a few 'chests' of Baroque recorders may reflect the continuity of a custom rather than the imperative demands of the music of the time. (Personal communication to the writer.)

[3] The term *d'amour* or *d'amore* seems to have been applied to this size of flute purely on the grounds of a pitch relationship parallel to that of the C and A oboes. The A flutes have never had any distinctive structure like the bulb-bell of the larger oboes which might have justified the name on a physical basis.

[4] See also pp. 170–71 above and Chapter 9, note 13.

[5] Illustrated respectively in Galpin, *Old English Instruments of Music*, and in Baines, *op. cit.*

Pierre, Constant, *La Facture Instrumentale à L'Exposition Universelle de 1889*, p. 283, mentions having seen there a *flûte basse* by Thomas Lot with a reflected head. Unfortunately, as Pierre observes, the catalogue of the exhibition gives no details of the antique instruments shown, but this example must have dated from the third quarter of the 18th century. Again, we have no sure information as to its provenance, but the majority of these exhibits came, it is believed, from the local museum of the instrument-making village of La Couture-Boussey in Normandy.

[6] Sachs, Curt, *The History of Musical Instruments*, New York, W. W. Norton and Co. Inc., 1940, p. 410. Sachs's reference to the second model with reduced bore is a little obscure, and it may be that he intended it to refer to the Rudall, Carte instrument. There appears to be no reason to hold the Albisiphon diagonally, and the writer has seen no example with this modification. As to whether the Albisiphon in its original form was really fatiguing to blow, opinions seem to differ. Professor Dayton Miller, who acquired Albisi's own instrument, reported that it was not at all difficult to 'fill' and had a full and free tone. In 1919 the instrument was played by Ary van Leeuwen at the production of Klose's *Der Sonnegeist* in Vienna, and attracted the favourable comments of Julius Schlosser of the Kunsthistorisches Museum there.

[7] In their latest catalogue the makers offered to build the instrument in plain Boehm, Carte 1867, Radcliff, or 'Guards' models.

[8] For the inventor's description see *Musical Opinion*, London, July 1953, p. 599. About 1940 the present writer devised a system of controlling the extension holes of the basset horn in a manner very similar to Moore's first arrangement, the idea being to relieve the right thumb or little fingers which are overburdened on the conventional modern instrument. Some experiments were made but the complete scheme was never realised due to other war-time preoccupations.

CHAPTER II

Exceptional Varieties

THE FLUTES which fall to be considered under this head range from the strictly utilitarian to the fantastic. Many of them show features of great merit, but they do not fit conveniently into the main categories which we have so far observed, and it has therefore been thought best to deal with them individually in a separate section.

Plate 9G shows an instrument which at first sight appears to be no more than a well made and handsomely mounted seven-keyed flute of the 'old' type, but when taken in the hand it reveals its secret at once. It is, in fact, the mirror-image of the simple concert flute of its time, built for a left-handed player. Unfortunately it bears no maker's mark and nothing is known of its history, but the workmanship is fine and it was evidently an expensive custom-made instrument. Incidentally, left-handed playing is by no means uncommon today in some parts of the world. Probably half the traditional flute players in the Irish Ceili bands use the one-keyed flute left-handed, and it is not unknown to see a young man playing on grandfather's—or great-grandfather's—six-keyed flute with the keys tied down with string, or even broken off and bound with friction tape.

In the category of custom-built flutes come also instruments designed to be controlled with less than the normal number of fingers, or even with one hand only. There have been several notable players who have overcome such disabilities.

Ever since the Baroque period flutes have tended in their external ornament to reflect the taste of their time, and this characteristic is sometimes useful in dating obscure specimens. *Musical* taste is less often illustrated in the construction of flutes, but one example is the so-called *Flauto di Voce* produced by Wigley and MacGregor, *c.* 1811. The instrument was built on the lines of MacGregor's patent alto flute of 1810 with the reflected head, and pitched in A♭. Nearly opposite the c″♯ hole was a large opening covered with a thin membrane whose vibration was intended to impart a reedy, romantic quality to the sound. The principle is found as an essential feature in the Chinese *ti tse* (see p. 62) where a nasal tone is admired, but it does not seem to have been pursued further in Europe.

The reflected head as an expedient in dealing with the great length of the deeper-toned flutes has already been dealt with in Chapter 10, but a version of it has also been applied at times to instruments of the normal sizes. It is difficult to account for this unless it was based on some idea of making all woodwinds consistent as to playing position, and it certainly made for extra work in construction with apparently little reward. In 1889 E. Wünnenberg of Cologne obtained a British patent for a head consisting of a barrel-shaped wooden *embouchure* mounted on a metal tube shaped rather like a '?' or a letter P which could be fitted to any normal flute and so allow of vertical playing. A few complete flutes on this system were built by Wünnenberg, but, apart from the novel position, they do not seem to offer anything special. An excellent specimen in box-wood is to be seen in the National Museum of Ireland, Dublin.

Some seventy years earlier W. Wheatstone—already mentioned as the author of a 'clip-on' device intended to assist the blowing of an ordinary flute (p. 106 above)—had produced a much simpler arrangement than Wünnenberg's. It consisted of a plain tube equivalent in length to a normal flute head, and closed at the top by a spherically hollowed plug perforated with a normal mouth-hole, and shaped comfortably to the lips on the outside. Little seems to have been heard of this idea after its first appearance, although it did receive another patent in the name of C. Bergonzoni of Bologna in 1878. Though the benefits of holding the flute in a vertical position are, to say the least, questionable—and probably no present-day orchestral flautist would consider it—the special heads mentioned certainly enabled a player to do so if he wished while enjoying all the advantages of his accustomed key-work, and in this last facility we may perhaps find a clue to Wünnenberg's reason for reviving an idea that had failed to 'catch on' before.

In 1896 considerable attention was attracted by the appearance of a much more limited instrument designed *ab initio* for vertical playing. This was the Giorgi flute—and flute it was by definition since it was sounded by a free air-reed and had no whistle device of any kind. It consisted of a plain cylindrical ebonite tube with a head similar to that designed by Wheatstone, and perforated with eleven holes so disposed about the body that they could be stopped by the fingers, thumbs, and certain intermediate joints of both hands. In the original design there were no keys so the compass did not go below d' (see

Plate 9H). This instrument was assiduously 'pushed' by the London firm of Wallis and Son, who both made and distributed in this country, and it was favourably noticed by several critics.[1] The originator, Carlo Tomasso Giorgi of Rome, played his instrument with great virtuosity, but the difficulty of its fingering to many people is shown by the existence in various collections of specimens with one to four added keys. Occasionally these appear to be an original part of the instrument, and the possibility of adding them was envisaged in the patent specifications, though the published fingering chart ignores them (see Appendix III). Giorgi seems to have had something of a 'fixation' about this, for in the Dayton Miller Collection there is a quite normal piccolo with the special head. This dates from the early years of the present century (D.C.M. No. 402).

While Giorgi's keyless flute remains today a collector's curiosity, an earlier patent, also in his name, was of considerable importance, and in other circumstances might well have become influential. In 1888 he, in partnership with a Florentine dentist named Schaffner, embarked on a series of experiments designed to reform the woodwind in general, and the next year they obtained French protection for the system proposed. Proceeding somewhat on the lines adopted forty years earlier by Boehm, they began by taking flute, oboe, and clarinet tubes of theoretical length. These they measured off according to the laws of physics for each note required, and at the divisions they placed a series of large rectangular holes of graduated size. Each hole was equipped with an appropriate cover and pad, and a complicated system of rods and bell-cranks brought them all under the control of the fingers. The fingering and playing position of all three instruments was intended to be identical, which might indeed have been of benefit, but the idea came into the field too late to compete with the other established systems. Whether the Giorgi–Schaffner flute had any advantages to offer over the Boehm instrument is difficult to judge, but as will be seen from Plate 9 the mechanism is much more complicated and has a multiplicity of adjusting screws. In France and Italy (outside the circle of open-key converts) it would seem to have been foredoomed because of the large holes, and this may account for the choice of England for a specifically flute patent in 1888. From that year the firm of Giorgi and Schaffner of Florence became active in the woodwind business, selling instruments of all sorts made for them by Maino and Orsi of Milan, but stamped with their own mark. In 1889 they gained a bronze medal at the Paris Exhibition.[2]

In addition to attempts to eliminate the 'transverse' from the transverse flute, there have been from time to time more or less disguised
efforts to help the would-be flautist who, for some reason, was unable
to achieve the normal embouchure. Wheatstone's clip-on 'mouthpiece'
was one such, but some makers went much further and discarded the
ordinary head entirely, replacing it with a flageolet-type whistle. Such
'flageolet' heads were fitted with a small ivory blow-tube at the side so
that appearances could be preserved, and externally they were made
to resemble an ordinary head as much as possible. It seems that these
affairs could be obtained to order specially, for a number of examples
figure in instrumental collections without any associated flute, but
they were also sometimes supplied as part of an outfit, as witness a four-
keyed flute by Wood and Ivy (1836–47) in the writer's cabinet. This
has two heads, mounted with identical ivory rings and caps, and from
the back they are indistinguishable.

A stage further still are the quaint instruments that have been described as 'flageolet-flutes'—flageolets pure and simple in their method
of blowing and in the distribution of finger-holes, yet built in transverse
form as if to claim an aristocracy which they did not naturally possess.
They have been made in all sizes, the most notable perhaps being the
'Chromatic Albion' or 'Albion flute' produced by Bainbridge and Wood
of London about 1815. This instrument was as large as an ordinary
concert flute, and was made in both side-blown and end-blown forms.
A similar instrument is illustrated in Diderot's *Encyclopédie*, Plate IX,
published *c.* 1751 (see Fig. 50). Bainbridge, and his successor Simpson,
carried flageolet making into the realm of real artistry, and their so-
called 'English Flutes', single, double, or even triple, have never been
surpassed. The association of the names of Bainbridge and of the Wood
family establishes an interesting link between what we may call the
ephemeral and the enduring, the fashionable and the eminently practical,
in English woodwind making, and the work of each in their own line was
magnificent.

It was a vagary of fashion which gave rise to the last of the unorthodox
instruments that we have to discuss in this chapter—the Walking-stick
Flute. During the latter part of the 18th century, and through the
period of the Regency in England, the more sophisticated centres of
Europe produced a considerable quantity of these *jeux d'esprit*, many of
them extremely handsome and elegantly made. Structurally they
consisted of the three or four joints of the simple flute of the time,
permanently fixed together, and with added length to make up a walk-

ing-stick of convenient size. Near the knob or handle there was a mouth-hole, then the six finger-holes, commonly a d'♯ key, and finally one or two large holes to terminate the air column. Plate 11 shows a typical example such as can be found in many collections of old instruments, and it will be noticed that the outside is turned to resemble the joints of a natural cane (see also Plate 4C). In the finest specimens great care was taken to simulate the 'clouded' Malacca canes so much admired by the 'Bucks' of the Regency period, and these often had silver or ivory knobs and an elegant thong and tassel. Specimens are also known with as many as six keys, and in these a more rustic type of stick is usually represented, the keys being made of wood also, and carved to resemble the natural growth of knots or truncated side shoots. In modern times the idea has been revived with the production of 'flageolet canes', but these do not seem to have the same charm.

The writer has not had the good fortune to find a really well tuned walking-stick flute, but there seems to be no reason why, with care, the intonation should not be as good as that of any one-keyed flute of the time. The same period also saw such notions as a walking-stick clarinet, and trumpet—even a walking-stick violin, rather like a stout 'Gampish' umbrella. We may perhaps smile at these fancies today, but at least they were more agreeable than the sword-sticks and gun-sticks of their age—and less lethal.

NOTES

[1] Standish, H., 'The Giorgi Flute' in *Proceedings of the Musical Society*, Vol. XXIV, London 1898, p. 57.

[2] There is obscurity about the relations of many of the Continental instrument makers at this period. For example, although the research connected with the Giorgi–Schaffner instruments appears to have been without question a joint effort, the British patent for the 1888 flute on this system was granted in the name of the former only. The late Geoffrey Rendall was inclined to the view that the basic conception was Schaffner's, and that Giorgi contributed mostly in the field of practical design. As regards the keyless flute patented in England eight years later, this was exclusively Giorgi's work. Further, there seems to have been some sort of association between Schaffner and the Florentine instrument maker P. Pupeschi at the same period, for Langwill quotes an oboe, No. 132 in the museum of the Milan Conservatoire, with the inscription 'Sistema Schaffner, secondo studio di Oboé di Pupeschi e Schaffner l'anno 1889'. There is much need of further investigation here.

CHAPTER 12

Materials and Manufacture

THE VARIOUS materials which have been used for the body of the flute make an interesting study, and one which has at times given rise to a deal of controversy. Nowadays for wooden instruments cocus— *Brya ebene* D.C.—is in almost universal use, though some Continental makers employ what appears to be a true ebony which was at one time very popular in spite of its tendency to 'break short'. These very dark and dense woods are extremely difficult to identify botanically without the preparation of microscope sections, and few enthusiasts are prepared to submit a cherished flute to this process. Curiously enough, African blackwood—*Dalbergia melanoxylon*—so much esteemed for clarinets, does not seem to have found much favour in the flute-making world. The only disadvantage of cocus, or 'Cocoa' as it is sometimes called in the older catalogues, appears to be that a few players are allergic to its contact and find that it causes an inflammation of the lower lip. These unfortunates are, however, very few and their problem, which can easily be met by the use of a metal head or inlaid lip-plate, has done nothing to offset the other advantages of the material.

Box—*Buxus sempervirens*—which is excellent for all sorts of turned work, was at one time the favourite wood for all the smaller musical instruments, and the so-called Turkish variety could be found with a beautiful curly grain which yielded a very handsome finish when polished. English box, which is perhaps a little softer and tougher than other growths, was formerly held in high esteem, and the older turners tended to attribute its virtues to the method of its preparation. This is said to have included burial underground to season for up to twenty years. At a time when crafts were handed down from father to son this sort of thing was of course possible, but material seasoned like this is quite unobtainable today and, in an ever-hastening world, it is unlikely that it ever will be again. One occasionally finds also flutes of the very beautiful wood called in France *Palissandre*—in England *violet-ebony*—king-wood, and true rosewood, but none of these have any special advantage as far as I am aware, and their identification (beyond general importers' terminology) is uncertain. Quantz, in 1752, wrote with some enthusiasm of *lignum vitae* and said that it was then much used, though he found it lacking in elasticity. He also found it liable to crack in use, though this does not seem to be consistent with the curiously inter-twined fibrous structure which renders this material so useful in many technical fields, from lawn bowls to the thrust-blocks for ships' propellers.[1]

From early in the 19th century we hear from time to time of flutes with metal tubes, and at the present day these seem to be in the ascen-dant; indeed only a few weeks ago a well-known London flute craftsman told the writer that the wooden flute is today 'a dead duck'. This may be an exaggeration, but certain it is that in France, Italy, and America the metal flute is used almost exclusively, while in Britain and Germany the traditional preference for wood is breaking down. Some reasons for this have been suggested in Chapter 1 and we need say no more about them here, but as the matter also has a bearing on the player's technique we shall return to it later.

The connection between the tone of a wind instrument and the material of its tube has deeply interested conscientious musicians for many years, and from time to time comparative trials have been made. Until fairly recently the consensus of scientific opinion has been that, provided it be dense enough, the substance of the resonating tube has no effect on tone quality. On this point, however, players have continued to outface the scientists, and recently their attitude has found some justification. Experiments with sets of organ-pipes of like dimensions and pitch have tended to show that different materials do reinforce different groups of partials.[2] The same may reasonably be expected to apply to orchestral instruments.

The metals preferred for flutes are silver, gold, and the various white bronze alloys the constitutions of which are usually the jealously guarded secrets of different manufacturers.[3] In recent years metallurgy has made amazing strides and there are now available alloys whose properties have eased the processes of drawing and swaging to a degree not imagined fifty years ago. Some of these have been adopted for manu-facturing reasons rather than musical ones, but there are others for which great tonal advantages are claimed. Probably, for those who can afford it, silver is the most favoured all round, lending itself well to delicate playing. Gold, by the few who have used it, is said to be equally sensitive and to have a warmer yet more solid tone, but here, we may suppose, the 'personal equation' plays a great part. The writer was once shown a flute made of platinum for a wealthy amateur who presumed

that with the densest of all metals generally available at the time he
would have the supreme instrument. Alas, it proved to have a dull,
uninteresting tone, and to be desperately heavy in the hand.

Of man-made materials ebonite alone is at present important in flute-
making. It is easily worked to a high finish, is more stable than wood in
bad climates, and is not subject to the great fluctuations of temperature
that are the major disadvantage of metal instruments in playing. Comparatively few orchestral players use it, however. Quite recently the
various plastics are finding increased use in woodwind making and they
would seem to offer many advantages, at least on the manufacturing side.
The initial cost of the necessary dies, etc., required for the process of
injection-moulding so complicated an object as a flute body must of
course be very heavy, but if setting up costs could be balanced by output, plastics might well revolutionise the woodwind industry. Much
detail that is at present produced by machining or hand work could be
incorporated in the basic dies and the final cost to the customer be
thereby reduced. As things are, it seems that the serious musician will
always insist on an instrument made by an artist-craftsman, with more
or less mechanical assistance, but in the cheaper market the plastics
industry will be well worth watching.

Although certain special woods have always been preferred for
instrument making,[4] the older flutes preserved in musical collections
show a surprising variety of material. That the woods favoured gave
satisfactory musical results can hardly be doubted, but it seems, nevertheless, that these may often have been selected in the first place for
their good turning and boring qualities. Mersenne, in regard to the
flute, writes of 'plum tree, cherry tree, and other woods that may be
easily bored', and goes on to say, 'It is customary to choose wood of
beautiful colour, that will bear a high polish, to the end that the excellence of the instrument may be combined with beauty of appearance.'
This conjecture is supported, in the case of the English makers at least,
by the fact that between 1694 and 1849 the Register Book of the
Company of Turners of London contains the names of many celebrated
wind-instrument makers, and shows that in youth all were bound
apprentice as turners pure and simple.

A survey of antique flutes listed in the principal European and
American collections is extremely revealing. Between 1690 and 1830
they were regularly made of the 'fruit' woods, pear and cherry; maple
and allied trees; and most frequently of box. Solid ivory was used only
for specially rich examples, though with greater frequency towards the

end of the period. After the first quarter of the 19th century we encounter ebony, cocus wood, and the rarer fancy woods; violet and rose woods; maple and box are still there, though the latter less frequently; finally metal and ebonite make their appearance. In addition cut glass and porcelain were occasionally employed, though these can hardly be regarded as common or practical materials for serious musical use and flutes made of them were probably mainly 'show' or presentation pieces. Possibly Laurent's glass flutes were more practical than most, and the intractability of the material certainly led to one or two interesting details of mounting which found further application. For the mounts that strengthened the sockets ivory was much the commonest material, with horn as a poor second on Continental instruments. Occasionally, in fine specimens, silver ornamental rings were placed over the ivory ones, and sometimes ivory concealed metal linings. In earlier instruments, and cheap later examples, the sockets were strengthened merely by external bulges on the tube. Of course such a list as the above does no more than indicate a sequence of trends, and there were always exceptions to the general. For example box stained to simulate the darker woods is known as early as 1769, and on the other hand there have been both oboe and clarinet enthusiasts within the last fifty years who have insisted on having box-wood instruments made, regardless of cost. I know of no really modern flutes in box-wood, the latest I have seen being of the Rudall and Rose period, i.e. c. 1850. Probably no present-day flautist would consider an all-ivory flute—the general opinion being that their tone is on the meagre side— but there are still players in Germany who believe in the virtues of an ivory *head*, and these are often allied with wooden or metal bodies. In fact there is probably no instrument which offers the player more possible alternatives than the flute, and among them he must try to choose the combination which suits him best both physically and in respect of the style of tone and playing he wishes to cultivate.

As regards the keys, brass, and silver for high-class work, were the usual thing till supplanted about 1830 by the white bronzes. These alloys were of course also used for the rims and strengthening rings. Today they are universally employed, either plain or plated, and their only rival is sterling silver. In view of the amount of wear to which key-work is subject it has been suggested that stainless steel might be used, but so far the difficulty (and hence the cost) of working this material has proved prohibitive. Some perspiration is extremely corrosive to copper-based alloys, and chromium plating, which is a good protection, has been used at times. Unfortunately many players find that burnished chromium makes the keys too slippery for comfort in playing.

Turning and Boring

In the early days the making of flutes involved no operations that were not the common currency of the master-turner's art. The joints were shaped externally on the reciprocating pole lathe, and the boring was done with long 'shell' bits, and reamers or D-bits of suitable shape, while the free end of the work was supported by a perforated steady or 'spectacle plate' attached to the lathe bed. After the advent of the fully rotary lathe these methods continued, and they still remain the essential basis of the much more complex modern technique. The special tools formerly used in instrument making are illustrated in some of the classic works on turnery, notably those of Plumier,[5] a contemporary of Dr Talbot, and of L. E. Bergeron.[6] These clearly show that, in their day, the work was regarded as within the province of the general turner, though probably only the most skilled undertook it. There are also four plates in the 'Luthérie' section of Diderot's *Encyclopédie* of 1747 *et seq.* which, for the details they give, are well worth study.

The piercing of side-holes is always a matter of some anxiety to instrument makers, on account of the risk of splitting a joint, and before the days of power tools this must have been even more acute. Some early makers are believed to have avoided the danger by burning out finger-holes with hot irons, but simple openings were usually made with a spear-point bit driven by the drill-bow. This, in skilled hands, gave fast, clean cutting and a sensitive control of direction (Fig. 52). In Vol. 2 of his great treatise on turning, Holtzapffel illustrates two special tools, one for boring simple holes, the other designed to form the seatings for key-pads. In this connection Holtzapffel says that the holes in flutes and clarinets were undercut when necessary by means of a stout knife.[7] In this, however, he seems to be behind his time, for thirty years earlier Bergeron had depicted a much more elegant tool which is used today with but little improvement. This implement, sometimes called a *fraise*, will be easily understood from Bergeron's engraving reproduced here (Fig. 53). It consists of two parts: a fluted conical cutter and a stem with a wooden handle like that of an awl. The stem has a screw thread at its end, and the cutter is pierced down the centre and tapped to correspond. In use the cutter is slid into the bore of the instrument and the stem passed through the hole to be treated. A turn

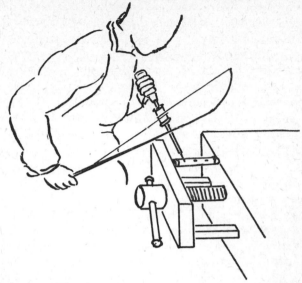

Fig. 52   The bow-drill in use

Fig. 53   The *fraise* from Bergeron's *Manuel du Tourneur* (1816)

or two serves to pick up the cutter, which can then be drawn up till its apex enters the hole. Since the stem has a *right-handed* thread and the teeth of the cutter face to the *right*, the resistance encountered in cutting tends only to screw the two parts more firmly together. A gentle pull on the handle puts the necessary feed on the *fraise*. Modern versions of the tool have certain refinements which make it easier to control, and the stem has even been adapted for use in the lathe chuck, but the operative principle remains exactly the same as it was in Bergeron's day.

Now let us consider a little the processes involved in making a modern wooden flute in an up-to-date factory. The rough timber, already seasoned in the open air for at least three years, is first cross-cut into billets slightly longer than finally required for the joints. These are up-ended on a chopping-block and *cleft* into pieces of suitable size.

This procedure, though much less economical than sawing, is essential in all the best-quality work, since it brings to light any incipient cracks and flaws which might open up later in the finished joints. The final cost of an instrument so begun is, of course, high, on account of the quantity of wood discarded, but the difference in price between first- and second-class flutes (whose joints are usually sawn from the log) is well spent in buying the nearest approach possible to a guarantee against future splitting. After cleaving out, the joints are roughly chopped to shape by hand, then rough turned, and bored with a small hole from end to end. There follows another period of seasoning, the longer the better, though it is to be noted that with air circulating through the central hole, the wood now comes into condition much more quickly. At the present time some instrument makers, especially those using maple or other of the more sappy woods, speak highly of artificial methods of seasoning in steam and then dry heat, but the old tradition is still followed by the smaller artist-makers. When judged ready, the joints are turned to their final shape and the bore is developed in stages with suitable bits and reamers. Formerly this part of the work took up a good deal of time, but the advent of modern super-hard tool steels has shortened the process considerably. At this stage there follows another prolonged seasoning, this time in an oil bath.

To the onlooker, the 'setting out' which comes next is probably the most interesting part of the whole business. For this are employed 'setting-out machines', which differ in detail according to the ideas of different makers, though all embody the same essentials, and all involve a great deal of capital outlay. In general such a machine consists of a short lathe bed carrying two poppet-heads between which the turned and bored joints can be mounted. One head carries a plain cone centre, while the other has a spindle fitted with a self-centring chuck to grip the work. The spindle can rotate freely or be rigidly locked, and its position is shown by an indexed dividing plate. The small bed slides longways upon a second rather larger bed, and this carries a longitudinal scale and lock. The third component is a sensitive drill-press mounted exactly over the axis of the two poppet-heads. By means of the two motions, rotary between the heads, and longitudinal on the main bed, any point on the surface of the blank joint can be brought accurately beneath the drill and maintained there by the locks. The combined readings of the two indices provide a formula which gives the precise location of every hole to be drilled, and enables the most perfect repetition work to be done. In cases where a large number of identical joints are required, as in the clarinet trade, some makers replace the bed index with a sort of 'master bar'. This is a metal cylinder full of holes so placed that when one of them engages with a small bolt attached to the travelling bed that member is held rigid, and in consequence the work-piece is automatically positioned as well. Near each hole in the master is stamped the corresponding reading for the dividing plate on the chuck spindle and the size number of the drill required. This arrangement speeds the work up greatly and each bar represents in fact the maker's own specification for a particular joint. A further refinement, used mostly by bassoon makers, consists in having the column of the drill-press movable through an arc so that holes can be drilled not only perpendicular to the work, but at any angle to it as well. The actual drills used nowadays for this work are double-edged fly-cutters, which at high speed cut extremely freely and leave virtually no 'burr'. As these cutters are made from flat steel stock—they are in fact only a develop-ment of the primitive spear-point drill—there is little difficulty in shaping them for special purposes. It is, for instance, the regular thing to bore a note-hole and cut out the surrounding seating for a key-pad with the same tool and so get them absolutely concentric. Certain of the cutters, too, are made with a stop to prevent them from penetrating the full thickness of the wood. These are used to make the blind holes, which are subsequently tapped with a coarse thread to take the key pillars. Others, again, are designed to mill out any surface recesses which the key-work may require, as, for instance, to accom-modate a ring-key. When the joint leaves the setting-out machine it is ready to receive the pillars and keys.

A modern standard Boehm flute body and foot joint finished to length and ready for mounting is shown in Plate 8, and it is at this stage that the beauty of its workmanship is perhaps best appreciated. Even this, however, is not the ultimate in wooden flute-making for such instruments are occasionally made to special order with thinned walls. As will be seen from the plate, the full diameter of the key-seatings is rather less than that of the tube itself and this makes it possible to turn most of the body down even further, till the two diameters nearly correspond. In the foot section, however, it is usually necessary to leave some substance around the holes, so this is secured by careful hand carving which merges imperceptibly into the general surface. In such cases it is customary to make body and foot in one piece for the thinned walls do not leave sufficient material to form adequate tenons. For the same reason the head tenon is replaced by a metal lining tube. Some extremely delicate workmanship is called for in the making of thinned heads too. The work-piece is first turned and bored as for a head of normal thickness, and this is then further turned down except in the region of the socket and the mouth-hole. Here a raised band the width of a lip-plate is left and the mouth-hole is formed in it. The surplus wood is then carved away leaving a shaped and raised area equivalent to the lip-plate of a metal flute (see p. 9 above). Fig. 54 illustrates the thinned wooden head as adapted to the ordinary wooden or metal flute.

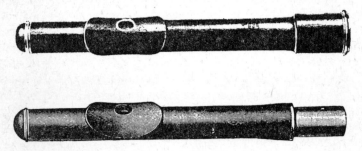

Fig. 54   Thinned heads

The last stages—pillar and key fitting, springing, and padding—are ones in which machinery cannot help, except perhaps in forming key components. Formerly these were shaped by hand from sheet or bar metal and finally assembled by soldering. In France, where by the end of the last century the cheap woodwind trade was most highly organised, this work was often farmed out. Workers turned out enormous numbers of keys in their own homes, and in certain districts the business became almost a domestic industry, as did chain-making in the Midlands of Victorian England. The French key-maker, in fact, seldom, if ever, saw the instrument to which his labours contributed. At the present day keys are often cast in comparatively soft metal in an effort to approach the cheapness of the former French product which used to be exported in quantity as well as used in the home industry. Recently, too, in high-class key-making, hand forging has largely given place to power pressing or hammering and milling. The metal so treated becomes 'work-hardened', and the makers claim this to be advantageous. Somehow, however, machine-formed keys never seem to be quite so elegant as the old hand-made type.

We have digressed, and must return to our half-finished flute. From the setting-out machine the joints pass to the pillar setter. The holes have been tapped, and the pillars are now screwed firmly home. Here occurs an interesting point of manufacturing technique which appears to be quite a modern invention. We know that Boehm invented a device to ensure the setting of pillars accurately on the radius of the tube. Today this is still essential but the setting-out machine should ensure it without further help. In order that the pivot-holes in corresponding pillars shall be perfectly aligned, these are fitted in the form of blanks with solid globular heads. A jig is then applied which supports both pillars rigidly, and a drill is passed through both heads together. The jig removed, the heads are faced off flat where the tube of the key will bear against them. All work on the actual wood of the tube being now finished, the bore is again checked and gauged for the last time. The keys, which have in the meantime been assembled, are mounted and padded. The actual fabrication is over, and the instrument passes to the tuner for the most subtle operation of all. A touch with a small hand reamer here, a *fraise* there, a hair's-breadth of adjustment to the rise of this key or that, and under his hands a beautiful mechanism becomes a work of art.

From the foregoing it is clear that the methods used by the modern woodwind maker are almost exactly those of his predecessor of two hundred or more years ago. Certainly the mechanism he provides is more reliable in some respects, and machinery has reduced the physical labour and time spent on some operations. Machinery has made some processes more exact, but it has done nothing to supplant the skill of the individual craftsman, nor does it seem likely to do so as long as natural wood remains the principal raw material. With metal instruments mechanisation has indeed gone somewhat further, and we must now look briefly at these.

It is evident that key-work for metal flutes will be made by the same methods used for wooden instruments, but the body will be a very different matter. The tubing employed for the earliest metal flutes was produced by the only method known at their time, i.e. by rolling up sheet metal, brazing or hard soldering the seam, and then hammering it on a polished steel mandrel. The final sizing was obtained by drawing the tube, still on the mandrel, slowly and with great force through a hole in a block of lead. This squeezed the two closely together and smoothed out all irregularities. While some very beautiful instruments were based on tubing of this description, it has one inherent weakness. The soldered seam sometimes tends to form a focus where chemical

P

action and corrosion can begin, and this can often be seen in, for instance, the head linings of old wooden flutes. Seamless drawn tubing, first produced about 1840, got rid of this particular problem, but another somewhat similar remained. Whereas the note-holes in a wooden flute are bored through comparatively thick walls in the substance of which the pad seatings are formed, the seatings in a metal instrument have to be in the form of rings raised above the surface. From before Boehm's time till early in the present century no other method was known than to fit rings of appropriate depth saddle-wise to the surface of the tube, and to solder them on. In order to give an adequate 'butt' for the solder to hold well between the rings and the body the former were often made of metal as much as five times as thick as the tube, and they were carefully rounded off and even bevelled to make a good surface for the pad to close down on. The solder was again a potential weakness, though in this case it was mostly on the upper part of the tube and outside and so less exposed to condensed moisture in playing.

Then in 1913 came a really revolutionary advance. In that year W. S. Haynes, the Boston flute-maker, obtained patents in several parts of the world for a method of deriving the rings literally from the substance of the tube itself.[8] In short, the process consisted of first cutting an oval slot in the tube on the same centre as the intended tone-hole (see Fig. 55). The tube was then supported on the outside by a saddle-shaped block of steel with a hole in it fractionally larger than the required ring (see Fig. 56). A slightly tapered plug was passed along the bore and its nose guided into the oval slot. A screwed rod was then passed through the saddle support and this picked up an internal thread in the plug. Powerful traction on the rod drew the plug up into the hole in the saddle, forming a raised ring on its way. A second parallel-sided plug was then passed in the same manner which gave a perfect internal finish to the hole. All that was now required was to smooth off the drawn up ring to make a level seating. In addition to the rigidity and relative lightness of tubes made in this way, the inventor claimed several acoustic advantages for them, pointing out in his specification that when suspended and gently tapped they would ring like a bell due to their homogeneity, while the older built-up type had a dull sound. Since the basic patents became generally available, Haynes's method has been adapted to metal instruments of all sorts and sizes—notably saxophones. In the course of time, too, improvements in detail have been introduced, and nowadays the edges of drawn holes are often rolled over on themselves to form a rounded bead to the pad-seating.

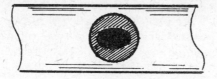

Fig. 55 Workpiece with preliminary oval hole punched out. Shaded area becomes the 'collar'

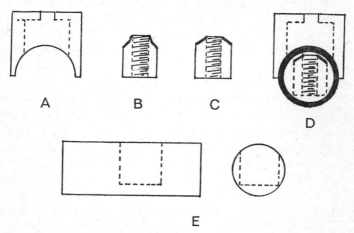

Fig. 56   Sectional views of
    A. The outer supporting saddle
    B. and C. Plugs
    D. Saddle, workpiece, and plug in position
       for drawing
    E. Inner guide block for locating plugs prior
       to drawing

It will have been noticed from these figures that the holes defined by raised rings in a metal flute meet the bore at an almost sharp right angle, and the thinness of the tube allows of no adjustment by undercutting or fraising. This, in turn, implies absolute accuracy in setting out and there is no 'second chance'. For this reason many quickly produced second-grade flutes may be of dubious intonation, and the student is advised to be careful if he buys one. He may well learn to correct automatically a doubtful note, but he may also acquire a permanent tendency to blow sharp or flat in some part of the scale.

There remain two cases in which the drawing process cannot well be applied. The first is the 'double-tube' type of metal instrument, where clearly it is impossible to do other than perforate both tubes according to measurement and solder in small connecting tubes. The other is the metal *head* in general. We have already pointed out (p. 9 above) that for any given flute the depth of the mouth-hole is a parameter, and the degree of under-cutting is largely a personal matter. To provide for both of these, then, it is necessary to supply some considerable body of metal in the 'chimney', and this is evidently a matter for soldering. It seems possible that a suitably tapered oval draw-plug and die might serve to form the actual blow-hole, but, even so, the lip-plate would have to be soldered in the usual manner. Again no adjustment would be possible and I am not aware of any maker who uses such a method.

The last point of difference we have to note between the making of wood and metal flutes lies in the mounting and keying, and here again soldering plays an important part. With a thin metal body it is of course not possible to screw the pillars into the substance of the tube, so soldering is inevitable—and here lies a particular danger. It is only too easy when setting up the pillars to overheat work already done, even to melt off a ring completely. One solution is to use high-temperature hard solder for the rings and then a lower melting tin-based solder for the later fittings, but with such tiny bearing surfaces the latter is not over strong. A better device is to set all pillars, stops, etc., on narrow straps of metal, either by riveting or hard soldering, and then to unite these, which provide a good contact surface, to the main tube with tin solder. This is done in the best class of work even in drawn-hole flutes, and it is commonly applied to wooden instruments also, since it obviates entirely the bugbear of a loosened pillar which can bind and put mechanism out of action at the most embarrassing moments. The protective beadings at the ends of the body, and the sockets, which in metal flutes are no more than short lengths of telescopic tubing, are of course also soldered—preferably with hard material.

It is an inescapable fact that in recent years mechanisation and mass-production methods have penetrated into many traditional crafts, and have tended to depersonalise them. In wind instrument making, where art and craftsmanship are so closely allied, this is particularly to be deplored. Today the Flutemakers' Guild of London, founded with the help of a former Lord Mayor, Sir Bernard Waley-Cohen, and Mr C. S. Padgett of the Worshipful Company of Goldsmiths, exists to preserve the traditional high name of English flute-making, and to enable young craftsmen to be suitably trained. Thus in this 20th century one of the old City Companies of London has in a way resumed its ancient function as the custodian of craft standards.[9]

NOTES

[1] Quantz, J. J., *Versuch einer Anweisung die Flöte traversiere zu spielen*, Berlin, Johann Friedrich Voss, 1752.

[2] Miller, Dayton C., in *Science*, 1909, Vol. 29. While his conclusions regarding the influence of materials on *timbre* remain unchallenged, Miller's experimental approach has recently been called in question (A. H. Benade, in a personal communication to the writer).

[3] Maillot and Chorier, two metallurgists of Lyons, devised one of the best known formulae for a white bronze *c*. 1820, hence the name *Maillechort* current in France, and sometimes incorrectly rendered as *Melchior*. In English speaking countries *German silver* is the common term for this group of alloys.

[4] Box is mentioned in the *Oeuvres* of J. P. Coutant, published in Poitiers in 1628. Constant Pierre points out that the reference concerns an industry that was then at least a century older.

[5] Plumier, Charles, Religieux Minime, *L'Art de Tourner en Perfection*, Lyons, 1701.

[6] Bergeron, L. E., *Manuel de Tourneur*, Paris, 1792 and 1816.

[7] Holtzapffel, C., *Turning and Mechanical Manipulation*, London, 1846, Vol. 2, p. 541.

[8] British patent 24483 of 23 Oct. 1913. German patent 279926, 1 Nov. 1913.

[9] We have already referred several times to the current enormous increase in the cost of first-class instruments of European or American make. In recent years developing countries in the Far East have entered the instrument trade with highly competitive prices. At the time of writing two firms, located respectively in Hong Kong and Tientsin, are producing flutes on the best European models which leave nothing to be desired as to accuracy of dimensions or finish. Older players express some doubt about the stability of the wood employed, but only time will prove this. Nevertheless, this source of instruments will be worth watching in future years.

CHAPTER 13

Some Notes on Key-work: Miscellanea

As THE flute, for reasons which appear in our earlier chapters, must be regarded as something of a pioneer in the acquisition of advanced key-work, and because it is hoped that this book may be of use to collectors of musical instruments as well as to the general student, it may be appropriate to give here some outline of the phases through which key-work has passed. The style of key-work can at times be a useful guide to dating an otherwise doubtful instrument, although this cannot always be accepted as absolute evidence. It must be remembered that fashion in musical instruments, as in other fields, has sometimes been conservative, and has outlived its period of origin. Furthermore, outdated styles have tended to survive in the cheaper classes of instruments, while improvements appeared first in the more expensive ranges.

Keys

Any key consists of three essential parts, the touch-piece, the shank, and the cover-plate (in later forms the 'cup') faced with some soft material that will ensure air-tight closure of the related hole. Together these elements form a simple lever of first, second, or third order, depending on the placing of the touch-piece and the cover in relation to the pivot or fulcrum about which the whole turns. According to whether they stop or open their associated holes when at rest, keys fall naturally into two groups, 'closed' and 'open', and the rest position is determined by a suitable spring. In identifying keys it is customary to label them according to the note sounded when they are pressed, so open-standing keys are named from the note spoken by the next open hole below, while closed keys take their names from the holes which they actually cover. An open key, if it be in one piece, must obviously have its pivot at one end, and there are many circumstances in which this is inconvenient. In such a case two simple first-order levers can be linked together (in French the *clef-à-bascule*) such as are used for the c′ and c′♯ keys of the common flute, and by a combination of several linked levers long spans can be covered. The disadvantage of the arrangement lies in the amount of lost motion entailed, even with the most careful construction when a little worn, and using the stiffest possible material for the levers. Nowadays long spans are almost always bridged by some form of the axle or pivoted tube mechanism which we have already described in connection with the Boehm 1832 flute (p. 122 above) and there is no need to say more of it here except to point out that mechanically it too is just a form of simple lever in which the pivot is greatly elongated, while the arms carrying the touch-piece and cover are kept very short. Fig. 57 illustrates in order of appearance three common methods of linking simple levers, and Fig. 58 shows the axle principle applied to open and closed keys, the touch-piece of the former in the form of a ring.

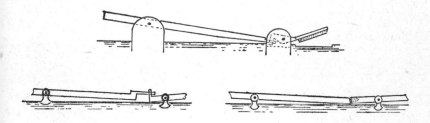

Fig. 57   Linkages of simple levers

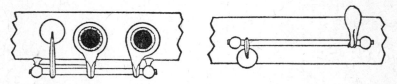

Fig. 58   Axle-mounted keys. Open and closed

The first clue towards dating an instrument that we can derive from key-work—albeit only a relative one—lies in the touch-piece. If this should be of 'fishtail' shape (Fig. 59) it usually indicates that the instrument comes from a period before discrimination began between right- and left-handed playing, for example the shawms of the 16th and 17th centuries. In the true oboes of the early 18th century, however, this no longer holds, and the fishtail survives as a 'hang-over' from the earlier instrument. We note also that all the earlier keys were open-standing. Closed keys intended to supplement the natural scale did not appear for at least another century. Fishtail touch-pieces are rare on transverse flutes and in most sizes they were clearly not necessary. On one-keyed flutes, d♯ keys shaped as in Fig. 60A are usually of early 18th-century date when associated with a plain rectangular cover. By the mid-century there appears a marked tendency towards a smoother 'fiddle-shaped' touch, and about the same time the cover shows sharp notches in each corner and a curved chamfer on each long edge. This form of cover lasted well into the 19th century on cheaper instruments, and can be found associated with a racquet shaped touch with a rounded surface. Occasionally the earliest cover-plates are curved to match the surface of the joint.

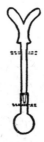

Fig. 59   The 'fishtail' key

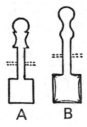

A   B

Fig. 60   Closed keys
A. Early 18th century
B. Late 18th and 19th centuries

The raw material of the earliest keys was simply sheet metal, brass or silver, cut and filed to shape, and with two small lugs bent down at right angles and drilled to take the pivot pin. Occasionally, where very long keys were required as in the bassoon and some clarinets, the sheet was bent into channel form to give added stiffness, but this was not common on other instruments. The cover-plates of open keys were constructed on the same lines, with an additional lug bent *up* and per-forated to mate with the end of the shank section. This hole had necessarily to be an easy fit with the result that there was much lost motion at the best of times, and a very firm pressure was needed to ensure good closing. With the acceptance of c' and c'♯ keys on the flute, sheet metal construction could not well provide the bent shanks required, and thicker metal, usually cast or forged and filed up, had to be used. In this case the pivot-hole could be drilled through the thick-ness of the metal, and by about 1770 such keys were in common produc-tion, though the sheet method served for simple closed keys for a long time after. There is some evidence that, in England at least, specialised key-makers were already beginning to supply more or less standard keys to general instrument makers much as was to become the modern French practice.

In the first part of the 19th century many modifications and improve-ments were made in key-work, some of them the patented ideas of individual makers, but the old flat cover-plate still survived, in a rounded form as late as *c.* 1850.

Pads and Seatings

It has been repeatedly said in these chapters that firm, air-tight closure of all holes is essential, and even today this remains a major worry with complicated key-work. With nothing better than flat covers the problem was ever present, and could only be met by facing them with a resilient substance, and making the seatings as flat as possible. Natural leather of suitable thickness, skin side outwards, was the obvious material, and this had to be kept in good condition and not allowed to get hardened by moisture. For this reason, glues were not good for attachment, and shellac or sealing wax was the chosen adhesive for leathers that must have required frequent renewal. In the last years of the 18th century some improvement was gained by lining the note-holes with small metal tubes which stood just proud of the pad seating and so made a permanent impression on the leather. This was not to come into general use, however, and some leading English makers were much opposed to it—presumably because of the possible danger of cutting the skin surface. In 1810 MacGregor included in his bass-flute patent a proposal for a 'valve' for wind instruments which seems to have consisted of a plate attached to the shank by a screw which also held on a slice of sponge faced with fine leather. Nothing much seems to have come of the idea, but soon after that date Monzani of London

began to adopt a sort of inversion of the idea. A slender screw permanently riveted to the shank carried, first, a small washer of some
resilient material, then the cover-plate, and finally the leather, all loosely
retained by a minute nut. This arrangement allowed of some latitude
in bedding down on the seating. About the same time Laurent and
Belissent, both of Paris, introduced cover-plates *hinged* transversely
to the shank, and in London James Wood was producing a rather crude
version of the same thing on his military clarinets. None of these arrangements, of course, gave quite the all-round flexibility of the Monzani
type key. The screw and nut are still used by some makers to attach
the modern thin pads to which we shall refer shortly. The shanks of
Monzani's keys were commonly marked with a crown, a veiled reference
to royal favour which some older-established English makers found a
trifle galling.

The various schemes we have looked at so far were all based on the
idea of getting air-tight closure by means of a more or less yielding
stopper, but in the last decades of the 18th century a totally different
principle was also tried out, and for a time had considerable success.
Among his several flute patents of 1785 Richard Potter included what
came to be known as the 'pewter plugs'. These were conical stoppers
of soft metal which fitted closely into a countersunk recess at the mouth
of the note-hole (sometimes bushed with metal) much in the manner
of the valves of an internal combustion engine. As long as these were
kept clean and occasionally smeared with oil they worked very well,
and trials have shown that they were much less noisy than one might
suppose. Potter had a high reputation as a general flute-maker, and his
plugs remained popular until nearly the mid-1800s, at which time they
were still being used for the c' and c'♯ keys. Their particular virtue
here was that, unlike plain leather, they could not lose their shape
while at rest out of contact with their seatings. The seatings themselves
were also improved by the use of flat countersunk plates screwed to the
surface of the tube instead of depending on the more vulnerable metal
linings. According to Rockstro, the pewter plug idea originated with
Boie of Göttingen who was active *c.* 1726, but whether Potter was aware
of this, or whether his was an independent re-invention—by no means
a rare phenomenon in many fields—will probably never be determined.

In spite of some opposition from the devotees of flat leathers, improved in one way or another perhaps, the really major advance came in
the early 19th century with the advent of the first stuffed pads which
had something of the softness and resilience of the natural finger tip.

They consisted of small circles of thin kid, drawn up by a running thread round the edge like an old-fashioned purse, and stuffed with a ball of fine wool—indeed they were often called 'purse-pads'. Of course these could not be easily attached to flat cover-plates, and the natural corollary to their appearance was the cupped key. At first such 'salt-spoon' keys were produced by casting in one piece, but very soon a lighter construction with a pressed or stamped-out cup soldered or riveted to the shank was adopted. A disadvantage of the first purse-pads was that they were somewhat unstable, especially if they got damp, and tended sometimes to bulge in the middle and so spoil the clarity of a keyed note. A stitch of thread through the middle proved only a partial solution.

On English flutes of the early to mid century the collector will sometimes find these pads made of *black* kid which at first sight looks a little strange. The alleged explanation reveals an interesting, if slightly macabre, association of trades. In Victorian times it was among the duties of a funeral undertaker to see that all participants were seemly clad, and a quantity of black gloves was therefore provided for loan or hire as required. After use these could hardly be returned to stock, so they were collected and sold in lots to the musical trade for pad making.

While it is evident that the stuffed pad was a vast improvement on what had gone before, it is equally clear that it did not provide all the answers, as we may deduce from the variety of seatings that we find associated with it. The simplest of these was a plain hemispherical countersink worked round the hole and large enough to accommodate the entire pad. This gave the largest bearing surface possible in the circumstances but it also increased the chances of sticking. Although such authorities as Rockstro insist that no oil should be applied to the bore of a wooden flute, and that after playing only excess moisture should be wiped out leaving the whole bore *uniformly* damp so as to avoid uneven stresses, this has not always been the general opinion, and many older players and makers obviously believed in a good deal of oiling. Linseed, especially the boiled oil, has the property of drying to a flexible gum (after all, it was for this reason that it was chosen as the basis of traditional varnishes) and an accumulation of such oil on a seating could easily stick down a pad, or even pull it away from the cup. A projecting metal lining tube, while giving good closure, did sometimes cut the surface of the pad, and probably the best type of seating for a purse-pad was the recessed type shown in Fig. 61. From that it was but a step to the modern form, produced by similar tools, and apparently quite satisfactory.

The next improvement in pads lay in the direction of flattening them, and this is reflected in the shape of the cups which got progressively shallower as the years passed. By Boehm's time the most advanced makers were producing cups almost flat with a definite rim, cut-out conical seatings, and pads consisting of a thin disc of felt, backed with card, and covered with fine kid. Indeed, without the existence of these Boehm's inventions could hardly have been realised. His book gives detailed instructions for setting and adjusting pads, and illustrates some useful tools he designed for the purpose. The pads provided by Boehm himself were perforated in the middle and were held in place by a washer and a tiny screw tapped into the thicker metal in the centre of the cup, a reversal of the Monzani scheme mentioned above. For the keys with large perforations introduced by the French makers about this time such an arrangement was of course not possible, and the ring-like pads required had to be cemented into place. From this period on, improvement has been concerned more with materials than anything else, and most pads today are surfaced with goldbeaters' skin or similar animal tissue, and synthetic waterproof materials similar to sausage casing have been tried out and are recommended by some makers. An attempt to replace composite pads with solid discs of a resilient plastic does not seem to have had much success so far, except perhaps in America.

Mountings and Pivots

To quote the late Geoffrey Rendall in the first volume of this series:[1] 'Of far greater importance to the player than the shape of the key is the mounting. The most elegant key is useless unless the mounting allows it to perform its function efficiently.' The sheet-metal keys of 16th- and 17th-century wind instruments were commonly pivoted on a piece of wire, either held down at each end by staples driven into the wood, or itself formed into a flat topped staple. This somewhat rickety arrangement was superseded in the later 17th century by a device in which the shank of the key worked in slot cut across a ring of wood left standing above the general surface of the tube. A fine hole was bored tangentially through both the ring and the key shank and this carried an axle pin of iron, brass, or silver wire. At the end, the axle wire was usually bent at right angles to form a tiny hook, and by this the pin could be withdrawn when necessary. This was the type of mounting found on the Baroque

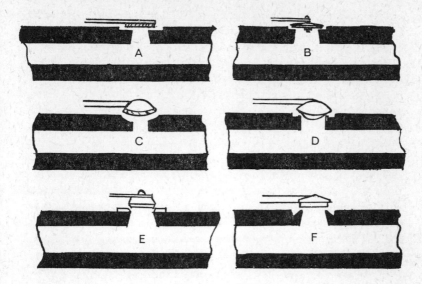

Fig. 61 Varieties of keys and seatings in section
A. Plain flat key. Flat seating
B. Monzani type loose riveted key. Leather retained by screw and nut
C. Cupped key (early type) 'Purse' pad. Hemispherical seating
D. Cupped key (later type). Inset metal tube seating (shows choking effect of bulging or deformed pad)
E. Soft metal plug. Countersunk metal plate seating
F. Modern flat cup with thin, felt-backed pad. Conical and recessed seating

conical flutes, and it was very often profiled to form part of the general ornament. When chromatic keys began to come in, however, and fashion decreed a less architecturally ornate style, a series of upstanding rings became something of an embarrassment, so the greater part of the ring was cut away, leaving only two blocks sufficient to support the axle pin. These were respectively the 'ring' and 'knob' mountings which are often mentioned in museum and makers' catalogues, and they give some basis for comparative dating, though here again we must be aware of the overlap of fashions and the persistence of older devices in the cheaper class of instrument. Military band flutes with knob mountings were listed

by one leading London maker, side by side with the most refined
Boehm instruments, at least as late as 1902.

The weakness of ring and knob mountings lies in the fact that the
fibres of the wood run naturally *across* the ring, so that there is relatively
little resistance to splitting through the cross-hole, and some of the later
makers have tried to strengthen things by putting in threaded wire pins
at strategic angles. And here a warning to the amateur who may want
to clean up an old instrument. The hooked type of pin should never be
pulled out with ordinary serrated pliers, which may well cut through
perished metal. Smooth jawed pliers can be obtained through jewellers'
supply men. A late refinement which, while no doubt elegant, is most
tiresome, was the filing off of the pivot wires level with the surface of the
wood. There is no way to remove such pins except by *pushing* them out,
and for this a tool similar to a bradawl, ground straight across the end,
smaller in diameter than the pin concerned and with *no taper* at all, is
essential. This must be applied absolutely in line with the pin. Many a
collector has split the knob of a cherished specimen through neglect of
these points.

In favour of the knob mounting it must be said that it wears well, the
surfaces exposed to friction being large, and when after a long time
looseness has developed, a slip of wood can be inserted and the original
fit restored. Further strength can be obtained by lining the cheeks of
the slot with thin metal. Rather later than the knob came the 'saddle'
type of mounting, which consists basically of a piece of channel-section
metal, either filed up from the solid, or bent up from sheet material,
and screwed to the surface of the tube. Additional stability was often
secured by sinking the saddle into the wood of the tube or by soldering
it to a curved base-plate. Saddles were frequently made quite long so as
to prevent wobble in long keys, but they could also be much smaller
than knobs and could be applied in cramped positions as, for example,
on the Monzani flute shown in Plate 7B. For this reason saddles are
often contemporary with knobs, and they do not always represent later
additions to an instrument—a mistake occasionally found in catalogues.
In fact it is not unknown for undoubted additional keys to be mounted
on knobs which have been beautifully dove-tailed into the tube, and in
the finest example of such work known to the writer the extra supports were actually turned to shape on the lathe, screwed into holes
in the body, and then slotted to receive the shanks.

The last form of mounting to arrive was the turned metal pillar which
we have already discussed in some detail. There is some doubt as to its

actual date of appearance, but examples are found on Laurent's glass flutes as early as 1806. It seems possible that this elegant device, now in universal use, was called into being by the practical difficulty of forming the conventional knobs in so intractable a material as glass, and it is perhaps significant that in conservative England it was for long called 'the French pillar'. As first made, pillars were always attached to oval base-plates, and this may also be traceable to the exigencies of glass-mounting. By about 1840, however, except in the highest class of flutes, the foot-plate had been dispensed with—presumably for the sake of economy—and at once a serious disadvantage appeared—the inevitable loosened pillar. Beyond the specialised field of flute-making, it has taken the woodwind industry till today to reintroduce the anchored pillar, and even now some firms make a special selling point of their pillars which are prevented from turning by a set-screw lying in a notch or passing through a pierced lug (see Fig. 62 and p. 212 above).

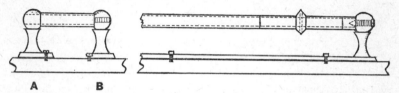

A   B

Fig. 62   Pillar and point-screw—profile and section.
Left: Pillars anchored by
        A. Perforated lug and screw
        B. Notched lug and screw
Right: Pillar   anchored   by   longitudinal
        strap

As a pair of pillars does not provide anything in the nature of a slot that can control side play, their introduction imposed one change on the general design of keys. This was a tube or barrel fitting closely between adjacent heads and turning without shake on the pivot. For this purpose only hard-drawn 'hinge-wire', as it is called, should be used, and it should be let into the shank and hard soldered. The use of soft tubing and solder here can only lead to vexation, for the cumulative effect of the thousands of tiny movements to which a key is subjected amounts to very considerable strain and mechanical wear. For the same reason the pivots if screwed into the pillars should be of hardened steel, accurately threaded, and with well formed shoulders. Soft material here though easier to work is a false economy. Exactly the same considerations apply to the long tubes and rods of the typical Boehm mechanism, and to the point-screws on which they turn. From time to time point-screws may require to be advanced fractionally to take up wear, so they should fit tightly in their pillars, and occasionally in very high-class work they have been provided with locking set-screws. This refinement is, however, seldom found, and is probably unnecessary if the original fitting has been done as it should.

Two final points—on older instruments with saddle mounts the student will very often, though not always, find screwed pivots rather than simple pins. On the other hand with pillared instruments of Continental make simple pins of hard brass or German silver are some-times preferred and seem to be quite satisfactory. An extreme case is the rather exceptional Boehm flute illustrated on Plate 8F, in which the longitudinal tubes turn on rods simply pushed into place and not anchored in any way. The action, after over a century, is perfect.

Springs

Without proper control the best of keys and mounts will be of no service, and this is provided by the springs. In wind instruments, above all the flute, the keys must open and close promptly and with the lightest touch possible, so the strength of the springs must be carefully adjusted. Two types of spring are now employed, the leaf and the needle. The former is the older, having been known since the beginning of key-work. In the 16th century leaf-springs made of hard hammered brass were the only type known, and usually they were attached to the body tube, the free end pressing upwards against the under side of the touch-piece. This arrangement survived on bassoons and other long instruments till into the 18th century. On other instruments the point of anchorage was early transferred to the key shank and the attachment was by riveting. As a spring material brass is not particularly efficient, being subject to both corrosion and fatigue, but until the advent of suitable forged steel c. 1800 nothing better was available. In this, again, Laurent of Paris seems to have been a pioneer. With the invention of German silver many Continental makers turned to this material, but, apart from non-corrosion, it seems to have little advantage over well hardened brass. As to riveting, there is no apparent reason why it should have continued as long as it did—it is found in first-class instru-ments until well on in the 19th century—unless it was retained for commercial reasons. Riveted springs are difficult to replace, and surely the technique of fitting small screws, as in clock-making, could have been generally applied much earlier.

With leaf-springs sluggishness due to the friction of the free end moving against the wood of the tube is often a problem. Today this is minimised by the insertion of polished steel studs on which the spring can bear. In the early 1800s Rudall and Rose provided an elegant arrangement in which a steel leaf attached to the key rested on another of brass screwed to the body of the instrument, thus taking advantage of the anti-friction properties of dissimilar metals. About the same time Brod of Paris fitted springs tipped with tiny rollers to some of his very beautiful oboes, but the writer is not aware of any flute so equipped.

The needle-spring is said to have been invented by Auguste Buffet in connection with his version of the Boehm 1832 flute (p. 122 above) and it was adopted by the latter in his next model. It consists of a curved springy wire anchored at one end in the neck of a pillar, and at the other bearing on a minute hook soldered to a key barrel. According to the bias of the spring it can serve to open or close the associated key, and springs of different power can even be arranged to oppose each other (see 'Dorus G♯ key', p. 124 above). Boehm himself at first used hard-drawn gold wire for this purpose, but later specified the best quality English sewing needles with the temper let down to 'dark blue'. The biassing of needle-springs calls for much experience, but they are highly satisfactory, and are now made in strengths suitable for all mechanisms from the lightest flute to the largest saxophone.

Miscellanea

There remain to be noticed one or two details which the flute enthusiast will sometimes encounter, but which do not seem to have any consistent story. These are the various arrangements that makers have devised to ease the purely mechanical difficulties of fingering. The advent of keys eliminated, more or less, the problem of poor intonation in chromatic notes, but their placing sometimes called for awkward finger movements, and this fact no doubt contributed to the early opposition they encountered. Transverse keys in particular were inconvenient; the cross F for the right ring finger, and the cross C♮ for the left thumb. The former was, as we have seen, the first and most desirable of all keys from the intonation aspect, but its use often involved a sliding movement from the adjacent hole to the touch-piece. Many old flutes show attempts to help this situation by widening the touch-piece and sloping it towards the hole, and making an excavation in the wood to accommodate the extension. Others have a roller attached, either as an original feature, or as an evident addition, and many

Q

modern 'reform-flutes' carry this fitting as standard. This appears to be the earliest application of roller-touches to the flute, and, though we cannot date it accurately, it certainly took place before 1817—by which time, of course, the alternative 'long F' was already well known, if not popular. Subsequently, rollers have been applied in many situations, particularly for the right little finger, as can be seen from several examples shown in our Plates.

The last chromatic key in sequence to be added to the simple flute was that for the higher C♮ which appeared during the last quarter of the 18th century (p. 98 above). It required a new hole between those for C♯ and B♮ and this naturally suggested the left thumb, but as that digit was already in charge of the B♭ key, things were bound to be somewhat uncomfortable. In 1828 the acoustician Gottfried Weber discussed this C♮ key in the pages of *Caecilia*, and suggested that it be replaced by a hole, with or without an open-standing key, directly under the thumb. He does not seem to have been aware of the earlier open C♮ hole, and to make his version as convenient as possible he arranged it to be bored through a swelling on the tube level with the touch of the B♭ key. The writer has never seen an actual example of Weber's scheme, but the drawings are reproduced here for any collector who may be so fortunate as to find one.

The curious object shown in Fig. 65, colloquially known as 'Boehm's

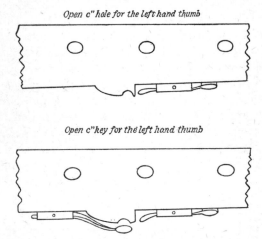

Open c" hole for the left hand thumb

Open c" key for the left hand thumb

Figs. 63 & 64   Gottfried Weber's proposals for the
high C♮ (left thumb)

Crutch', was a support designed to transfer the weight of the flute to
the space between the left thumb and forefinger, its function being
therefore slightly different from that of a rather similar accessory
sometimes used by bassoon players (see also p. 140 above). The inventor
used and advocated his device, claiming that it helped the freedom of
the left-hand fingers. Other players have found the reverse to be the
case, and few if any make use of the support today.

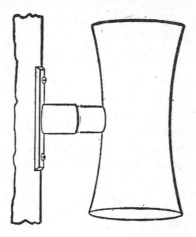

Fig. 65 'Boehm's Crutch'

Finally, under this heading, the reader's attention is drawn to the
flute shown in Plate 7E, which has several interesting features. It is
by the celebrated maker Streitwolf of Göttingen and dates from before
1837. In appearance this seems to be a normal cone-flute of its time,
with small holes, and extended down to the low B♮, but it embodies a
number of unusual features which are typical of the inventive genius of
its designer. From the head downwards these are: (1) the screw-cork;
(2) a C♮ key pivoted *above* the hole and opened by alternative touches
for the left thumb and the right first finger; (3) B♭ key to the right
forefinger only; (4) the cross F♮ bored through a swelling set well to
the *front* of the instrument, so that a long lever for the left little finger
can open the same key and replace a separate long F key; Tromlitz's
invention of 1800; (5) the long lever for the low B♮ is detachable by
pulling out the pivot pin which has a ring-shaped head. The touch-
piece has an adjustable extension to suit different hands. On p. 105 we
spoke of Monzani's characteristic omission of a tuning slide in the

head, and of his occasional use of metal tubes instead of wooden tenons between the joints. These features are carried much further in the Streitwolf instrument. The two middle joints are fitted with metal tubes, lapped with thread, and so accurately fitted that they can be pulled out for tuning with complete stability. That at the head end is long enough to represent the tuning slide of an ordinary flute. The great beauty of these tenons lies in their construction, however. Instead of being merely tubes inserted in the bore and retained in the common way by roughening and cementing in, these have each a circular flange which is held to the end of the wood by three tiny wood-screws, making an uncommonly strong joint. One of these flanges can be seen in the plate just behind the C and C♯ touch-pieces, and this reveals the final secret of the instrument—the ivory mounts are only thin ornamental shells, but made deep enough to conceal the inner tubes even when drawn out to the practical limit. Unfortunately the history of this obviously very superior instrument is unknown except for one fact— it was obtained during the 1914–18 War by a son of the late Canon Galpin in exchange for a packet of English cigarettes.

NOTE

[1] Rendall, F. G., *The Clarinet*, in Instruments of the Orchestra, London, Ernest Benn Ltd., 1954.

CHAPTER 14

Capabilities and Technique

IT HAS been repeated almost *ad nauseam* in textbooks and works on orchestration that, of all the wind instruments, the flute is the most agile; that it is capable of almost every conceivable nuance, style of ornament, *arpeggio* or *batterie*; and that its tones range from a velvety langour in the lower register to a bird-like clarity at the top which can float above the orchestral ensemble and impart a shimmering brilliance to the whole. What is less often stressed is that unless the composer is careful the low notes, which have relatively little power, can often be lost and do no more than contribute to a general muddiness of effect, while the top register can easily get harsh. Nor are any of the flute's great virtues to be elicited without assiduous practice and constant attention by the instrumentalist. A well-known wind player once said to the writer, 'the clarinet is a good friend but an infernal master', and the same might well be said of the flute. Yet no instrument gives greater satisfaction and pleasure to the even moderate performer, as witness the thousands who belong to amateur orchestras and flute societies all over the world. There is also no instrument in which the personal charac- teristics of the player, both in physique and in temperament, are more influential, and in his student period the would-be professional flautist must find out what these are and train himself accordingly. Much help will be got from a discerning teacher in the early stages, but the final result will rest with the player himself. No two flautists do exactly the same in similar circumstances, and for this reason it is nearly impossible to define flute technique in a few words. All flautists, however, agree broadly on fundamentals, and these we shall try to outline here.

Fingering

It goes without saying that complete familiarity and fluency in finger- ing all scales is a first necessary, but the idea that with modern instru- ments all scales are equally easy or difficult is quite false. So is the notion that today all shakes and graces are easy. Even with the most modern supplementary mechanism, some are difficult—especially those involving the alternation of adjacent fingers. Formerly some shakes were regarded as quite impossible, and a glance at the tables in some of the tutors listed in our Bibliography will show what might be expected of the flautist at different periods. The choice of extra facilities is nowadays a wide one, and it is almost impossible to have them all on any one instrument—*pace* the late James Mathews of Birmingham (p. 133 above) who managed to get no less than twenty-eight keys on to his gold flute. The player must decide for himself which of a limited number are of the most service to him personally, and it may well be that he cannot make this decision until he has gained considerable experience. In this matter too, the advice of a good teacher will be valuable at the outset. The young player will be able to make his choice later, as he gets to know himself, and what he can accomplish with the standard equipment. If he should opt for something a little out of the ordinary he will do well to understand how it works, but unless he is a skilled mechanic, he should leave adjustment to the expert. The writer once knew an oboist who used a slightly unusual combination of keys with great skill, and he asked with some diffidence if he might examine the instrument. The reply was startling—'Of course you may look at my oboe—you can borrow it if you like—but don't ask me how it works. If it goes wrong I just chuck it in to the repair man.' That oboist was probably wise in his generation, and he attempted nothing beyond routine care of his instrument. The reader will find a few notes on general care and maintenance of the flute in Appendix IV. Fork-fingering and its *raison d'être* have been mentioned so frequently in these pages that there is no need to notice it again, except to point out that it remains an indispensable part of the technique of all flutes based on the so-called simple system. In the various modern cylinder flutes the acoustic problems that could only be got round by 'forking' have been overcome by mechanical means, but even so a similar action of the fingers is often called for, as for example in the third octave of the Boehm instrument (see Appendix III, p. 247). It follows that the flautist must cultivate just as much suppleness as the pianist, and may encounter similar difficulties. Supporting the flute must never be allowed to interfere with the freedom of the fingers, so a good position is essential from the first.

Embouchure

The heart and soul of flute playing lie in the embouchure and it is here that we meet the curious paradox of general agreement on principle and widely divergent individual practice. Broadly speaking, flautists recognise two types of embouchure—*tight* and *relaxed*—and these are generally associated with wooden and metal flutes respectively. The wooden flute naturally yields a more powerful and dense tone than the metal, and it requires generally a stronger attack and more forceful blowing. Lightness and delicacy of control come with practice. These requirements give rise to a muscular embouchure, with the lips firmly braced sideways. The flute is pressed rather strongly against the lower lip and the corners of the mouth are often turned up producing the traditional 'fluteplayer's smile'. This conformation results in a rather flat 'air-reed', and with it the sound can be made wonderfully rich, and, in the lower notes, powerful. In this we can still recognise the typically English tradition of Nicholson—more refined now perhaps—but very distinctive, as exemplified by the late Robert Murchie and his pupils, first among them Gareth Morris. Their work has created a very definite 'school' of playing. In Germany and Russia today 'solid' tone seems to be preferred, but to English ears it seems less rich than our own. The compromise instruments which are perhaps lighter to blow, yet possess something of the density of wood tone, have already been noticed in our descriptive section (pp. 8–10 above).

The *genius* of the metal flute is of a lighter and more ethereal sort, and these instruments respond best to the relaxed embouchure. This is effected by turning the lips more or less loosely outward and pulling them somewhat inward at the sides, forming a rounder aperture than with the tight style. Control of the air stream is obtained by varying tension at the sides of the mouth and by an in-and-out movement of the lower jaw. The resultant tone is most distinctive, clear and limpid— if required, penetrating—in the upper registers, but in the low octave rather hollow and short of overtones. Detractors of the metal flute have sometimes described this sound as 'wind-in-the-chimney', but French players, who are the great exponents of the style, do much to make it telling by a lavish use of *vibrato*. The relaxed style had its origin in France in the latter part of the 19th century, when Paul Taffanel, then Professor in the Paris Conservatoire, was probably the most influential teacher in Europe. Since Taffanel's time, the style has become widely appreciated through the concert tours of his successor and pupil, Louis Fleury, and later those of Marcel Moyse, René Le Roy, etc. The delicate performance and control of tone colour shown by these artists have done much to popularise the metal flute, which today must rank as the world-favourite, and which has a growing list of devotees even in England and Germany.

To make the flute speak, it is held horizontally (normally to the player's right) and supported by the lowest joint of the left forefinger, the right hand, and the front of the lower jaw. The mouth-hole is placed centrally with its near edge against the vermilion border of the lower lip, and the aperture formed according to whichever style of embouchure is adopted. The air stream is directed towards the far edge of the mouth-hole. Thus is sounded the first octave. The second octave is produced by some increase of air pressure, and by directing the stream a little upwards by a slight movement of the lower lip or jaw—but not by consciously turning the tube. This action causes the second harmonic to become dominant, and the fundamental to drop out; indeed, the harmonic is already present with some power in the complex tone of the first octave (p. 40 above) and many students at first have difficulty in keeping it sufficiently subdued for the fundamental to be really telling. Hence also the difficulty sometimes experienced by the listener in distinguishing the true pitch of low flute tones in the orchestra. It is interesting to note here that while the great majority of important teachers, from Quantz to Nicholson, advocated that the mouth-hole should be turned its own width inwards from the line of the finger-holes, Boehm insisted that all should be on one line.

The first and second octaves being mastered, the player then further increases the pressure, at the same time opening one or other supplementary hole to encourage appropriate sub-division of the air-column, and the super-octave or fourth harmonic appears and gives the third register. On the modern flute the third harmonic (twelfth) is not used in the normal scale, except that of g' which gives d'''. Otherwise these twelfths are in general too flat to be used as sustained notes, but may occasionally serve as passing notes in ornaments. It is in eliciting the harmonics that the flautist's individuality becomes most evident, and few are able to describe exactly what they do to produce any given note. Practice is all.

The relaxed embouchure, quite apart from *style* pure and simple, presents certain technical advantages in that it eases *crescendo* and *diminuendo* in the high registers, and slurring at low dynamics over wide intervals. These facilities *can*, of course, be cultivated with the wooden flute, just as a metal one *can* be played tightly and made to give a truly solid tone if desired, and the above remarks only indicate the inherent *bias* of the two varieties.

It is extremely difficult to describe in words the behaviour of so complex a group of small muscles as those which contribute to the flautist's embouchure, each of which has to be educated in its function as the instrument is learnt. The two sketches in Fig. 66 may be of some help in visualising this point. In addition to forming and controlling the air stream, the player must also consider all the time his intonation. A note may easily be blown sharp or flat even though the instrument is intrinsically well tuned, and Rockstro, for one, insisted strenuously that

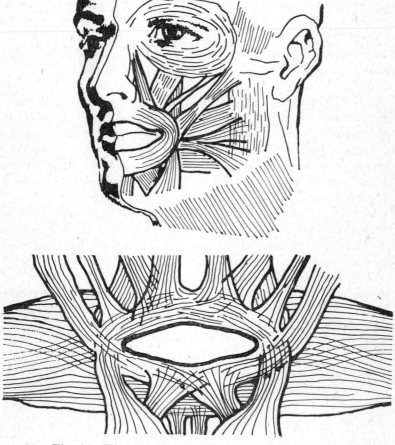

Fig. 66 The muscles involved in forming the flautist's embouchure
A. General three-quarter view
B. Orifice of mouth. Front view (*after Porter. British Dental Journal*)

the student must learn to blow his flute automatically at its *mean* pitch. The artist-player will turn this property to advantage, for example, to sharpen the leading-note, or to make hair's breadth enharmonic distinctions. All this is done by minute muscular control, by 'covering' the *embouchure* more or less, and by slight turning movements of the tube, and it is this capacity which makes the flute perhaps the wind instrument *par excellence* in chamber music. In the end things still come down to the old advice to all wind players—'First imagine the sound you want to hear—then make it.'

Vibrato

Vibrato has been a bone of contention among wind players for centuries, and no doubt its excessive use can lead to vulgarity of style. On the other hand, used with discretion, it adds life and expressiveness to *legato* playing, provided always that the player has a good basic *cantabile* which is the foundation of everything. Although *vibrato* was recommended as long ago as Agricola's time, it has not, as far as I am aware, ever become part of academic wind teaching, and it remains a matter for the taste of the individual musician, and his understanding of the composer's intention. It should never become a mere habit. As a rule, flautists are the chief exponents of the device, as we have mentioned in regard to the French School, though reed players, too, employ it a good deal. There is some speculation as to the whys and wherefores of this, for today even the clarinet—traditionally played quite 'straight'— has submitted.[1]

In flute playing *vibrato* is sometimes engendered with the lower lip, but better by the breath controlled by the diaphragm. The method is not easy to learn, and is best begun by practising slow rhythmical pulses, increasing in speed as facility is gained. As in good singing, deep breathing from the diaphragm is necessary for proper control in all wind playing, and the shallow 'top-of-the-lungs' method can only yield a monotonous *mezzo-forte* without reserves.

Articulation

In these pages we can hardly begin to discuss the manifold phrase and expression marks which the wind player may encounter in the course of his work. Their intention, and how they are to be treated, will be part of his basic musical education, but we may perhaps point out that they have at different times been used to different degrees, and proper interpretation implies some understanding of periods, styles, and customs in music. The most generally useful thing we can say to a wind student is probably, 'look at the marks as a violinist would at his bowings', for, after all, in initiating and shaping the sounds the breath is surely the equivalent of the bow.

In flute playing the tongue is used to give a clean start to a note or phrase, and as a general rule every note is to be somewhat tongued unless expressly marked with a slur from the one before. Most commonly the flautist does this by forming the letter T with the tongue against the palate behind the upper teeth, but many obtain a similar effect by touching the upper lip with the tongue and withdrawing it smartly. The labial P, to start a note, is also possible on the flute, and it is sometimes recommended to beginners who are learning to produce the top register softly. It is evident that the consonants of speech offer a convenient method of naming the different articulations, and there are several others which are useful in special circumstances, *viz.* K, L, and the trilled R—even the French glottal R is occasionally used.

Like all good rules, that about general tonguing has some exceptions. When a long slur mark is placed over a group of repeated notes it is usually intended to indicate an overall smoothness with only a very light separation; and when dotted or barred notes occur under a slur mark they are still to be lightly tongued, but the breath allowed to fall away on each note in the first case, and slightly forced in the second. These should give the effects of *semi-staccato* and *semi-legato* respectively. Arrow-head accents under a slur indicate that separation is to be made by breathing only and no tongue attack. It may seem that in the above there are more distinctions than differences, but it is just the observation of such fine details that separates musicianly playing from mere blowing.

At fast *tempi* a sequence of repeated 'Ts' can become very tiring to keep up, and this leads to irregularity or even breakdown. In such circumstances *double-tonguing* is employed, using the tip and back of the tongue alternately, T–K–T–K. The exact alternation will be dictated by the phrasing of the music, i.e. for triplets T–K–T—K–T–K, or for dotted triplets T–T–K—T–T–K, etc. With the flute doubletonguing is very efficient (rather less so with reeds which properly require an actual touch of the tongue on each note) and it is regarded as part of normal technique. Indeed, some composers will even call for it by special directions in the score. Writing in 1889 Rockstro stated that some players within memory—among them the great Nicholson—were accustomed to use the T–L articulation, but this he regarded as then quite out of date.[2] The writer has been told, but can

offer no proof, that a few players still use this formula as 'too-tle' or
'too-tle-too' (or its German form 'didd'l-didd'l'), and it is recorded that
Quantz made use of both T and D as occasion dictated.

Mention of Quantz leads us to another point we must observe here,
which is that in the 'period' revivals of early music so much in vogue
at the present time, the flautist, though he may not see his way to
making a special study of the obsolete instrument, should at least be
aware of former methods. Up to about the beginning of the 19th century
double-tonguing was not in use solely as an expedient to ease the
difficulty of fast articulation, but was employed to give life and expression even in quite moderate *tempi*, and to reproduce this calls for much
study and critical assessment of scores. It seems that the K syllable,
which came into use about 1820, was regarded in earlier times as too
explosive in character, and in 1582 Agricola, in his doggerel verse
instructions, wrote of the piper's 'diridiride'. This may be interpreted, a
little later, and in France, as T–R–T–R–T, and may be found in
instruction books for flute, cornett, trumpet, and even oboe, throughout
the 18th century. The slur, incidentally, is not so far recorded before
the time of Mersenne (1636). It is said that Drouet, the famous French
flautist of the Beethoven period, taught his English pupils by the use of
the word 'territory', presumably using the English trilled R. The French
glottal R has some place today in the special effect of 'flutter-tonguing',
though the tip of the tongue can flutter equally effectively.

It is surely a sign of a healthy and vital art that musicians are turning
their attention at this time not only to the authentic performance of
ancient music, but to increasing the capacity of existing instruments.
Even within the last year, some extremely interesting effects have been
achieved, though as yet they can hardly be recognised as part of accepted
technique. As regards the four standard woodwinds the new work is
concerned with the ability of a single instrument under certain conditions to sound chords. The horn player's trick of occasionally producing
chords by sounding a note in the normal way while humming a related
note and so generating a 'resultant tone' is well known. Though it is
quite possible to vocalise while blowing a flute (and no doubt some
advanced jazz players do so) the new woodwind effects seem to be
something rather different. Readers will recall that in Chapter 2 we
noticed that nearly all musical sounds are complex and contain an
assemblage of frequencies whose total effect is to produce a characteristic *timbre*. The simplest explanation of the new effects would appear
to be that some players, by a combination of special fingerings and a

very sensitive control of the tone generator (be it air-reed or cane reed), have found a method of reinforcing certain partial tones to a strength comparable with that of the fundamental. This, however, does not seem to be the whole story. Some players are able to maintain one of the frequencies while trilling another. It will be remembered, also, that some partials are dissonant with respect to their fundamental, and dissonance is a characteristic of some of the one-instrument chords. Others seem to contain frequencies not related to the fundamental in any recognised way. The work done so far has been written up by Bruno Bartolozzi in his *New Sounds for Woodwinds* (London, O.U.P., 1967) which is published together with an illustrative record. It is impossible at present to foresee how far this new technique may come to be accepted as orthodox, but certain *avant-garde* musicians are already writing for it, notably Niccolo Castilioni. This composer's *Alef* for solo oboe, which has been broadcast a number of times by the admirable oboist Heinz Holliger, though strange at first to the conventionally trained ear, has a very considerable appeal.

NOTE

[1] Originally found only in dance band circles, *vibrato* with the clarinet finds limited use today in the orchestra, but to be acceptable calls for a basic tone of great quality. Reginald Kell, principal clarinet with the famous pre-war London Philharmonic Orchestra, was probably the first symphony clarinettist to use *vibrato* in England, and in that organisation was associated with Leon Goossens, the celebrated oboist, who also uses *vibrato* with great taste and artistry.

[2] Rockstro, *The Flute*, Article 909, Notice of Charles Nicholson.

The Boehm-Gordon Controversy

The writer's reasons for adding one more account of this distasteful business to the already overburdened corpus of flute literature have been set out in the main text of this book (p. 115). As the documents, letters, and commentaries in the case can all be read in the original languages and in translation in Rockstro's *The Flute*, and in Christopher Welch's *History of the Boehm Flute*, together with the curious arguments and special pleadings that some parties have based on them, it seems that all that is required here is a summary of the situation as it appears now, over a century after the *affaire*, and seventy-seven years after Rockstro's renewed attack on the memory of Boehm. For the advanced student Karl Ventzke's book *Die Boehmflöte* (1966) re-surveys Boehm's entire life and work, and introduces some fresh matter which was not available to the earlier writers. This very able treatise brings to light nothing but what is to the credit of Boehm as an honourable gentleman.

The contact between Captain Gordon and Boehm began in 1831 in London, where the latter was appearing as a concert virtuoso. Both men, before this date, had ideas of improving the standard flute of their time, and Gordon, whose profession as an officer in Charles X's Swiss Guards vanished in the disastrous Revolution of 1830, conceived the idea of turning his amateur enthusiasm for the instrument into a means of livelihood. He had already by 1826 designed several flutes which had been constructed for him by a Swiss watchmaker, but the exact details of these are not known. In 1831 Gordon visited London where flutes were made for him by Rudall and Rose and by Cornelius Ward. (Ward, though he was a Gordon partisan in the later quarrels, wrote in 1844 that the Captain was thought even then to have been mentally disturbed by his horrible experiences in the Louvre massacre.)

During 1831 Gordon made the acquaintance of Boehm and the two men showed each other their instruments with complete amity and mutual respect. At this time, we recall, Boehm was using his first improved model (Fig. 30, p. 118) which did not fully realise the open-keyed theory, though it did have a *ring-key* associated with the F♯ hole. Gordon's earliest flutes (though we have no contemporary drawings of them) seem to have had a completely open-keyed mechanism. In the application of this principle, then, Gordon does appear to have been ahead of Boehm at this time, though of course the idea did not originate with him, it having been set out by Pottgeisser as early as 1803 and re-stated by him in 1824. Our knowledge of the Gordon flute as at 1831 we owe to Boehm's description written many years later (1847), a point that his detractors were not slow to seize on, but there is no reason to doubt its accuracy or objectivity. He says that the instrument differed greatly from the common flute, that it had a ring- and crescent-key, and that the mechanism was ingeniously arranged, though complicated and not well conceived for efficiency. These are points that would at once be evident to the experienced mechanic, however kindly disposed. The lay-out of the holes Boehm criticised as unscientific, which need not surprise us in the light of what other writers who knew him tell us of the 'trial and error' methods to which Gordon's lack of acoustical knowledge limited him. Nevertheless, a sight of this instrument may possibly have canalised the ideas of reform which Boehm already harboured, and which were realised to a great extent in 1832.

The two parts of Fig. 67 are illustrations of Gordon's flute as depicted in 1839 and 1846, the first said to come from his first prospectus of 1833 (see next paragraph) and the second from some earlier source not yet positively identified. It will be seen that the placing of the holes, though still irregular, is improved in the later figure. The most notable points, however, are the means employed to

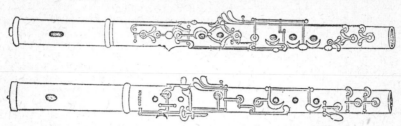

Fig. 67   Two versions of the Gordon flute. There is
some uncertainty as to the original sources of these
engravings

enable one finger to govern more than one hole, and the spanning of long distances by a system of bell-cranks connected by tracker-wires. To close an open hole and a key at the same time Gordon used a crescent-shaped touch-piece lying close to the edge of the hole. Boehm, in 1832, used rings for the same purpose, but there is no reason to suppose (as Rockstro contended) that the one was derived from the other. Neither device was new, Pottgeisser again having proposed the crescentic touch in 1824, and Nolan the ring in 1808. Boehm, be it noted, never claimed the ring-key as an invention, but wrote specifically in his first pamphlet (1847): 'je me fixai au système des clefs à anneaux comme répondant le mieux à toutes les exigences, système que j'avais déjà médité dès avant 1831'; that is, 'I decided on (chose) the system of ring keys, etc.'

Early in 1833 Gordon, still unsatisfied with the progress of his flute, went specially to Munich to obtain the help of one of Boehm's best workmen, whose services had most generously been placed at his disposal. Boehm himself was again in London at the time. After several failures in Munich, Gordon succeeded in producing an instrument that pleased him, and in July of the same year he sent prospectuses of it to London, Paris, and Germany. In 1834 Gordon published a scale for the instrument, and in this acknowledged the use of Boehm's F♯ and 'd″ shake' keys by express permission. The new flute, however, failed to commend itself, and in bitter disappointment the Captain retired to Lausanne, where he continued his experiments until a total mental breakdown brought his work to a sad end in 1836. The above sketch summarises the relations of the two men over a period of five years, during which we have no evidence that either ever thought of the other but with appreciation and regard. We may perhaps think that there was no great element of *invention* in the mechanism of either flute; both Gordon and Boehm adapted freely the crude devices of earlier workers, but it was the latter who transmuted them into an elegant and practical key system.

The attack on Boehm came in 1838, and from a direction which must have been surprising. The year before (or some say in 1835) Camus, who was friendly to Boehm, adopted his instrument with enthusiasm and, as his agent, brought a specimen to Paris, handing it over to the excellent maker Buffet. The latter copied it carefully, and shortly devised the mechanical improvements mentioned on p. 121, for which he secured French patents. The Buffet version was now taken up by Victor Coche, by this time a professor in the Paris Conservatoire; the very man who had made such a show of apparent friendship to Boehm in 1832 when he was trying to get his new instrument before the French Academy of Sciences. In the intervening years professional success and overweening personal vanity had made Coche many enemies in musical circles, though it must be admitted that, as a performer, he deserved the position he had gained. By 1838 the Boehm flute had attracted general attention in Paris, and in the month of March, at the invitation of the Minister of the Interior, the instrument was brought to the attention of the Royal Academy of Fine Arts. But in the event—and one wonders how far professional jealousy between Coche and Camus affected the matter—the subject examined by the Music Committee was 'the improvements introduced into the manufacture of the flutes called "flutes on the Boehm system by M. Coche"'. High praise was accorded to the professor, but as to Buffet, his name was recognised only as the maker of the instrument. His very practical contribution was ignored.

The report of the Royal Academy had been issued but a short time when whispers began to be heard among Paris musicians to the effect that Gordon and not Boehm was the true inventor of the new flute, and Coche—if he was not responsible himself for the innuendos—saw in them an opportunity for further personal aggrandisement. He therefore first addressed himself to Gordon, and, hearing from Mme Gordon that her husband was then in a mental institution, embarked on a considerable correspondence with that unfortunate lady. From the tone of her letters it is clear that he presented himself as a disinterested friend, concerned only to see justice done, but it is to be noticed that in quotations from the correspondence published later he suppressed his own letters. Having had his first reply from Mme Gordon, Coche then wrote a malicious letter to Boehm in the following terms: 'It is said in professional society that the flute that bears your name was discovered and invented, with all its present improvements, by a person of the name of Gordon; that this Gordon, after devoting several years to experiments and labours, has given up, on account of illness, occupying himself with his flute; and that your discovery, in a word, is no other than his.' No credit given, we observe, to Buffet for 'present improvements'. Boehm at once repudiated the charge, but most unfortunately in giving his account of his past relationship with Gordon made a mistake of one year in regard to Gordon's visit to Munich. This error has been dealt with satisfactorily by later investigators, but at the time it was a gift to Coche, who used it as a basis to attack Boehm's general veracity. Sweeping aside Boehm's denial, Coche then proceeded to issue an *Examen Critique de la flûte ordinaire comparée à la flûte de Böhm*, which he dedicated to the members of the Royal Academy of Fine Arts, and in which he claimed priority for Gordon. Finally he published a *Méthode pour servir à l'enseignement de la Nouvelle Flûte, inventée par Gordon, modifiée par Böhm et perfectionée par V. Coche et Buffet, jeune*; an excellent practical instruction book with a title that must be hard to equal for grandiloquent impudence.

In England the Gordon cause was espoused by the maker Cornelius Ward in a pamphlet called *The Flute Explained* (1844), and by Prowse, who was then enjoying the fruits of the 'Nicholson's Improved' eight-keyed flute (p. 112). Ward, it will be recalled, was one of those makers who failed to satisfy Gordon in 1831, but he may have felt some sense of obligation to him, as well as to

Pottgeisser, for certain features of his own 'patent' flute produced in 1842. On the other hand, Clinton, then influential as Professor at the Royal Academy of Music in London, gave lavish credit to Boehm in his *Theoretical and Practical Essay* (1843) and his *Practical Instruction Book* (1846). A better reasoned, though less flamboyant, supporter of Boehm was the leading London flautist Richard Carte (1845). Other players, both amateur and professional, took up either side, and, in the pages of *The Musical World* for 1843, letter after letter appeared, some well informed, others merely silly. Finally the correspondence was closed when many readers pointed out that their interests in the journal were other than flute-oriented.

With the advent of Boehm's cylinder flute in 1847, the matter lost importance—except in so far that his honour had been maliciously impugned—and nothing further was heard of it till, on his death, certain Continental journalists revived it in their search for obituary material. The *London Figaro* of 28 December 1881 carried a particularly nasty comment, which was firmly crushed by W. S. Broadwood, an enthusiastic flautist and personal friend of Boehm, in the same columns; and in *The Musical World* for January 1882. Von Schafhäutl also wrote a paper at that time which appeared in translation in the same journal for February the following year.

There, one might have hoped, the affair would be allowed to rest. In 1890, however, R. S. Rockstro chose to revive it again, taking a bitterly prejudiced view and losing no opportunity to denigrate all Boehm's work. In his otherwise valuable *Treatise on the Flute* Rockstro chose to accept Coche's self-portrait as the disinterested seeker after justice, and himself always referred to even the classic *cylinder* flute as 'Gordon's Flute'. The cause of Rockstro's prejudice is difficult even to guess at, but at least it had one good result—it led later workers to re-examine the original documents, to interview surviving parties, and to publish conclusions that are fairer to all.

Named Flute 'Systems'

In the foregoing text some account has been given of the major systems, either acoustical or mechanical, which have been applied to the transverse flute. Some of these have contributed important features to the present-day instrument, but there are many which are of historical interest only. Most are no more than variations on one or two basic ideas, but hopeful originators have attached their names to them for one reason or another, and have even at times secured patents.

The following list contains both those which have been regarded as important within the compass of this book, and those which the reader may encounter from time to time in general flute literature. The significance of the latter will depend on the purpose and scope of his studies, but their number will give some idea of the amount of work that has been lavished on the flute over many years.

Alberti
Albisi
Badger (an experimental system with all keys independent)
Barett
Berteling
Boehm 1832
Boehm 1847
Boehm-Julliot (Boehm with supplementary keys)
Burghley (open-hole theory; wooden keys)
Briccialdi (a modified 'old system'; not to be confused with the Briccialdi B♭ mechanism)
Card
Carte 1851
Carte 1867
Carte 'Guards' Model'
Clinton 1848
Clinton 1857
Clinton 'Equisonant'
Colonieu (Boehm and 'old system' fingerings combined)
Giorgi
Giorgi and Schaffner
Julliot (modified Boehm)
McAvoy (modified Boehm)
MacGregor
Piazza
Pratten 'Perfected'
Radcliff
Rampone
Rockstro
Siccama
Tulou (modified 'old system')

Uebel
Van Everen (modified Boehm)
Ward
Welch (modified 'old system')
Willoughby

Specimens of most of the above are to be found in the Dayton C. Miller Collection, now in the Library of Congress, Washington, D.C., and two- or three-line descriptions of the more unusual ones in the invaluable Check List recently published.

In addition, the student will from time to time come across single examples which have been built to the special requirements of individual flautists. These vary from the simplest to extreme complication, as, for example, the gold flute with silver keys and ivory *embouchure*, used by James Mathews, founder in 1856 of the Birmingham, England, Flute Trio and Quartett Society. Some of these are of considerable merit, but they are difficult to categorise.

Some Important Fingering Charts

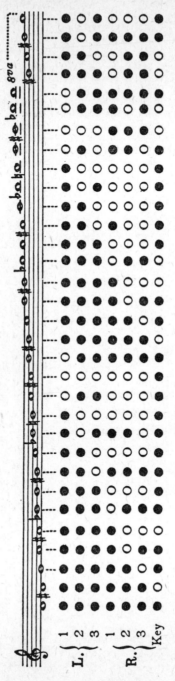

App. III, Fig. 1 *Echelle de tous les tons, etc.* From Hotteterre's *Principes* (1707). Adjusted for comparison of enharmonic fingerings

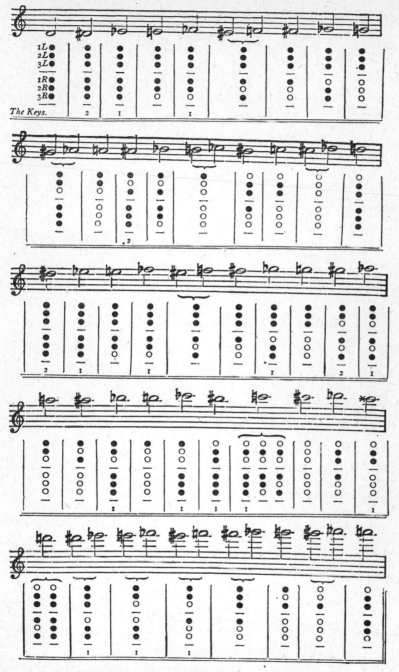

App. III, Fig. 2 Scale for Quantz's Flute with d♯ and e♭ keys. Adjusted from the original Table for comparison of the enharmonic fingerings

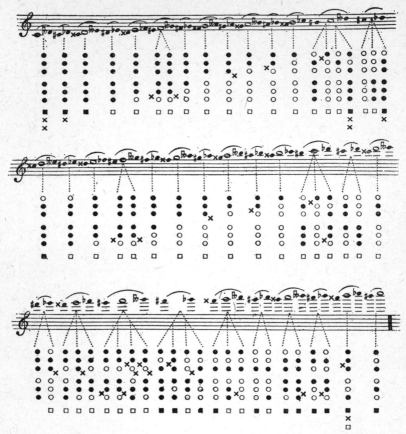

App. III, Fig. 3 Scale for six-keyed flute from
Clinton's *Universal Instruction Book* (*c.* 1864). Illustrating alternative fingerings recognised at the period

App. III, Fig. 4 Basic fingerings for Boehm Flute of 1847 from *Die Flöte und das Flötenspiel* (1871)

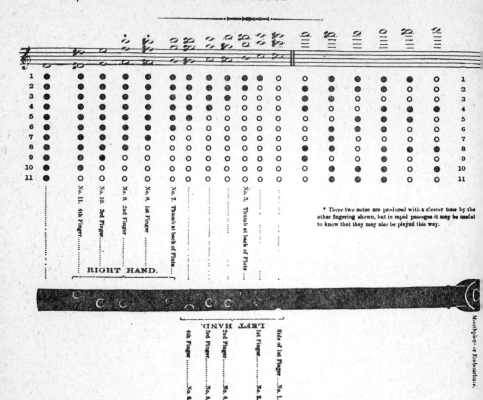

App. III, Fig. 5   Fingering of the Giorgi Flute from
Wallis' pamphlet of 1896

Care and Maintenance of the Flute

The most common mistake that the inexperienced owner of a flute makes is to try to dry it out completely after playing. This, of course, arises from anxiety to preserve the instrument, but it is impossible to achieve, and is, in fact, deleterious. After playing, the condensed moisture which might flow on to the pads should be wiped out with a loosely fitting mop or pull-through, so as to leave the bore *evenly* moist. Unequal absorption of moisture at different parts of the bore may lead to unequal expansion of the wood and so to splitting. Of course metal and ebonite flutes are not subject to this trouble, but surplus moisture can still damage the pads.

It is surprising how dirty the head of any flute can get, and this part should be gently cleaned from time to time, taking the greatest care not to damage the sharp edge of the mouth-hole. If the cork is removed in the course of cleaning it should be replaced at once in the correct position. Boehm recommended a wooden plug-gauge for this purpose, but today many makers supply a cleaning stick which has appropriate gauge marks at one end and at the other an eye through which a cleaning cloth can be threaded.

Occasionally a joint becomes uncomfortably stiff. This should not happen if the tenons are kept clean, and lubricated occasionally with *lapping grease*, as supplied by instrument makers. Traditionally, spermaceti ointment, a stand-by of the older dispensing chemists, was the lubricant of choice, but today this is hardly to be obtained. A joint that is too loose can be rectified by wrapping a few turns of lapping thread—in the trade known as 'hemp'—around it. 'Hemp' is a loosely twisted yarn impregnated with a mixture of beeswax and tallow. In the old days it was the only lapping applied to wooden tenons, but if left too long unrenewed it tended to dry out and form a hard waxy mass. Today thin sheet cork lapping is the usual thing. The joints of metal flutes are often un-lapped, and require very little lubrication, but much care not to distort them.

It goes without saying that in putting a flute together the parts must be held so as not to apply undue pressure on the long rods. The slightest bending of an axle may cause the key tubes to bind on it. A player may be able very gently to straighten a bent axle, but this is best left to the professional repair man. Occasionally a key will stick down, although it is quite free on its pivot. In this case the pad and its seating should be cleaned with spirit on the corner of an old handkerchief. A pad that adheres to the seating through damp may be dried with French chalk.

One of the most tiresome things that can befall the flautist is the breaking of a spring—and it always happens at the most embarrassing moment. If the mechanism is occasionally treated to a drop of the finest clock oil the springs should never rust, which is the prime cause of breakages, but this can some-times happen unnoticed. As a makeshift the flautist should carry a few of the smallest size of elastic bands. It is surprising how often one of these can be passed round the neck of a key and some anchorage be found so as to make an improvised spring.

From time to time keys leak due to worn pads, to accidental bending, or to the loss of one of the tiny slips of cork which are interposed between bearing surfaces in the mechanism to quieten the action. The cork buffers can easily be replaced, but pads are more difficult. Instrument dealers supply assorted pads, and these can be fitted by the player himself if he is neat-fingered. The old pad should be carefully removed and the cup cleaned out. A fragment of sealing-wax is melted into the cup, or a drop of French cement placed in it. The new pad is placed level and centrally in the cup, and while the adhesive is yet soft (with sealing-wax the cup may have to be re-warmed with a match) pressed lightly and evenly down on to the seating. Flute pads attached by a central screw may have to be brought up to height which can easily be done with discs of paper placed behind them.

Sometimes a leak is very difficult to locate, and here the smoke test will be useful. Stuff up the foot of the tube with a handkerchief, and while closing all the keys with no more than normal pressure, blow cigarette smoke in at the other end. Notice where the smoke comes out. An independent observer is a great help. To test if a flute is 'stopping' properly all over plug up the foot and, with all keys closed, suck gently at the other end. The slightest leak will reveal itself.

Finally, every flute should pay a periodical visit to the professional repair man. The expense is well repaid by freedom from anxiety.

A Selective Bibliography of the Flute (Short Title)

The fullest bibliography of the flute that is now available is certainly that compiled by Professor Dayton C. Miller in the years up to 1941. In 1935 he issued a privately printed list which at that time comprised 115 closely set quarto pages. The material is now in the Library of Congress, Washington, D.C., and the original list has been reissued. Since Miller's death important items have been added to the collection.

The following list has been divided for convenience into four sections: A. Instruction Books (a limited number, since these tend to repeat each other, or to be mere reprints under varied titles); B. Works valuable mainly for their historical or descriptive matter; C. Technical Works; D. Catalogues of Collections and Exhibitions, and Commentaries thereon. No claim is made as regards completeness, but all works I have found of most general interest under each heading are included. In a number of cases specialist references will be found in the chapter notes. With one or two important exceptions articles printed in foreign languages other than French, German, or Italian are not included. Wherever known, dates and the names of publishers are given.

As fingering charts sometimes afford clues to the state of development of contemporary instruments, the Tutors listed below (other than anonymous issues) have been placed in datal order. Otherwise the customary alphabetical arrangement has been adopted.

A. Tutors and Fingering Charts

Anonymous

The Compleat Tutor for the German Flute. (A large number of instruction books appeared under this title between 1730 and 1800. Two volumes published respectively by C. S. Thompson, London, and by Jonathan Fentum, both in 1770, contain the first references to the 'additional keys'.)

New Instructions for the German Flute. (This, again, is a title which was repeated many times. One such, issued by Thompson, London, in 1790 mentions 'Potter's Patent German Flute'. Potter's patent of 1785, to which this presumably refers, included the 'pewter plugs', graduated tuning slide, and 'register' on the foot joint. Many similar works appeared on the Continent under fanciful titles during this period. Few shed any particular light on the development of the instrument.)

B(anister), J(ohn), Gent. *The Most Pleasant Companion.* London, John Hudgebutt, 1681. (A Tutor for the recorder only, there denominated *Flute.* The copy in the Dayton Miller Collection appears to be unique, though its publication is recorded elsewhere.)

Hotteterre-le-Romain. *Principes de la Flûte Traversiere—et du Haut-bois.* Paris, Christophe Ballard, 1707, 1713, 1722; Amsterdam, Estienne Roger, 1708; a new edition with added tablature for clarinet and bassoon, Paris, Bailleux, c. 1765; reprinted in fascimile from the Amsterdam version with a German translation by H. J. Hellweg, Cassel, 1941. (Instructions are given for both the transverse flute, for which this is the earliest known Tutor, and the *flûte-à-bec*, as well as the oboe.)

Prelleur. *The Modern Music Master*. London, Cluer or Dicey, 1731. (According to Dayton Miller the flute matter was taken direct from Hotteterre *via* an English translation of *Les Principes* published by Walsh and Hare in 1729.)

Eisel. *Musicus Autodidaktos*. Erfurt, 1738.

Minguet y Yrol. *Reglas, y Advertencias Generales que ensenan el modo de taner todos los instrumentos mejores . . ., etc.* Madrid, 1754, 1774.

? Charles. *Apollo's Cabinet or the Muses' Delight*. Liverpool, published by Mr Charles, 1754, 1757. (Doublets of *The Modern Music Master*.)

Granom, L. C. A. *Plain and Easy Instructions for Playing on the German-flute*. London, T. Bennett, *c.* 1770.

Heron, Luke. *A Treatise on the German Flute, etc.* London, W. Griffin, 1771. (The copy of this most important work in the Dayton Miller Collection appears to be unique. It is dedicated to the Earl of Westmeath, and was to be obtained of the Author 'at his house in Great Britain-street, Dublin,' as well as at all the Music Shops in London. Miller suggests that it may have been inspired by Quantz but is in no way a copy of his treatise. Another indication of the high cultivation of flute playing in Ireland in the 18th century.)

Lorenzoni, A. *Saggio per ben sonare il flauto traverso . . ., etc.* Vicenza, F. Modena, 1779.

Gunn, John. *The Art of Playing the German-Flute on New Principles . . ., etc.* London, Birchall, 1793. (An important work, and advanced for its time.)

Tromlitz, J. G. *Flötenschule*. Leipzig, 1791, 1800.

Wragg, J. *The Flute Preceptor*. London, published by the Author. (Wragg's name is to be found on the longest series of Flute Preceptors known, running from 1792 to 1860. The later editions carry the names of various well-known publishers in London, Philadelphia, Boston, etc. The 20th edition, 1802, mentions the eight-keyed flute.)

Hugot et Wunderlich. *Méthode de Flûte du Conservatoire*. Paris, Conservatoire de Musique, 1804. (Begun by Hugot and completed by Wunderlich, both professors in the Paris Conservatoire, this was long regarded as the best *Méthode* of its time. Valuable for the light it sheds on French playing at the turn of the century.)

Nicholson, C. *Nicholson's Complete Preceptor for the German Flute, etc.* London, Preston, 1816. (The first of several instruction books by this celebrated flautist published successively until 1836. Contains data for flutes with one, four, and six keys including the c′ and c′♯ foot-keys. A second edition of this work, revised by Richardson, appeared *c.* 1840. In 1875 Harrington Young used the title 'Charles Nicholson's School for the Flute' for a composite work based on the original Preceptor plus selections from his 'Preceptive Lessons' of 1841, and adapted for the Boehm, Carte and Boehm, and Radcliff flutes.)

Furstenau, A. B. *Flöten-Schule*. Leipzig, Breitkopf and Härtel, 1826.

Drouet, L. *Méthode pour la Flûte*. Anvers, A. Schott, 1827. (Contains both French and German texts. Fingerings for one-, four-, and eight-keyed flutes plus a page of music specially for flutes with the extended foot joint to b or g.)

Gerock and Wolf. *Scale and Description of Boehm's Newly-Invented Patent Flute*. London, n.d., *c.* 1831.

Coche, V. *Méthode pour servir à l'enseignement de la nouvelle Flûte inventée par Gordon, modifiée par Boehm et perfectionnée par V. Coche et Buffet, Jne.* Paris, Schonenberger, 1838. (The justice of the above grandiose title is discussed in Appendix I.)

Tulou, J. L. *Méthode de Flûte*. Paris, Chabal, 1835.

Carte, R. *A Complete Course of Instruction for the Boehm Flute*. London, Addison and Hodson, 1845. (This work is addressed to beginners and those already acquainted with the old flute. It covers both the open and closed G♯ keys.)

Siccama, A. *Theory of the New Patent Diatonic Flute*. London, Cramer, Beale and Co., 1847.

Radcliff, J. *School for the flute*. London, Rudall, Carte and Co., 1873. (This is a revision, with acknowledgement, of Nicholson, and is adapted to the Radcliff model.)

Tillmetz, R. *Anleitung zur Erlernung der Theobald Böhm'schen Cylinder- und Ringklappen-Flöte, mit konischer Bohrung*. Leipzig, Fr. Kistner, 1890.

Schwedler, M. *Katechismus der Flöte und des Flötenspiels*. Leipzig, J. J. Weber, 1897. (The first of three works by this eminent teacher, which may be regarded as the 'great' instruction books for the old system flute.)

Lorenzo, L. de. *L'Indespensable. A Complete Modern School for the Flute*. New York, Carl Fischer, 1912. (A Tutor of average distinction, but valuable for the inclusion of biographical notices of some five hundred eminent flautists, etc.)

Moyse, M. *Enseignement complet de la flûte*. Paris, 1921. (May be regarded as the authoritative work on the French School of today.)

Langey, O. *Tutor for the Flute*. London, Hawkes and Son, modern. (One of a long series of Tutors for wind instruments of all kinds appearing under the same general editorship. Much used for basic instruction, it contains charts for almost all fingering systems.)

Potter, H. *Flute Tutor for B flat Flute, etc*. London, H. Potter and Co., modern. (Standard Tutors for the flute band instruments in all sizes.)

B. HISTORICAL AND DESCRIPTIVE

Agricola, M. *Musica Instrumentalis deudsch*. Wittemberg, 1528, 1532, 1542, 1545.

—— *Musica Instrumentalis deudsch*. (Reprint in facsimile.) Leipzig, Breitkopf, 1896.

Apel, W. *The Harvard Dictionary of Music*. Cambridge, Mass., 1954.

Baines, A. C. *Woodwind Instruments and their History*. London, Faber and Faber, 1957.

European and American Musical Instruments. London, Batsford, 1966.

Boehm, Th. *Die Flöte und das Flötenspiel*. Munich, Joseph Aibl, 1871.

—— *An Essay on the Construction of Flutes*. Edited, with the addition of correspondence and other documents by W. S. Broadwood. London, Rudall, Carte and Co., 1882.

Bonanni, F. *Gabinetto armonico*. Rome, 1722.

Brancour. *Histoire des Instruments de Musique*. Paris, H. Laurens, 1921.

Burney, Dr. C. *A General History of Music*. London, 1776.

—— *The Present State of Music in France and Italy*. London, 1771.

—— *The Present State of Music in Germany and the Netherlands*. London, 1773.

Carse, A. *The History of Orchestration*. London, Kegan Paul, 1925.

—— *Musical Wind Instruments*. London, Macmillan, 1939.

—— *The Orchestra in the 18th Century*. Cambridge, Heffer, 1940.

—— *The Orchestra from Beethoven to Berlioz*. Cambridge, Heffer, 1948.

Carte, Richard. *Sketch of the progressive improvements made in the Flute, etc*. London, Rudall, Rose, Carte and Co., 1851.

Catrufo, J. *Traité des Voix et des Instruments*. Paris, 1832.

Clinton, John. *A Treatise upon the Mechanism and General Principles of the Flute*. London, H. Potter, 1852.

Closson, Ernest. *La Facture des Instruments de Musique en Belgique*. Brussels, Commissariat Général près l'Exposition de Bruxelles, 1935.

Cobbet, W. W. *Cyclopedic Survey of Chamber Music.* Oxford, 1929.
Comettant, O. *Histoire d'un Inventeur (Ad. Sax).* Paris, 1860.
Cucuel, G. *Etudes sur un orchestre au 18ᵐᵉ siècle.* Paris, Fischbacher, 1913.
Dalyell, J. G. *Musical Memoirs of Scotland.* London, Pickering, 1849.
Diderot and d'Alembert. *Encyclopédie.* Paris, 1767, 1776.
Donington, R. *The Instruments of Music.* London, 1949.
Doppelmayr, J. *Historische Nachricht von den Nürnbergischen Mathematicis und Kunstlern.* Nürnberg, 1730.
Euting, E. *Zur Geschichte der Blasinstrumente im 16 und 17 Jahrhundert.* Berlin, 1899.
Farmer, H. *Rise and Development of Military Music.* London, W. Reeves, 1912.
Fétis, F. J. *Biographie Universelle des Musiciens.* Paris, Firmin-Didot, 1868.
Fitzgibbon, H. M. *The Story of the Flute.* London, W. Reeves, 1914; 2nd edn. (amplified), 1928.
Francoeur, L. J. *Diapason général—des instruments à vent.* Paris, 1772.
—— *Traité général—des instruments d'orchestre.* (Revised by A. Choron.) Paris, 1813.
Galpin, F. W. *European Musical Instruments.* London, Williams and Norgate, 1937.
—— *Old English Instruments of Music.* (3rd edition.) London, Methuen, 1932.
Geiringer, Karl. *Musical Instruments. Their History from the Stone Age to the Present Day.* London, Geo. Allen and Unwin, 1943.
Gerber, E. L. *Historisch—biographisches Lexikon.* Leipzig, Breitkopf, 1792.
Fevaert, F. A. *Nouveau traité d'instrumentation.* Paris, Lemine, 1885.
Grove, G. *Dictionary of Music and Musicians.* (5th edition.) London, Macmillan & Co., 1954.
Hawkins, C. *A General History of Music.* London, 1876.
Heckel, W. *Der Fagott.* Leipzig, Merseburger, 1899. Revised edn. 1931.
—— English translation by L. G. Langwill, 1931. (Typescript.)
Heckel/Waples Ex. *Journal of Musicology*, Vol. 11 Ohio, U.S.A., 1940.
Hipkins and Gibb. *Musical Instruments, etc.* Edinburgh, Black, 1888, 1921.
James, W. N. *A Word or Two on the Flute.* Edinburgh, C. Smith and Co., 1826.
Junker. *Musikalischer Almanach.* 1782.
Kappey, J. A. *Short History of Military Music.* London, Boosey & Company, c. 1890.
Kastner, G. *Manuel Général de Musique Militaire.* Paris, Firmin-Didot, 1848.
Kinsky, G. *A History of Music in Pictures.* London, Dent, 1930–37.
Kircher, A. *Musurgia Universalis.* Rome, Corbeletti, 1650.
Koch, H. *Musikalisches Lexikon.* Offenbach, 1802.
Koch-Dommer. *Musikalisches Lexikon.* Heidelberg, 1865.
Laborde, J. B. de. *Essai sur la Musique.* Paris, 1780, 1781.
Langwill, L. G. *Two Rare Eighteenth-century London Directories.* (ex. *Music and Letters.*) London, January 1949.
—— *London Wind-instrument Makers—17th and 18th Centuries.* (ex. *The Music Review*, Vol. VII.) Cambridge, Heffer.
Lavignac, and de la Laurencie. *Encyclopédie.* Article 'Flûte' by Taffanel and Fleury, Paris, Delagrave, 1927.
Lavoix, H. *Histoire de l'instrumentation.* Paris, Firmin-Didot, 1878.
Lorenzo, L. de. *My Complete Story of the Flute.* New York, Crescendo Publishing Co., 1952.
Luscinius, O. *Musurgia.* Strassburg, Joan Schott, 1536.
Majer, J. *Neu eröffneter Musik Saal.* (2nd edn.) Nürnberg, Kremer, 1741.
Mattheson, J. *Das neu-eröffnete Orchester.* Hamburg, 1713.

Mersenne, M. *Harmonie universelle*. Paris, Baudry, 1636.
Miller, Dayton C. *The Flute and Flute Playing*. Cleveland, Case School of Applied Science; London, Rudall, Carte and Co., 1922. (A scholarly translation of Boehm's great work of 1882 with a valuable commentary)
—— *Bibliography of the Flute*. Cleveland, privately printed.
Miller, G. *The Military Band*. London, Boosey & Co., 1912.
Norlind, T. *Musikinstrumentenhistoria i ord och bild*. Stockholm, Dordish Rotogravyr, 1941.
Parke, W. *Musical Memoirs*. London, Colburn and Bentley, 1830.
Pierre, C. *Les facteurs d'instruments de musique*. Paris, Sagot, 1893.
—— *La Facture Instrumentale* . . . Paris, Librairie de l'Art Indépendant, 1890.
Pontécoulant, L. G. le D. *Organographie*. Paris, Castel, 1861.
Praetorius, M. *Syntagma musicum*. Wolfenbüttel, E. Holwein, 1619.
—— Reprint. Berlin, Trautwein, 1884.
Prestini, G. *Notizie intorno alla storia degli strumenti, etc*. Bologna, Bongiovanni, 1925.
Profeta, R. *Storia—degli strumenti musicali*. Florence, 1952.
Quantz, J. J. *Versuch Einer Anweisung die Flöte traversière zu spielen*. Berlin, J. F. Voss, 1752.
Redfield, J. *Music, a science and an art*. New York, Knopf, 1928.
Ribock, J. J. H. *Bemerkungen über die Flöte, etc*. Stendal: bey Dan. Christ. Franzen und Grosse, 1782.
Riemann, H. *Musik—Lexikon*. (Various editions.) Mainz, Leipzig, Berlin, 1882–1922.
Rockstro, R. R. *A Treatise on the Flute*. London, Rudall, Carte and Co., 1890, 2nd edn., 1928 (revised). Reprinted 1967 by Musica Rara, London.
Sachs, Curt. *The History of Musical Instruments*. New York, W. W. Norton and Co. Inc., 1940.
—— *Handbuch der Musikinstrumentenkunde*. Leipzig, Breitkopf, 1930.
—— *Real-Lexikon der Musikinstrumente*. Berlin, 1913.
Schlesinger, K. *Modern Orchestral Instruments*. London, W. Reeves, 1910.
Schmidl, C. *Dizionario universale dei musicisti*. Milan, 1928–38.
Schneider, W. *Historisch-Technische Beschreibung, etc*. Leipzig, Hennings, 1834.
Southgate, T. Lea. 'The Evolution of the Flute', ex. *Proceedings of the Musical Association*. London, 1908.
Speer, D. *Grund-richtiger Unterricht der Musikalischen Kunst*. Ulm, 1687, 1697.
Sundelin. *Die Instrumentirung—Militar Musik-Chöre*. Berlin, Wagenführ, 1828.
—— *Die Instrumentirung für das Orchester*. Berlin, 1828.
Tans'ur, William. *The Elements of Music Displayed*. London, 1772.
Terry, C. S. *Bach's Orchestra*. London, O.U.P., 1932.
Teuchert, E., and Haupt, E. *Musik-Instrumentenkunde in Wort und Bild*. (Vol. II.) Leipzig, Breitkopf, 1911.
Tromlitz, J. G. *Kurze Abhandlung vom Flötenspielen*. Leipzig, Breitkopf und Härtel, 1786.
—— *Ausfürlicher und gründlicher Unterricht die Flöte zu spielen*. Leipzig, A. F. Böhme, 1791.
Ventzke, Karl. *Die Boehmflöte*. Frankfurt am Main, Verlag Das Musikinstrument, 1965.
Vester, Frans. *Flute Repertoire Catalogue*. London, Musica Rara, 1967. (A catalogue of over 10,000 music titles.)
Virdung, A. *Musica Getutscht*. Basle, 1511.
—— Reprint in facsimile. Berlin, Trautwein, 1882. Kassel, 1931.
Ward, Cornelius. *The Flute Explained, etc*. London, the author, 1844.

Weckerlin, J. B. *Nouveau Musiciana*. Paris, 1890.
Welch, Christopher. *History of the Boehm Flute*, London, Rudall, Carte, and Co., 1883.
—— *Six Lectures on the Recorder and Other Flutes*. London, Hy. Frowd, O.U.P., 1911.
Wetzger. *Die Flöte*. Heilbronn, c. 1897.
Winternitz, E. *Musical Instruments of the Western World*. London, Thames and Hudson, 1966.

C. TECHNICAL

Andries. *Aperçu théorique de tous les instruments de musique*. Ghent, 1856.
Bartolozzi, Bruno. *New Sounds for Woodwinds*, trans. R. Smith Brindle. London, O.U.P., 1967. With Record.
Benade, Arthur. *Horns, Strings, and Harmony*. New York, Doubleday and Co. Inc., 1960. (Also various extremely important papers in *Journal of the Acoustical Society of America*, see p. 48, note 6.)
Berlioz, H. *Traité de l'instrumentation*. Paris, Schonenberger, 1844.
—— *Instrumentationslehre. Erganstz u. revidiert von Richard Strauss*. Leipzig, 1905.
Buck, Percy. *Acoustics for Musicians*. London, O.U.P., 1918.
Bonavia-Hunt, N. A. *What is the Formant?* (ex. *Musical Opinion*.) London, December 1948, January 1949.
Chapman, F. B. *Flute Technique*. London, 1936.
Forsyth, Cecil. *Orchestration*. London, Macmillan, 1922.
Hague, B. *The Tonal Spectra of Wind Instruments*. (ex. Proc. Roy. Mus. Ass. Session LXXIII.), 1947.
Helmholtz, H. L. F. von. *The Sensations of Tone*, trans. A. J. Ellis (2nd edn.), London, Longmans, Green & Co., 1885.
Hopkins and Rimbault. *The Organ*. (3rd edn.) London, Robert Cocks, 1877.
Lloyd, Ll. *The Musical Ear*. London, O.U.P., 1940.
Mackworth-Young, G. *What Happens in Singing*. London, Newman Neame, 1953.
Mahillon, V. *Elements d'acoustique*. Brussels, Mahillon, 1874.
Miller, D. C. *The Science of Musical Sounds*. New York, Macmillan, 1922.
—— *Sound Waves*. New York, the Macmillan Co., 1937.
Porter, M. M. *The Embouchure*. London, Boosey and Hawkes, 1967.
Richardson, E. G. *The Acoustics of Orchestral Instruments*. London, Arnold, 1929.
Smith, Robert. *Harmonics*. Cambridge, T. and J. Merrill, 1757.
Wood, Alexander. *The Physics of Music*. London, Methuen, 1944.

PERIODICALS

Acoustical Society of America Journal. Menasha, 1929.
Allgemeine Musikalische Zeitung. Leipzig, 1798–1849, 1863–1882.
Cæcilia. Mainz, 1824–48.
Royal Musical Association, Proceedings, London. London, 1875.
Galpin Society Journal. London, 1948.
Monatsheft für Musikwissenschaft.
Musical Opinion. London, 1877.
Woodwind Magazine. New York, 1948.
Zeitschrift für Instrumentenbau. Leipzig, 1880.
Zeitschrift für Musikwissenschaft.
Sitzungberichte der Preuss. Akad. der Wissenschaft. Berlin, 1882.

D. Catalogues of Collections and Exhibitions (including Commentaries)

AMSTERDAM. Rijksmuseum—Musiekinstrumenten uit het Rijksmuseum te Amsterdam, 1952. (Exhibition in The Hague.)

BASLE. Historisches Museum, Basel. *Katalog* No. IV, KARL NEF, 1906.

BERLIN. Sammlung der Staatlichen Hochschule. *Beschreibender Katalog.* CURT SACHS, 1922.

BOLOGNA. Esposizione internazionale di Musica in Bologna, nel 1888. *Catalogo ufficiale.* (Parma 1888.)

BOSTON, MASS. Boston Museum of Fine Arts, Boston, Massachusetts. *Ancient European Musical Instruments, An Organological Study of the Musical Instruments in the Lesley Lindsey Mason Collection at the Museum of Fine Arts, Boston.* N. BESSARABOFF, Harvard University Press, 1941.

BRESLAU. Schlesisches Museum. *Catalogue.* EPSTEIN-SCHEYER, 1932.

BRUSSELS. Musée instrumental du Conservatoire Royal. *Catalogue descriptif et analytique.* V. C. MAHILLON, 5 vols., 1893–1922.

BIRMINGHAM. Birmingham and Midland Institute. *Catalogue*, 1953 (cyclostyled).

COLOGNE. Musikhistorisches Museum von Wilhelm Heyer in Cöln. *Kleiner Katalog.* GEORGE KINSKY, 1913.

COPENHAGEN. Music History Museum. *Das Musikhistorische Museum, Kopenhagen.* ANGUL HAMMERICH, 1911. German translation of Danish text, Erna Bobe, pub. Breitkopf, Leipzig. (179 illustrations.)

—— Claudius Collection. *Catalogue* 1900 and enlarged edition. Danish and German texts, 1921.

EDINBURGH. The Galpin Society Exhibition held in Edinburgh in 1958. *Catalogue* (cyclostyled).

—— The Galpin Society 21st Anniversary Exhibition held in Edinburgh in 1968. *Catalogue* edited by G. Melville-Mason.

FLORENCE. *Catalogo de Instrumentos antigos de Leopold Francolini.*

—— R. Istituto L. Cherubini. *Gli strumenti raccolti nel Museo* etc. Leto Bargagna, 1911.

—— Collezione Etnografico-Musicale Kraus. *Catalogo Sezione Instrumenti Musicali.* A. KRAUS FIGLIO, 1901.

GHENT. Collection d'Instruments de Musique Anciens ou Curieux formée par C. C. Snoeck. *Catalogue*, 1894. (This collection was subsequently divided between the Berlin Hochschule and the Brussels Conservatoire Museums but certain specimens mentioned in the Catalogue are no longer to be found in either of these.)

GLASGOW. Kelvingrove Art Gallery and Museum. *The Glen Collection of Musical Instruments.* HENRY GEORGE FARMER, 1943. (ex. *The Art Review of the Glasgow Gallery and Museums Association.*)

HAGUE, THE. D. F. Scheurleer Collection. *De Muziek-Historische Afdeling.* Gemeente-Museum, 's-Gravenhage, DIRK J. BALFOORT, 1935.

HAMBURG. Museum für Hamburgische Geschichte. *Verzeichnis der Sammlung alter Musikinstrumente.* HANS SCHRÖDER, 1930.

INNSBRUCK. Museum Ferdinandeum. *Catalogue.*

LEIPZIG. Instrumenten-Sammlung von Paul de Wit. *Perlen aus der I-S* etc. German, French, and English texts in parallel columns and 16 plates in colour, 1892.

LISBON. Museu Instrumental em Lisboa. *Catalogo summario.* MICHEL'ANGELO LAMBERTINI, 1914.

—— Collecções Keil. *Breve noticia dos instrumentos de musica antigos e modernos.* ALFREDO KEIL, 1904

S

LIVERPOOL. Rushworth and Dreaper Collection. *General Catalogue*, 1923.
LONDON. Exhibition 1852. *Exhibition Lecture on the Musical Department.* W. W.
CAZALET.
—— *Douze jours à Londres. Voyage d'un mélomane à travers l'Exposition Universelle.* COMTE AD. DE PONTÉCOULANT, 1862 (Paris).
—— South Kensington Museum. *Descriptive Catalogue of the Musical Instruments.* CARL ENGEL, 1870.
—— South Kensington Museum. *Catalogue of the Special Exhibition of Ancient Musical Instruments* (1872), published 1873.
—— Victoria and Albert Museum. *Catalogue of Wood-wind and Strings.* A. C. Baines. H.M.S.O. 1968.
—— International Inventions Exhibition, 1885 *Guide to the Loan Collection and List of Musical Instruments, etc.*
—— Royal Military Exhibition, 1890. *Descriptive Catalogue of the Musical Instruments.* C. R. DAY, 1891.
—— Crystal Palace Exhibition. *Catalogue*, 1900.
—— Loan Exhibition, Fishmongers' Hall, 1904. *Illustrated Catalogue.* Various contributors, published Novello, London, 1909. (This and the R.M.E. are probably the most important of all English catalogues.)
—— The Horniman Museum. *The Adam Carse Collection of Musical Wind Instruments.* A list published by the London County Council, 1947.
—— As above a *Catalogue*, illustrated. Published by the L.C.C. 1951.
—— The Galpin Society. British Musical Instruments, an Exhibition by arrangement with the Arts Council of Great Britain, *Catalogue*, 1951.
—— Boosey and Hawkes Collection. *Catalogue*, 1939. (Typescript, privately circulated.)
LUTON. Luton Museum. Exhibition 1947. 'Growth of Music.' *Catalogue* (cyclostyled 1947.)
MILAN. Museo del Conservatorio. *Gli strumenti musicali nel Museo.* EUGENIO DE GUARINONI, 1908.
MILAN. Esposizione musicale, sotto il patrocinio di S.M. la Regina. Atti del congresso dei Musicisti italiani, riunito in Milano dal 16 al 22 Giugno, 1881.
MICHIGAN. University of Ann Arbor. The Frederick Stearns Collection. *Catalogue.* A. A. STANLEY, 1921.
MUNICH. Baierisches Nationalmuseum. *Catalogue.* K. A. BIERDIMPFL, 1883.
NEW YORK. Crosby Brown Collection. The Metropolitan Museum of Art. *Catalogue*, 1902.
PARIS. Musée du Conservatoire National. *Catalogue raisonné.* G. CHOUQUET, 1884. Supplements 1894, 1899, 1903.
—— Conservatoire des Arts et Métiers. *General Catalogue* in course of reprinting in 1948.
—— *Catalogue du Musée instrumental de M. Adolphe Sax*, 1877.
—— L'Industrie. *Exposition de 1834.* STEPHEN FLACHAT.
—— *Histoire illustrée de l'Exposition Universelle, par catégories d'industries, avec notices sur les exposants.* 1855. (Vol. I refers to the musical section.) CHARLES ROBIN.
—— *La Musique à l'Exposition Universelle de 1867.* COMTE DE PONTÉCOULANT. Published 1868.
—— *La Musique, les Musiciens, et les Instruments de Musique . . . Archive complètes . . . l'Exposition Internationale de 1867.* OSCAR COMETTANT. Published 1869.
—— *Exposition Universelle de Paris, en 1855. Fabrication des Instruments de Musique, rapport.* F. J. FÉTIS. Published 1856.

PARIS. *La facture instrumentale à l'Exposition Universelle de* 1889 . . . *etc.*
CONSTANT PIERRE. Published 1890.
—— Exposition universelle internationale de 1878 à Paris. *Les instruments de musique etc.* G. CHOUQUET. Published 1880.
—— Exposition universelle internationale de 1900 à Paris. *Instruments de musique. Rapport.* E. BRIQUEVILLE.
PRAGUE. National Museum. An exhibition of musical instruments. *Catalogue.* ALEXANDER BUCHNER, 1952.
SALZBURG. Museum Carolino Augusteum. *Catalogue.* C. GEIRINGER (Leipzig), 1931.
STOCKHOLM. Musikhistoriska Museet. *Catalogue.* J. SVANBERG, 1902.
VERONA. *Catalogo de Instrumentos do municipio de Verona.*
VIENNA. Die Sammlung Alter Musikinstrumente. *Beschreibendes Verzeichnis.* J. SCHLOSSER, 1920. (A most important work with many magnificent illustrations.)
—— Sammlung der K. K. Gesellschaft der Musikfreunde in Wien. *Catalogue.* E. MANDYCZEWSKI, 1921.
—— *Rapport sur les Instruments de Musique à l'Exposition de Vienne en 1837* LISSAJOUS. Published 1895.
VIENNA. International Exhibition of Music and Theatre, 1892. *Catalogue* edited by G. Adler, 1892.
WASHINGTON, D.C. *The Dayton C. Miller Collection.* A Checklist of Instruments. W. LICHTENWANGER and LAURA E. GILLIAM, 1961.
YORK. The Castle Museum. Musical section. *Catalogue.*

Condensed Subject Index

(Principal References)

Index of Names

(Principal References)

Proper names in the following table are arranged alphabetically. Celebrities are indicated by surname only. In other cases where pre-names are known, these are either printed at length or represented by initials, according to whichever is the commoner usage in conversational reference.

Index of Instruments

(Confined to first references and principal ones in the text)

Printed in Great Britain by
The Camelot Press Limited, London and Southampton